John Henry Middleton

Engraved Gems of classical Times

With a Catalogue of the Gems in the Fitzwilliam Museum

John Henry Middleton

Engraved Gems of classical Times
With a Catalogue of the Gems in the Fitzwilliam Museum

ISBN/EAN: 9783337177249

Printed in Europe, USA, Canada, Australia, Japan

Cover: Foto ©ninafisch / pixelio.de

More available books at **www.hansebooks.com**

THE ENGRAVED GEMS OF CLASSICAL TIMES

WITH A

CATALOGUE

OF THE

GEMS IN THE FITZWILLIAM MUSEUM.

BY

J. HENRY MIDDLETON,

SLADE PROFESSOR OF FINE ART, DIRECTOR OF THE FITZWILLIAM MUSEUM,
AND FELLOW OF KING'S COLLEGE, CAMBRIDGE;
AUTHOR OF "ANCIENT ROME IN 1888."

CAMBRIDGE:
AT THE UNIVERSITY PRESS.
1891

[All Rights reserved.]

MEMORIAE

VIRI CARISSIMI

CAROLI WILHELMI KING.

TABLE OF CONTENTS.

PREFACE AND LIST OF AUTHORITIES. Page ix to xv.

CHAPTER I. Page 1 to 16.
SCARABS, CYLINDERS AND OTHER EARLY SIGNETS.

CHAPTER II. Page 17 to 34.
GREEK GEMS.

CHAPTER III. Page 35 to 46.
GREEK GEMS (CONTINUED) AND ETRUSCAN SCARABS.

CHAPTER IV. Page 47 to 58.
ROMAN GEMS.

CHAPTER V. Page 59 to 65.
CAMEO GEMS.

CHAPTER VI. Page 66 to 83.
INSCRIPTIONS ON GEMS.

CHAPTER VII. Page 84 to 96.
INSCRIPTIONS ON GEMS (CONTINUED).

CHAPTER VIII. Page 97 to 102.
THE CHARACTERISTICS OF ANCIENT GEMS.

CHAPTER IX. Page 103 to 120.
THE TECHNIQUE OF GEM-ENGRAVING.

CHAPTER X. Page 121 to 128.
GEMS IN MEDIAEVAL TIMES.

CHAPTER XI. Page 129 to 139.
THE MATERIALS USED FOR ENGRAVED GEMS.

CHAPTER XII. Page 140 to 157.
THE MATERIALS USED FOR ENGRAVED GEMS (CONTINUED).

APPENDIX.
CATALOGUE OF THE GEMS IN THE FITZWILLIAM MUSEUM
Page i to xxv.

INDEX.

PREFACE.

IN the following pages I have attempted to give a brief account of the engraved gems and other forms of signet which were used by the chief classical races of ancient times. The book is intended for the general use of students of archaeology, and has been written with the hope that it may in some cases lead the reader to a more detailed and practical study of this most fascinating subject.

The various tools and technical processes used by the ancient gem-engravers have been discussed at some length, since a close attention to these points is specially desirable as a much-needed help in the frequently difficult task of distinguishing between gems of different origin and date.

With regard to the Appendix containing the catalogue of the gems in the Fitzwilliam Museum, I have attempted to indicate the period to which each gem seems to belong, in spite of the great difficulty there is, very frequently, in attaining to anything like certainty on this point.

Even though in many cases my judgment may be erroneous, yet, on the whole, the attempt to distinguish periods of workmanship has its use, in giving the reader a notion of the general style and character of the gem in question.

The gems which are described in this catalogue were, with very few exceptions, collected by Colonel Leake, the distinguished author of valuable works on the *Topography of Athens* and other kindred subjects. They came into the possession of the Fitzwilliam Museum in the following manner. By his will, dated Jan. 17, 1859, Colonel Leake bequeathed to his wife for her life his whole collection of books, coins, gems, bronzes, vases and other antiques, with the provision that at her death, the whole collection should be offered to the University of Cambridge for the sum of £5000.

Colonel Leake died in 1860, and his widow died in 1863. It was then decided, by a vote of the Senate on Feb. 4, 1864, that Colonel Leake's testamentary offer should be accepted and that £5000 out of the funds of the Fitzwilliam Museum should be devoted to this important acquisition.

The actual value of the whole Leake collection was probably double of the sum paid for it, and its value has largely increased since 1864. The coins alone are now worth considerably more than the £5000 which was paid for the whole collection.

In 1870 a catalogue of Colonel Leake's gems was published by the late Charles William King, M.A., Senior Fellow of Trinity College, Cambridge, the well-known author of many works on antique gems, which are full of interesting matter illustrated by the widest reading and the most copious learning. At this time, however, Mr King's eyesight had begun to fail, and in consequence of that a certain number of inaccuracies crept into his descriptions which make it desirable that another catalogue should be prepared, illustrated by a photographic process which gives the actual character of each gem better than the woodcuts in Mr King's work.

Mr King's chief works on gems were the following— *Antique gems*, 1866; *Precious Stones and Metals*, 1865; reprinted in Bohn's Series in 1883; *Handbook of engraved gems*, 1866; *Antique gems and rings*, 2 vols. 1872; *The Gnostics and their remains*, enlarged edition, 1887. And also a large number of articles on gems published in the

Archaeological Journal, Vols. XVIII., XIX., and others. All these works are full of valuable matter, and are written in the most interesting style.

Mr King's own collection of gems, consisting of 330 examples of various dates, was formed by him between the years 1845 and 1877.

In 1881 it was sold to an American gentleman, Mr J. T. Johnston, who presented the whole collection to the Metropolitan Museum in New York City. A descriptive catalogue, written by Mr King in 1878, was published by the New York Museum in 1882.

Mr King died suddenly in London on the 26th of March, 1888. Of his loss as a friend it is impossible to speak —

" aeternumque
Nulla dies nobis maerorem e pectore demet."

J. HEN. MIDDLETON.

KING'S COLLEGE,
CAMBRIDGE.

WORKS ON ANTIQUE GEMS[1].

A large number of the most valuable monographs on gems are scattered through the volumes of the chief archaeological periodicals of England, France, Germany and Italy; with the names of which classical students will be familiar.

Books on gems of the 17th and 18th centuries are now of but little value except for the records they supply, showing, in certain cases, that a special gem is not, at least, one of quite modern production.

The chief works of this class are these:

Agostini, *Gemme antiche figurate*, 2 vols., Roma, 1686.

De la Chausse, *Gemme antiche di Michelangelo Causeo de la Chausse*, Roma, 1700.

Maffei, *Gemme antiche di Dom. de' Rossi colle sposizioni di P. A. Maffei*, Roma, 1707.

Stosch, *Gemmae antiquae caelatae*, Amsterdam, 1724, and the same collection described by

Winckelmann, *Pierres gravées du feu Baron de Stosch*, Florence, 1760.

Zanetti, *Dactyliotheca*, Rome, 1747.

Mariette, *Traité des pierres gravées*, Paris, 1750; and *Museum Odescalchum, sive thesaurus gemmarum*, Rome, 1751.

Gori, *Museum Florentinum*, Florence, 1731—1762.

Natter, *Traité des pierres gravées*, London, 1761.

---

[1] The most important works in English on engraved gems are those written by C. W. King, a list of which is given in the Preface on page x.

Gori, *Dactyliotheca Smithiana*, Venice, 1767.

Worlidge, *Antique gems*, London, 1768.

Cipriani, *Drawings of 100 gems in the Marlborough Collection*, engraved by Bartolozzi, 2 vols. folio, 1780—1791.

Raspe, *Catalogue of gems cast in paste by James Tassie*, London, 1791.

Many other large and costly works with illustrations of antique gems were published in the 18th century, but the engravings of that time give little or no notion of the real character of the gems they represent, the main object of the artist being to give a pretty picture rather than a faithful copy.

Among more recent works the following are the most valuable—

Toelken, *Erklärendes Verzeichniss der antiken vertieft geschnittenen Steine*, Berlin, 1835.

Köhler, *Gesammelte Schriften, herausgegeben von L. Stephani*, St Petersburg, 1850—1853.

Panofka, *Gemmen mit Inschriften*, printed in Abhandlungen der König. Akad. der Wissenschaften zu Berlin, 1851, pp. 385—519.

Brunn, *Geschichte der Griechischen Künstler*, Brunswick, 1859, Vol. II., pp. 444—637; and new edition, 1889, Vol. II., pp. 303—433.

Chabouillet, *Catalogue des camées et pierres gravées de la Bibliothèque Impériale*, Paris, 1858.

Stephani and others, *Compte-rendu de la Commission Impériale Archéologique*, St Petersburg, 1860 to the present time; and, dealing with the same subject, *Antiquités du Bosphore Cimmérien*, St Petersburg, 1854.

Gerhard, *Gesammelte akademische Abhandlungen und kleine Schriften*, Berlin, 1866.

Müller-Wieseler, *Denkmäler der alten Kunst*, Theil II., Göttingen, 1869.

H. N. Story-Maskelyne, *Catalogue of the Marlborough gems*, privately printed, London, 1870.

Milchhoefer, *Die Anfänge der Kunst in Griechenland*, Leipzig, 1883, pp. 78 to 90.

Furtwängler and others, *Mykenische Vasen*, Berlin, 1886.

A. H. Smith, *Catalogue of gems in the British Museum*, with an Introduction by A. S. Murray, London, 1888.

Other works are referred to in the following text.

LIST OF ILLUSTRATIONS.

Page 4, fig. 1; Babylonian cylinder of c. 2600 B.C.
Pages 7 to 11, figs. 2 to 12; Various forms of "Hittite" signets.
Page 14, fig. 13; Phoenician scarab of mixed Egyptian and Assyrian style.
Page 19, fig. 14; Glandular gem with rude figure of an ibex.
Page 19, fig. 15; Lenticular gem, with two goats of heraldic style.
Page 25, fig. 16; Satyr and wine-cup; Greek gem of the 6th century B.C.
Page 26, fig. 17; Hero with bow and arrow; Greek scarab of the finest style.
Page 30, fig. 18; Lion and stag: fine Greek work of the 5th century B.C.
Page 41, fig. 19; Portrait head of Eumenes I., king of Pergamus.
Page 66, fig. 20; Jewish signet with owner's name; 9th or 8th century B.C.
Page 105, fig. 21; Gem showing a man working with the drill and bow.
Page 107, fig. 22; Etruscan scarab, with rude drill-work.
Page 108, fig. 23; Lenticular gem, showing the use of the tubular drill.
Page 110, fig. 24; Lenticular gem showing the use of the wheel.
Page 112, fig. 25; Head of Zeus; Greek scarab of finest style, showing the use of the diamond-point.

APPENDIX.

PLATE I.

Greek gems in the Fitzwilliam Museum, to face p. xxvi.

PLATE II.

Roman gems in the Fitzwilliam Museum.

CHAPTER I.

SCARABS, CYLINDERS, AND OTHER EARLY SIGNETS.

IN early times, when writing was a rare accomplishment practised by few except professional scribes or members of a priesthood, hard stones or jewels engraved with a name or a device were of special importance from their use as signets, the impression of which gave that authenticity and authority to a document which in modern times is more usually conferred by a written signature. The signet of a king was commonly regarded as an authoritative symbol of his power, which he could delegate to a subject by entrusting to him the royal seal, with permission to use it: as, for example in ancient Egypt, when the Pharaoh of the time invested Joseph with vice-regal power over his kingdom, "Pharaoh took off his signet ring from his hand, and put it upon Joseph's hand," *Gen.* xli. 42, Revised Version. In the same way a duplicate of Augustus' signet was entrusted to a friend in Rome for use during the Emperor's absence on military expeditions; see below, page 49; and cf. Dio Cass. LIII. 30. *Use of signet.*

It was not until a comparatively late period, about the 4th century B.C., that engraved gems were commonly treated as personal ornaments. At first they were made and used simply for the practical purpose of signets.

SCARABS: The earliest class of signets which now exist, with the exception of some Egyptian rings made wholly of gold, are in the form of the sacred *scarabaeus* beetle of Egypt, the symbol of the Sun-god Ra, the Fertilizer of *Scarabs set as rings.*

the World[1]. The back of the scarab is cut into the beetle form, and the signet-device, usually a hieroglyphic inscription, is cut on the flat underside of the scarab. A hole drilled longitudinally through the scarab allowed it to be set in a simple ring (δακτύλιος) of gold or other metal, with a wire or swivel passing through the perforation, so that, when required for use as a signet, the scarab could be revolved, and its flat side brought outwards and pressed on wax, clay or other soft plastic substance.

Revolving mounts.

Some of the signet-scarabs which are too large for setting in a ring were worn on a string round the neck; a method which appears to have been one of the earliest ways of wearing any kind of signet.

Materials of scarabs.

It should however be noticed that the scarabs of Egypt were made for many other purposes besides that of signets[2], and the majority of them are not cut in hard stone or crystal, but are moulded in clay or worked out of the comparatively soft steatite, a vitreous glaze being applied by the maker both to steatite and clay scarabs[3].

In point of date the oldest scarab-signets of Egypt go back to a very remote period: examples have been found with the names of kings of the 4th Dynasty, dating about 3700 years B.C.

In later times the scarab form of signet was adopted by the Phoenicians, the Greeks and other races, who either directly or indirectly came under Egyptian influence.

Cylinders.

CYLINDERS: another very early class of signet is the cylinder of Assyria and Babylon, measuring most commonly from ¾ of an inch to 1½ inches long, and about half an inch to an inch in diameter. These are not made of clay, like so many of the Egyptian scarabs, but are cut out of hard stones,

---

[1] The scarabaeus beetle (Egyptian *Kheper*) was adopted as this symbol on account of its moulding large balls of clay, round like the world, in which it encloses its eggs. The heat of the sun hatches the eggs, and the young beetles burst forth from the clay ball.

[2] The great bulk of them, especially those made of pottery, were sacred charms or amulets rather than signets.

[3] The Fitzwilliam Museum possesses a good collection of this class of scarab: they are described in the forthcoming catalogue of Egyptian objects in the Museum by Mr Budge.

such as green jasper, rock crystal, chalcedony, haematite, carnelian, or more rarely amethyst and lapis lazuli. These cylinders are drilled longitudinally with a hole of sufficient diameter to receive a woollen or linen cord instead of a metal wire, and they were worn as a bracelet on the wrist, or else strung round the neck[1]. Though used primarily by the powerful races of the Euphrates Valley, these cylinder signets were not unknown among other nations, such as the Semites of Phoenicia and Palestine, and even in the early island colonies of the Phoenicians. The "signet and the cord," mentioned in *Genesis* xxxviii. 18 and 25, Revised Version (or "signet and bracelets" of the Old Version) are examples of this use of the cylinder. So also in *Canticles* viii. 6, the phrase occurs "set me as a seal upon thine arm."

Method of wearing cylinders.

A very large number of these Babylonian and Assyrian cylinders still exist; they appear to have been used by all except the very poorest classes. They are usually engraved with the name of the owner in cuneiform characters, together with figures of various deities, accompanied frequently by attendant genii or worshippers. A very favourite subject, especially among the earliest cylinders, is a deity or a king slaying a lion. The sacred tree (Hôm) between two guardian beasts or winged figures of human form occurs very often. This latter is the most characteristic of the designs used by the inhabitants of the Euphrates valley; from them it was adopted by the Phoenicians, and thus spread over an area as wide as the whole range of Phoenician trade, that is throughout the whole of the shores and islands of the Mediterranean. This very early and widely popular design was largely used by the Tyrian builders of Solomon's temple, as we read in 1 *Kings*, chaps. vi. and vii., and in 2 *Chronicles*, chaps. iii. to v., where the device is mentioned as being repeated again and again in various materials under the name of "the palm-tree and the winged cherubim[2]."

Designs on cylinder.

Palm tree and Cherubim.

[1] In a few cases the cylinder is mounted on a metal pin with a boss at each end to hold it fast, but this is quite exceptional.
[2] The Phoenician scarab illustrated in fig. 13, page 14, has examples of the winged Cherubim of Assyria.

The cylinder signet of a private person commonly has a figure of his special deity, and often a representation of the owner standing by in the attitude of worship. The inscription usually gives the name both of the deity and of the owner; as, for example, a fine haematite cylinder in the British Museum which is inscribed thus, "Abum-ilu the scribe, son of Nur-Martu, the servant of the god Martu (Rimmon)."

Dates of cylinders. Examples of these cylinders exist extending over a very wide period of time, from about 2600 B.C. to 200 B.C. or even later. Some of them are very fine examples of ancient Oriental art, designed with much spirit and executed with wonderful minuteness and delicacy of touch in the highly decorative and conventional style which is common to all the best Assyrian sculpture, whatever its scale may be.

Those of early date are the finest and most powerful in style; as, for example, a magnificent Babylonian cylinder of jasper in the British Museum, the signet of a scribe, dating about 2600 B.C., on which is cut a very noble figure of the deified hero Gistubar strangling a lion[1]: see fig. 1.

FIG. 1. Impression from an early Babylonian cylinder of the finest style; with the name of the owner and his deity in cuneiform characters, between two representations (reversed) of the same subject—Gistubar strangling a lion: *real size.*

Sargon I. The equally fine cylinder of Sargon I. (in Paris) is closely similar in style to this, and seems to be the work of the same engraver. The very decorative treatment of the hair, both of the heroes and of the lions, is specially noticeable.

[1] On the fine cylinders of this early period the most frequent subjects are Gistubar and his companion Hea-bani slaying lions or bulls, sometimes separately and sometimes together, like Heracles and Iolaos in early Greek art.

The date of Sargon I. is not known with any certainty. According to some archaeologists his reign was as early as about 2800 B.C. If so, the date of the cylinder shown in fig. 1 would probably be two centuries earlier than is suggested above.

In later times, under the Persian conquerors Darius and Xerxes, Babylon produced cylinders of very minute and delicate workmanship, showing the influence of Greek art, but inferior in spirit and vigour to the engravings of earlier date. The most remarkable example of this, dating from the end of the 6th century B.C., is the signet of Darius Hystaspes, a jasper cylinder engraved with the king in a chariot hunting lions, and with the cuneiform inscription, "I am Darius, the Great King" thrice repeated in the Persian, Median and Assyrian languages. This also is in the British Museum. Lastly, the cylinders of the 3rd century B.C. are very rude in design and of the coarsest, most clumsy workmanship.

Persian cylinders.

The cylinder form of signet was also used, though not commonly, in Egypt. The Egyptian cylinders are, as a rule, not made of crystal or jasper, but of pottery or steatite covered with a blue glaze, exactly like the scarabs: on them are cut or moulded, not large figure subjects, but hieroglyphic inscriptions. They appear to have been usually worn round the neck.

Egyptian cylinders.

The custom of wearing the cylinder-signet as an ornament appears to have led to the use of plain unengraved cylinders, strung on necklaces like large beads. A great many of these in rock-crystal and glass have been found in the tombs of Camiros in Rhodes and elsewhere in the Greek islands and sea-port towns.

When used as a signet the cylinder was rolled over a soft lump of wax or clay, which was thus flattened out over the surface destined to receive the seal, and at the same time received the impress of the cylinder[1]. The fine clay used for sealing not only with cylinders, but also with other forms of

Use of cylinder.

---

[1] See *Book of Job*, xxxviii. 14, where Heaven, with its night and morning, is described as being "changed as clay under the seal."

engraved gems, was called γῆ σημαντρίς (σημαίνω to seal). Herodotus (II. 38) describes the Egyptian priests using this clay to mark with their signets the animals which were accepted for sacrifice. Many examples of these clay seals have been found in Egypt, used for many different purposes, both religious and secular; see page 37.

Stamps on pottery.

The method of sealing by rolling an engraved cylinder over soft clay appears to have suggested a form of decoration, which was largely used by the potters of Etruria for the shoulders of their colossal jars (*pithoi*), of which a great number of examples, mostly dating from the 6th or 5th century B.C., still exist.

The patterns on these were moulded in relief on the plastic clay, after the jar was "thrown" on the wheel, but before it was fired, by rolling along a cylinder or disc, on the edge of which the design was sunk. These discs were usually about 9 or 10 inches in circumference, and therefore the pattern repeats regularly at that interval.

The subjects on these bands are rows of animals, Tritons and the like, often very similar in design and style to the sculptured reliefs on the architrave from the Temple at Assos, now in the Louvre.

Cones.

CONICAL SIGNETS: in Assyria, even at an early period, signets of conical form, of the same materials as the cylinders, were sometimes used. These cones, with the device sunk on the broad end, were pressed on rounded lumps of clay in which a piece of string was embedded for the attachment of the seal to a document. The mediaeval system of sealing was similar to this, pendant seals of wax being fastened to parchment deeds by a cord embedded in the wax. Many of the so-called Hittite signets are conical in form, see pages 7 and 8, figs. 2 and 3.

The later Persian signet-gems, from about the time of Alexander downwards, were also very commonly cut, not in the form of cylinders, but of truncated cones. These belong to a period of artistic decadence, and are usually poor in design and coarse in execution; a great contrast to the magnificent vigour of the figures on the early Assyrian cylinders of about 2600 B.C., and also to the delicate minuteness of the Persian cylinders of the 5th century B.C.[1]

"HITTITE" GEMS, so-called.

The name "Hittite" has been given to a very remarkable and primitive class of signets, which appear to have been made by some powerful race, whose influence extended throughout a considerable portion of Northern Syria and Asia Minor, at a very early period, perhaps fifteen or sixteen centuries B.C.   *"Hittite" signets.*

These signets do not, strictly speaking, belong to the class of gems; as they are mostly cut out of the softer stones, such as steatite and fine limestones, marbles and serpentine of various colours—black, white, red and brown; a few are on an inferior variety of pale green jasper. They are however of very great interest to the student of early gems, since many of them appear to be prototypes of the lenticular "Island gems;" and others of various forms seem to show the gradual modification of the cylinder into the cone-signet, and the further change from the cone to the hemispherical or annular seal.   *Changes of form.*

The variety of the shapes of these "Hittite" gems is very great, but none of them appear to have been set in rings; all were suspended in some way by a cord, probably round the neck of the owner.

The following are the chief forms of these signets:

1. Rude *cylinders* of the Assyrian shape.

FIG. 1.

2. *Cones*, with the principal device on the base, and the hole or groove for suspension near its smaller end; see fig. 2.

[1] For an account of cylinders and other Oriental gems, see De Vogüé

8 VARIOUS FORMS [CHAP. I.

Cone signets.

If the cone is pierced the hole is drilled at right angles to its axis, not longitudinally as in the cylinders. Some of these conical signets are engraved with figures, not only on the base, but also round the sides of the cone, thus forming a link with the cylindrical shape of signet.

Another variety of the cone is very short in proportion to its diameter, almost hemispherical in shape; see fig. 3.

FIG. 3.

This variety, with its hole for suspension enlarged, leads to the *annular* form of signet.

Ring signets.

3. A *ring-like stone*, in which the perforation is not large enough for the signet to be worn on the finger; it must therefore have been suspended in the usual way by a cord; see fig. 4.

FIG. 4.

A further development of this shape, which rarely occurs,

FIG. 5.

Mélanges d'Archéologie Orientale; Paris, 1868; Levy, *Siegel und Gemmen mit aramäischen &c. Inschriften,* Breslau, 1869, and Menant, *Recherches sur la glyptique Orientale,* Paris, 1886.

is an actual *finger-ring* cut out of stone, with one side flattened to form the bezel for the signet device; see fig. 5.

4. Another form among these signets is a *rectangular tablet*, flat on the lower side where the device is cut, and shaped like a low-pitched roof on the other side, giving in section a triangle with one obtuse and two acute angles, the latter being rounded off; see fig. 6. The perforation runs longitudinally through the tablet. *Gable form.*

Fig. 6.

5. A great many of these signets have the bean-like, *lenticular* shape of the so-called "Island gems," usually with a longitudinal perforation, but sometimes, instead of that, with a groove cut all round the rim of the disc, allowing a cord or wire to be securely wrapped round the signet. *Bean form.*

A few of the conical signets also were suspended in the same way (see fig. 2), not by means of a hole drilled through them, but by a groove cut round the smaller end of the cone. Out of this form the *handled signet* was developed, class no. 7, described below.

6. Another less frequent variety seems to have developed out of the cylinder by slicing its round sides off, making it *square or polygonal* in section, and thus giving four or more surfaces for separate devices, instead of the continuous band of the cylinder.

7. *Handled signets*; a large proportion of these signets are cut into various shapes with handles worked out of the same piece of stone. The flat surface where the device is cut is of many forms, circular, oval, square, rectangular or lobed. The handles too vary greatly in shape, some being short projections, only sufficient to receive the perforation for the suspension of the seal, see fig. 7. Others have tall handles, in some cases moulded into ornamental forms at the place *Signets with handles.*

Fig. 7.

where the cord passed through the handle: see figs. 8, 9 and 10.

Fig. 8.   Fig. 9.   Fig. 10.

Chester collection.

Like the seals shown in figs. 2 to 12, the finest and most elaborate of these handled signets is among the very fine collection of "Hittite" gems, the most important in the world, formed by the Rev. Greville Chester, and now in the Ashmolean Museum at Oxford.

This is a large cubical signet cut out of a fine piece of black magnetite, with minutely engraved figures of deities on five sides of the cube. The pierced handle is elaborately moulded, in a fashion which suggests metal-work rather than hard stone. The workmanship of this remarkable signet is very delicate and skilful, a striking contrast to the usual very coarse figures on the "Hittite" seals. Though resembling in general form the handled signets of the "Hittite" class, it is most probably the work of a Phoenician gem-engraver: it was found in or near Antaradus on the coast of Phoenicia[1].

[1] It has been described and illustrated by Professor Sayce, *Arch. Journ.* Vol. XLIV. 1887, pp. 347 to 350.

The devices on the "Hittite" signets are usually extremely rude and coarsely cut, most of the sinking being done with large drills and wheels, with but little help from subsequent re-touching.

Animals, such as goats and stags, and others too coarsely drawn to be distinguished, together with very rude human figures frequently occur.

Other signets have simple geometrical patterns, formed mainly by combinations of wheel-cut straight lines, (see figs. 11 and 12) closely resembling the semé patterns which fill up

FIG. 11.

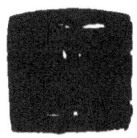
FIG. 12.

the backgrounds of early Greek pottery of the so-called "Oriental" and "Dipylon" types. Some of these signets have no more elaborate device than rows of drill-sunk holes, like the sixes on ordinary ivory dice; see figs. 5 and 10.

There is however in the Chester collection (Ashmolean Museum) one remarkable circular signet, with a rounded handle cut out of hard whitish limestone, the device on which is a much more skilful piece of work. Within a circular, hatched border is a double-headed eagle "displayed," very like the heraldic eagle of mediaeval Austria, designed with much spirit and decorative power. The same device occurs on some of the rock-cut reliefs of Asia Minor, which have been attributed to the same "Hittite" race. This double-headed eagle was adopted as his badge by the celebrated Moslem conqueror Saladin, who may possibly have taken it from some of these early reliefs. It is to be seen over one of the gates of the citadel of Cairo, which is said to have been built by Saladin, or more probably by one of his successors. It certainly was copied and introduced into Western Europe by the Crusaders of the 12th century A.D., and thus the familiar "displayed eagle" of Austria may have originated in the device used by some chief of the once powerful eastern race[1], which used these very interesting and primitive signets.

The name "Hittite."
With regard to the word "Hittite," as applied to signets and sculpture of uncertain date and origin, it should be observed that the name is a somewhat misleading one, since although monuments of the people who are so called have been found in the country of the Hittites, that is, in the district inhabited by the Canaanites of Coele-Syria, yet they are also largely found in regions with which, as far as is known, the true Hittites had no connection.

Nevertheless, the name which was given to this class of objects at their first discovery may be provisionally retained, until further researches have led to more accurate information on the subject.

PHOENICIAN GEMS.

Egypto-Phoenician scarabs.
A large number of scarabs made of pottery or steatite in the Egyptian form, but with almost meaningless copies of Egyptian designs with blundered hieroglyphic inscriptions, coarsely executed, are found in Rhodes, Cyprus and other islands of the Mediterranean; some of them apparently are as early as the 14th to the 10th century B.C. These imitations of Egyptian work were probably made by Phoenician settlers[2]. In some cases these Phoenician copies are made of *paste* or glass, and have the back simply rounded, instead of being shaped like the sacred beetle, a form which is usually called the *scarabaeoid*, from its having the general outline without the detail of the true scarab.

---

[1] I have to thank Mr A. J. Evans, keeper of the Ashmolean Museum, for ample opportunity to examine the gems at Oxford, both those in the Museum, and in his own very valuable private collection, and also for many useful suggestions on the subject.

[2] The Fitzwilliam Museum possesses a good collection of these "Island scarabs."

No. 3 in the Catalogue of the Fitzwilliam gems, from Camiros in Rhodes, is a good example of this class (see Pl. I.), and, though small in scale, it is a characteristic specimen of Phoenician art, which most commonly combines the types of Assyria and of Egypt, fusing them into one design, with very little admixture of any forms which are of purely Phoenician origin. In other cases Phoenician gems are either wholly Egyptian or wholly Assyrian in style; and even when Phoenician deities are represented, such as Baal-Melkarth or Baal-Moloch, they are usually treated to some extent after the fashion of either Egypt or Assyria.

Symbols of Egypt and Assyria.

One remarkable signet in the Ashmolean Museum at Oxford consists of a steatite scarab of Egypto-Phoenician style, set in an open bronze frame with a small ring for suspension, very much like a form of seal which was commonly used in the last century. In most cases, however, the Phoenician scarabs which, like those of Egypt, have a longitudinal perforation, were set in a swivel mount, not in a handled setting.

In later times, from the 8th to the 4th centuries B.C., a large number of scarabs and scarabaeoids of very superior workmanship were made by the Phoenicians, both for their own use and for purposes of trade. These gems, engraved in the harder stones, such as jasper, chalcedony and carnelian, are commonly found in Phoenicia itself, throughout Syria, and in the islands of the Mediterranean.

Later Phoenician scarabs.

Some of these scarabs have engraved devices of great beauty and most delicate execution, arranged and treated with that remarkable decorative skill for which the Phoenician artists were so celebrated. The finest of these, cut in chalcedony or sard, have Egyptian deities and sacred symbols arranged, not with any special meaning, but simply so as to fill up the space in the most decorative and graceful way. One or two examples in the Ashmolean Museum are among the finest which exist: they were brought from the coast of Phoenicia by Mr Greville Chester, and probably are considerably earlier in date than the scarabs from Tharros. Their minute workmanship and very high finish is as remarkable as their graceful design. Fig. 13 shows one of the

FIG. 13. Phoenician scarab of exceptionally delicate workmanship, dating probably from the 8th century B.C. The device consists of various sacred Egyptian and Assyrian symbols, arranged, without regard to meaning, simply as a decorative device. In the centre is the Egyptian god Horus seated on a lotus flower, between two winged cherubim of Assyrian style; at the top is the winged orb of the sun, the symbol of the sun-god Ra. *One and a half times the real size.*

finest of these, with devices of Egyptian and Assyrian style arranged in a very decorative way, and most delicately worked in all its details.

Tharros scarabs.

One of the finest collections, now in the British Museum (nos. 155 to 221), came from the cemetery of the Phoenician colony of Tharros in Sardinia, in most cases associated with objects which range in date from the 5th to the 3rd century B.C. It is however more than probable that in some cases the scarabs are much older than the date of the tomb in which they were buried.

These later Phoenician scarabs frequently have, in addition to the earlier designs borrowed from Egypt and Assyria, other subjects and forms of purely Greek origin; the tide of influence having turned during the days of Phoenician decadence, with the result that Phoenician art was modified by that of the Greeks; whereas some centuries earlier it was Greek art that received the influence of Phoenicia.

Scarab of Kreontidas.

No. 4 in the Fitzwilliam collection is a specially interesting example of a scarab of this later type; it was found in a Greek tomb in the island of Aegina, and is inscribed with the name of its owner Kreontidas; see below, page 67. The design on it, the sacred beetle with outspread wings, is of purely Egyptian origin and the whole character of the scarab

closely resembles some examples which are certainly of
Phoenician workmanship. It is however possible that it was *Græco-*
the work of a Greek engraver settled in the Hellenic trading *Egyptian*
city of Naukratis in the Delta of the Nile, where many objects *work.*
of Greek workmanship but of Egyptian style have been found.
Nothing is more difficult than to attain to any certainty either
as to the date or the origin of works of art of this class. As
is usually the case with the art of Oriental races, the same
hieratic forms survive for many centuries without any serious
alteration; and even technical peculiarities and details of
style remain unchanged for very long periods.

In the later class of Phoenician scarab-gems the design is *Guilloche*
very frequently surrounded by a peculiar border usually called *border.*
the "cable border," or in French the *guilloche*. This ornament evidently originated in a sort of plaited design, forming
a series of circular loops, which is one of the commonest
patterns used in the early sculpture, painting and jewellery of
Mycenae and other primitive Hellenic sites. It survived in
Greek art on painted vases, and as a sculptured decoration
for buildings, throughout the whole period of Greek autonomy.
Both as a painted and as a carved pattern it occurs very
frequently among the architectural fragments of pre-Persian
date, which have been recently discovered on the Acropolis
of Athens. In most cases, when used as a border for scarabs
or scarabaeoids, the pattern has lost its curved lines, and has
degenerated into a band with a succession of straight or
sloping cross strokes, mainly owing to the technical difficulty
of cutting a curved as compared with a straight line on a
hard stone or jewel[1].

A similar *guilloche* border occurs on the large thin di- *Borders on*
drachms of Metapontum, Sybaris and other cities of Magna *coins.*
Graecia during the 6th century B.C., those, that is, which have
an incuse design on the *reverse*.

Among the Sardinian scarabs found at Tharros and others
of that type a great many have been found in their original

[1] Owing to its frequent occurrence on the scarabs found in the tombs of
Etruria, this *guilloche* pattern was once commonly called the "Etruscan border;"
it is not however a design of Etruscan origin.

Mounted scarabs.

mounts; this is usually a simple gold swivel-ring, which allows the scarab to revolve on the wire which passes through the longitudinal perforation. In some cases the scarab itself is fixed in a gold mount or border of very delicate workmanship, which, of course, revolves with it.

In the 6th and 5th centuries B.C. and even later, signets of cylinder form, usually in magnetite, crystal, or chalcedony, were made by the Phoenicians, and engraved with figures of Assyrian style.

Later still, during the extreme decadence of Phoenician art in the 4th and 3rd centuries B.C., signet-gems of conical form, pierced for suspension through the smaller end of the cone, were commonly used.

The device engraved on the base of these cones is usually of the rudest and coarsest workmanship, a remarkable contrast to the very beautiful engraved scarabs made by the Phoenicians some centuries earlier.

Collections of scarabs.

With regard to collections of Phoenician gems, those in the British Museum and in the Ashmolean Museum have been already mentioned. A very fine collection of scarab gems from tombs in Phoenicia and Syria was made by the Duc de Luynes, and was presented by him to the Bibliothèque Nationale of Paris.

Many Phoenician gems are illustrated by Perrot and Chipiez, *History of Art in Phoenicia*, 1885 (translation), Vol. II. p. 227—260: see also Cesnola, *Cyprus*, 1877, Pl. XXXI—XLI; De Vogüé's *Mélanges d'Archéologie Orientale* has been already referred to. A good description of Oriental cylinders and cones is given by Perrot and Chipiez, *History of Art in Chaldaea and Assyria*, 1884 (translation), Vol. II., pages 251 to 280. In the main the literature of this subject is scattered through the pages of many different archaeological periodicals, chiefly published in Germany and France.

CHAPTER II.

GREEK GEMS.

AMONG the earliest signets found on Hellenic soil, though clearly not of Greek workmanship, are the massive gold rings found in the tombs of Mycenae, which have figures of Oriental or Egyptian type deeply cut on the broad gold bezel of the ring. The date of these is certainly not later than the 12th century B.C., and may possibly be earlier. As they are cut on metal, not on hard stones, they do not (strictly speaking) come under the class of gems. In style they are very different from the gems which were found with them, and it is most probable that these gold signets were not the productions of native artists, but were Oriental imports. They are remarkable for the great size of the gold bezel, and for the complicated and pictorial character of their devices, very unlike the simplicity of early Greek gems. *Gold signets.*

On one is cut a hunting scene of very Assyrian character; two men in a two-horse chariot pursue a stag, at which one of the hunters is aiming an arrow. Another of these rings has a battle scene, in which the figures resemble those on the elaborate bronze daggers inlaid with gold from the same tombs within the Acropolis of Mycenae. A third is quite different in style, being more like mediaeval or modern Hindoo work than the production of any classical country. The subject is this—a female deity in Oriental costume is seated under a tree; two women and a girl present flowers to her. The field is filled up with various scattered devices. The whole is bad in drawing, and weak and spiritless in design—very *Rings from Mycenae.*

unlike the vigour of the figures of Assyrian style on other works of art from Mycenae.

Though sunk on a gold bezel, the design is sharply cut with gem-engravers' tools, exactly as if the work had been on a hard stone, instead of on soft, unalloyed gold.

Mycenae gems.

In addition to these gold signets, a considerable number of engraved gems were found at Mycenae. These were of the class described in the following section, namely, gems of *lenticular* form, cut on various hard stones and crystal.

Recent discoveries in Egypt have shown that pottery of exactly similar type to that found at Mycenae was imported into Egypt about 1400 B.C.; this is a valuable piece of evidence with regard to the probable date of the gems and other objects found in the Acropolis of Mycenae.

"ISLAND GEMS:" examples of the earliest class of engraved gems of Greek workmanship have been found in great numbers, within recent years, on many early Hellenic sites, and more especially in the islands of the Aegean Sea, hence their usual designation of "Island gems." Their chief peculiarity is that they are engraved on rounded pebble-like stones, mostly shaped like a circular bean (*lenticula*), and hence called "lenticular gems;" less frequently they are of oblong form, like a bluntly pointed oval. Stones of this form are usually called "glandular gems" from their resemblance to the ordinary lead sling-bullets (*glandes*). These two forms appear to be referred to by Pliny (*Hist. Nat.* XXXVII., 196) when writing of the favourite shapes for gems, engraved or plain, "Figura *oblonga* maxime probatur, deinde quae vocatur *lenticula*." Nos. 1 and 2 in the Fitzwilliam catalogue are examples of the *glandular* form, with characteristic animal devices; see also fig. 14 from a glandular gem in the British Museum. They are always pierced with a hole drilled longitudinally through them, but in many cases they are too large to be set in swivel-rings, like the scarabs, and were probably worn by a string round the neck.

Forms of Island gems.

Plate I.

Pebble gems.

These shapes seem often to have come naturally from the form of the nodule of chalcedony or the water-worn pebble, which was polished, and had the signet device engraved on it, with very little cutting away of its natural surface. This is suggested by a common Greek word used for engraved gems, ψῆφος or δακτυλική ψῆφος.

FIG. 14. Characteristic example of an early glandular gem, representing the long-horned goat or ibex, which inhabited the mountains of Crete and other islands, cut in steatite. The use of the drill is evident in forming the border, and the hair and horns of the animal, which appears to be dead or wounded; *real size*.

Gems of this type[1] must have been common during the Homeric period; and Pliny (*Hist. Nat.* XXXIII. 12) is wrong in arguing that, because Homer does not mention the use of signets, therefore they were unknown among the Greeks of the Homeric age.

The devices cut on these early Greek gems consist chiefly of animals, such as lions, goats, deer, bulls, eagles, dolphins and others, very frequently arranged in a sort of heraldic way—two similar animals being set face to face or back to back, forming a stiffly conventional design like the beasts

Earliest Greek devices.

FIG. 15. Characteristic example of a lenticular gem of heraldic type, cut in rock crystal, with two goats on their hind legs, very skilfully designed so as to occupy fully the whole area of the gem; Brit. Mus. No. 57; *real size*.

sculptured over the "Lion gate" of Mycenae (see fig. 15 and fig. 23 at page 108). Somewhat similar animals of heraldic character occur very commonly on the round shields of

[1] See Milchhöfer, *Die Anfänge der Kunst in Griechenland*, 1883, pp. 78—90.

warriors on Greek painted vases of the 6th and 5th centuries B.C.

Oriental style.

These "Island gems" are obviously of various dates, from the Bronze Age of Mycenae and Tiryns down to the 7th or 6th century B.C; they are most commonly cut in steatite, but harder stones are also used. In style they are usually rude and coarsely worked, showing little artistic refinement, but their designs are frequently very decorative and well arranged to suit the shape of the gem. In many cases a very distinct Assyrian influence appears, some of the lenticular gems having figures which are rude copies of those on the cylinders of Babylon and Assyria, probably owing to the trade and artistic influence of the Phoenicians. The earlier examples of the *lenticular* and *glandular* gems seem, like the pottery of Mycenaean type, to have been produced not only in the Greek islands, but also all along the extensive coast-line of Hellenic territory, where a certain unity of artistic design seems to have prevailed in spite of the wide extent and scattered position of the different portions of these maritime colonies and settlements.

Spartan basalt.

One of the finest lenticular gems of this class, in the collection of Mr A. J. Evans, at Oxford, is remarkable from being cut out of the fine green feldspar or basalt from Mt Taygetus in Laconia, which was so largely used for decorative purposes by the Romans of the Empire—the *marmor Lacedaemonium* of Pliny, *Hist. Nat.* XXXVI. 55.

The device on this remarkable signet, which, judging from its material, was probably cut in the Peloponnese, is a bull, and, behind it, that curious monster resembling a sea-horse which frequently occurs on works of art of this early type. The exceptional material in which this gem is cut is strong evidence in favour of its being the work of a Laconian artist, as it is very improbable that a piece of basalt from Taygetus would have been exported for use at any far-away place. The British Museum possesses three or four gems of similar style cut in the same stone.

A large number of fine gems of the early lenticular class, probably of local fabrique, have recently been discovered in a bee-hive tomb of the Mycenae type at Baphion, near Sparta: they are identical in design and technique with those found in the Greek islands, at Mycenae and elsewhere on Hellenic soil: see Ἐφημ. Ἀρχαι. 1888—9, Pl. 10, p. 175; and 1889—90, Pl. 10, p. 163.

Baphion gems.

The commonest material used for the "Island gems" is steatite (soapstone), but some of them are engraved on much harder stones, such as rock crystal, carnelian and chalcedony. The fine lenticular gem, for example, which is shown in fig. 15, is cut out of rock crystal of very good quality, and that shown in fig. 23 is of carnelian; see *Brit. Mus. Cat. of Gems*, Nos. 57 and 106. It evidently was not, as was the case with the Hittites, on account of defective technical skill that the softer steatite was so often selected by the earliest Greek gem-cutters. The very bold and spirited character of many of the designs which are cut on very hard materials shows a complete command of the most effective tools, such as the engraver's wheel and drill—instruments which in skilful and patient hands will work even more refractory stones than rock crystal or carnelian.

Materials of early gems.

LATER GREEK GEMS.

In the 6th and 5th centuries B.C. Greek gems were usually cut in the scarab or scarabaeoid form, partly, no doubt, on account of the commercial intercourse with Egypt, which was fostered by the Greek settlement at Naukratis in the Delta, a town which appears to have been at the height of its prosperity during the 6th century B.C.

Greek scarabs.

A large number of the existing gems of this time, mostly in the form of scarabs, have been found in the tombs of Etruria, whither they must have been exported in large number, by Greek and Phoenician traders.

It is noticeable that scarabs were used by the Greeks, not only for signets, but as personal ornaments. Antiphanes, an Athenian dramatist of the 4th century B.C., in his *Boeotia* (quoted by Athenaeus, *Deipn.* XI., 48 ad fin.) mentions the κάνθαρος or scarabaeus beetle as a woman's ornament—Ὅτι

Scarabs as ornaments.

δὲ καὶ γυναικεῖον κοσμάριόν ἐστι κάνθαρος, Ἀντιφάνης εἴρηκεν ἐν Βοιωτίᾳ—but no indication is given of the material of which the scarab was made.

Statuette with scarab.

That the scarabaeus was an ornament worn also by men is shown by a fragmentary statuette in marble about ten inches high, from Cyrene, now in the British Museum.

It is a draped male figure of the Asklepios type; round the neck is a cord or necklace from which hangs a pendent in the form of the sacred beetle, with long outspread legs.

The importance of the signet-gems of this period, as a means of securing property and giving authenticity to documents, is borne witness to by Diogenes Laertius (I. 57) who states that one of Solon's Athenian laws (about 600 B.C.) forbade gem-engravers (δακτυλιογλυφοὶ) to keep an impression of any gem they had sold, for fear of another being made exactly like it.

Law of Solon.

Cf. page 34.

Among the Greeks it appears to have been the custom for men to send impressions of their signets to give authenticity to messages, or as pledges for a bargain. The former use is mentioned by Sophocles (*Trachin.* 614),

Καὶ τῶνδ' ἀποίσεις σῆμ', ὃ κεῖνος εὐμαθὲς
Σφραγῖδος ἕρκει τῷδ' ἐπὸν μαθήσεται[1].

Compare also Euripides, *Iph. Aul.* 155.

Seals as pledges.

Plautus, in his *Pseudolus*, mentions how the Macedonian soldier Harpax, when buying a slave-girl, deposited with the first instalment of money an impression of his signet (symbolum), as a pledge for the completion of the bargain. And again when he forwarded the rest of the money he sent a letter with another seal from his signet to testify that he was concluding the transaction; see *Pseud.* II. ii. 53 and IV. ii. 44.

Among the later Greeks and also among the Romans it was not unusual for the writer of a letter to state at the end of it what device it was sealed with, as a security against the letter being opened and re-sealed.

---

[1] On this use of the word σῆμα for a signet device see the inscription on a scarab given at page 67.

An example of this is quoted in the Appendix, *Catalogue of Fitzwilliam Gems*, no. 2 p. iii.

In one of the letters to the Emperor Trajan written from Nicomedeia by Pliny the younger while he was Propraetor of the province of Pontica, 103 to 104 A.D., we have another instance of this precaution. *Letter to Trajan.*

Pliny states that he delays sending to Rome a certain prisoner named Callidromus in the hope that a gem may be found which, the prisoner asserted, had been stolen from him.

The gem was engraved with a portrait in royal robes of its former owner, Pacorus, king of Parthia, whose slave Callidromus had been.

Pliny concludes by saying that he sends with the letter a nugget of ore, said to have come from a mine in Parthia, and that the packet is sealed with his own signet, the device on which was a quadriga : see Pliny, *Epis.* X., 74 (16). *Own signet.*

The *talismanic rings*, with devices of magical curative or protective power, which the Romans were so fond of, were not so largely used among the less superstitious Greeks; but such things were not unknown. Aristophanes (*Plut.* 883) alludes to signets which were a safeguard against poisonous reptiles, when he mentions the *Just man's* ring, which would protect him against the venom of the public informer— *Talismanic signets.*

Δικαῖος. Οὐδὶν προτιμῶ σου· φορῶ γὰρ πριάμενος
       Τὸν δακτύλιον τονδὶ παρ' Εὐδάμου δραχμῆς.

Again in a fragment of a play by Antiphanes (quoted by Athenaeus, *Deipn.* III. 96 (123)) the miser says

            Ἐὰν δ' ἄρα
Στρέφῃ με περὶ τὴν γαστέρ', ἢ τὸν ὀμφαλόν,
Παρὰ Φερτάτου δακτύλιός ἐστί μοι δραχμῆς.

These rings, which only cost a drachma, must have been set with *paste*, not real gems.

Many Greek signet-gems bear the badge (ἐπίσημον) of the owner, a sort of heraldic charge which was used to distinguish between various individuals of the same name. Thus we find on the celebrated inscribed bronze plates from *Personal badges.*

Heraklaea in Magna Graecia (*Tabulae Heraclaeenses*) each magistrate's name is followed by the name of his distinguishing badge, such as a dolphin, an ear of wheat, a bunch of grapes or the like.

Badges on Greek coins.

On Greek coins, from the 4th century B.C. downwards, magistrates' names are very frequently indicated by the addition of their ἐπίσημα to the usual device either on the *obverse* or *reverse* of the coin.

It is probable that in some cases the name of the artist who engraved the coin-die is represented by a symbol of this kind, instead of by an inscription or monogram, but no example of this can (as yet) be pointed out with any certainty. Great skill and taste are frequently shown by the way in which the badge of the individual is combined and blended with the main design on the coin.

Roman denarii.

So on the early Roman denarii of the third century B.C., before the actual name or monogram of the Mint official was used, the identity of the magistrate was indicated by some object which he used as his device, placed in the field of the *reverse* by the side of the usual figures of the Dioscuri on horseback.

Greek vases.

Greek vases, especially those of the 6th and 5th centuries B.C., have countless examples of warriors bearing on large round shields their personal heraldic badge; cf. Aeschylus, *Sept. con. Theb.* 384, and 427.

Some very beautiful and exquisitely minute examples of these heraldic shield-devices are to be seen on that wonderful little vase from Thebes, which was given to the British Museum by the late Malcolm Macmillan. The principal band on the vase has a row of fighting warriors, each bearing a device on his circular buckler. See *Jour. Hell. Stud.* Vol. XI., 1890, Plate I. and p. 167.

Subjects on gems.

The subjects on Greek gems of the 6th to the 4th century B.C., are very largely scenes from poems of the Homeric cycle, and the achievements of divine heroes, such as Herakles, Theseus and Perseus, and also athletes in various postures. Dionysiac subjects also frequently occur—Satyrs, Fauns, Maenads and the god Dionysos himself. Heads or busts on gems appear to have been rare till about the end of the 5th century B.C.

Fig. 16 shows one of the finest known gems of archaic

FIG. 16. Greek scarab of the 6th century B.C. of the finest archaic style, representing a satyr dancing with a wine-cup in his hand; skilfully designed so as to fill the whole field; *one and a half times the real size*.

style, dating from about the middle of the 6th century B.C. This is a large scarab of *striped chalcedony* in the British Museum, No. 289, representing a bearded Satyr dancing, with a wine-cup in his hand, within a "cable" border. The figure is bent to bring it within the oval field of the scarab: at his feet is a large amphora. The design of this gem is a good example of the pains taken by the Greek engravers to occupy very fully the whole field. The workmanship, in spite of its archaic stiffness, is very spirited and sharp in treatment. The use of a large drill for the body of the amphora, and of minute drills for the hair is plainly visible. The tail of the Satyr is put in with delicate strokes of the diamond point[1].

Archaic Satyr.

Plate I. no. 5 (described in the appendix) illustrates a fine scarabaeoid in the Fitzwilliam collection, cut in rock crystal, with a figure of a nude hero fitting on his greaves, dating about 500 B.C.

Crystal scarabaeoid.

One of the finest gems which has ever been discovered, dating from about 460 B.C., is now in a private collection in Scotland; see fig. 17. The design is a nude figure of

---

[1] This Satyr has previously been published as a recumbent figure, but there can be no doubt that Mr A. H. Smith (in his *Catalogue of the British Museum Gems*, No. 289, page 63 and Pl. E.) has given it rightly in an upright position.

Scarab of finest style.

a youth with a bow; he holds in his right hand an arrow, and tries the sharpness of its point with the other

FIG. 17. Greek scarab-gem of the best period of art, and of the finest workmanship: *one and a half times the real size.*

hand. He wears long hair, tied up behind his head like the marble statues of athletes, which have recently been found on the Athenian Acropolis among the débris caused by the Persian sack of Athens. The general design of the figure and the modelling of the nude flesh are magnificent in style, combining truth to nature with nobility of treatment in a way that could hardly be surpassed even in work on a much larger scale. As an example of largeness of style combined with extreme minuteness and accuracy of detail, nothing could surpass this wonderful scarab.

Style of work.

In both the last-mentioned gems the relief, as is usual in work of this period, is rather shallow, but treated in the most skilful way, with admirable spirit and delicacy of touch. This shallowness or, more correctly, flatness of relief (French *méplat*) is one of the characteristics of early Greek intaglio and relief work of the best period. The figure is not treated like a statue sawn in half and then applied to a background, but, like the best Florentine reliefs of the 15th century, is modelled with a peculiar delicacy of surface, and more relief than actually exists is, as it were, suggested. In some cases

Shallow sinking.

the edges of the design are, what is called "stilted," that is to say the intaglio or relief outline is bounded by a flat rim at right angles to the ground, as if the whole figure had been slightly pushed out from behind, so that the depth of sinking at the outline is nearly as deep as in the central part of the figure.

This delicacy of treatment is to be observed in gem no. 10, as well as in no. 5 of the Fitzwilliam Catalogue.

Plate I.

Gems of the 5th century B.C., the finest period of Greek art, are very scarce in comparison with those both of earlier and later times. Work as fine as that on the most beautiful Greek coins is extremely rare on gems of contemporary workmanship.

Gem of 5th century.

In the British Museum collection which, though not the largest, is on the whole the finest in the world, from its widely representative character, the number of gems of this period is comparatively small. Among the most notable are these— no. 464, a very beautiful and noble bearded head of Zeus[1], cut on a scarab of *green jasper* within a 'cable' border — a work of the finest style with a slight trace of archaic stiffness or rather dignity. No. 555, cut on the section of a *sard* cylinder, has a seated figure of a man draped below the waist, playing on a lyre of triangular shape.

Head of Zeus.

Musician.

The general design and motive of this gem are very beautiful, but the nude part of the figure is badly modelled and the general proportions defective.

A more skilfully drawn design is on a fragment of a very brilliant *sard* (No. 556), with a female draped figure seated in a chair reading from a scroll, possibly a representation of the poetess Sappho. In front of her, on a pedestal is a lyre: the word ΕΡΩϹ is lightly scratched on the pedestal. The lower part of the gem is missing. This is a work of extraordinary grace and refinement of detail; it appears not to be later than about 400 B.C.; the very faintly scratched inscription must be a later addition, judging from the rounded forms of the Є and the Ϲ (Σ) and its slight, careless execution.[2]

Sappho reading.

Another gem of very great beauty, which seems to date from the middle or latter part of the 5th century B.C., is

---

[1] This gem is illustrated in fig. 25 at page 112.

[2] Several gems with copies or *replicas* of this design exist, but none are as apparently authentic and fine in execution as that in the British Museum.

A painted vase of the fifth century, found in Athens, has a picture of Sappho reading one of her own poems from a scroll, very similar in design to the gem.

Lion and stag.

a scarabaeoid of *rock crystal* (No. 125), with a lion devouring a stag, within a 'cable' border; a work of remarkable delicacy of execution : see fig. 18 on page 30.

No. 557, a fragmentary gem cut in *chalcedony*, has a figure of a wounded centaur, which, as Mr A. S. Murray has pointed out, is of special interest from its resemblance to the centaurs on the *metopes* of the Parthenon, and probably dates from about the same time.

On all these very beautiful gems the use of the diamond-point rather than the drill is clearly visible; see page 111.

Age of Pheidias.

Among the few gems which can be attributed to the age of Pheidias and his pupils some are slight and even almost rude in execution.

Careful work by a really skilful artist on a gem of this time is rarely to be seen, but when it does occur it is an object of very great delicacy and dignified beauty.

Plate I.

The Fitzwilliam collection possesses a very noble example of this class (No. 10), which is of special interest from its design being similar to that of some of the finest Athenian

Attic stelae.

sepulchral *stelae*, of which so many (though in most cases of rather later date) have been found in the cemetery outside the Dipylon Gate in the outer Cerameicus. The subject on this gem, a large scarabaeoid of clouded chalcedony, is a nude figure of a youth, leaning on his staff and caressing his dog—the dog and horse, man's most faithful animal companions, being of frequent occurrence on the sepulchral reliefs of the 5th and 4th centuries B.C. In style this gem is of the noblest type, with a slight trace of archaic flatness of execution, but with the most skilful modelling of the nude form, and remarkable grace in the whole design and pose of the figure.

Sepulchral subject; Plate I.

Another gem in the Fitzwilliam collection (see No. 11) of rather later date, with the signature of its engraver, *Dexamenos*, is also engraved with a subject which occurs very often on the Athenian sepulchral *stelae*, namely, a lady seated, with an attendant girl assisting to complete her mistress' toilet, very like the beautiful sepulchral relief of Hegeso from the Dipylon cemetery. This very important gem is described in the Catalogue below, where other examples of gems signed by the same artist are mentioned; see page viii.

Some of the most beautiful gems of this period, 5th and 4th century B.C., were produced by the engravers of Sicily and Magna Graecia, where it appears to have been common for the same artist to be an engraver of gems and also of coin-dies. In style many of the finest coins of these districts show clearly the touch and minute execution of detail which come naturally to a man who is accustomed to work in a harder material than either bronze or iron: as, for example, that wonderful tetradrachm of Syracuse with, on the *reverse*, a quadriga and above it a flying Victory holding a small tablet or *pinax*, on which is engraved in microscopic letters the artist's name, Euainetos, ΕΥΑΙΝΕΤΟ.

Engravers of coins and gems.

Signed coins.

The same gem-like treatment is visible on the obverse of another Syracusan tetradrachm with an almost full face of Athene, on whose helmet is cut, in the most inconspicuous way, the signature Eucleidas, ΕΥΚΛΕΙΔΑΣ.

Gem like coins.

One of the peculiarities of this most beautiful class of coins is the frequency with which they bear the name of their artist: see the list given by B. V. Head, *Historia Numorum*, 1887, p. 785; and also a valuable monograph by A. J. Evans, "*Horsemen*" *of Tarentum*, 1889. A more recent paper by Mr Evans is mentioned below, see page 90. A good monograph on the signed coins of Sicily is that by Rudolf Weil, *Die Kunstlerinschriften der Sicilischen Munzen*, Berlin, 1884. The subject of signatures on gems and coins is further discussed in Chapter VII.

A good many fine gems exist which reproduce various coin-types of Magna Graecia and Sicily, as, for example, the already mentioned gem, No. 125, in the British Museum, with a lion devouring a stag; see fig. 18. This design occurs on silver didrachms of Velia, in Lucania, with the signature (more or less contracted) of the die-engraver ΦΙΛΙΣΤΙΩΝ or, with ΕΡΓΟΝ understood, ΦΙΛΙΣΤΙΟΝΟΣ. No. 356 in the same collection, with Heracles and the Nemean lion, reproduces a coin-reverse of Heraklaea, also in Lucania; and No. 443 has the man-headed bull crowned by a Victory,

Coin types on gems.

which occurs on the well-known didrachms of Neapolis (the modern Naples). The same connection between gems and

FIG. 18. Very fine work of the 5th century B.C.: one and a half times the real size. Cf. the description of gem No. 7 in the *Fitzwilliam Catalogue*.

Copies of coins.

coins is illustrated by a paste cameo in the British Museum, No. 646, which, as Mr A. H. Smith points out in his catalogue, p. 97, is moulded from a tetradrachm of Syracuse with the front face of Athene; see *Brit. Mus. Cat. of Coins of Syracuse*, No. 199: this is the coin mentioned above as having the signature of the die-engraver Eukleidas.

Gems objects of luxury.

The usual superiority of the coins, as compared with the gems of Greece proper, during the best period of Greek art, may possibly be due to the fact that the coins were intended for public use, while the gems were objects of private luxury. So in the case of architecture, painting and sculpture, we find that all the chief efforts of the greatest artists were devoted, during the great period of Athenian supremacy, to the service of the State, not of private individuals.

In Magna Graecia and Sicily, on the other hand, personal pomp and luxury were developed at an earlier time; and this may explain the frequently superior quality of the gems of those countries.

Coins of Sicily.

It should also be observed that the art-development of the Sicilian and Italian colonies was many years in advance of that in the mother country. The magnificent Syracusan decadrachms of Kimon and Euainetos, executed several years before the close of the 5th century B.C., are in style quite as advanced as the work of the artists of Attica fully half a century later.

The soft beauty and richly decorative treatment of the noble heads of Persephone and Arethusa on the *obverses* of these coins, and the almost realistic treatment of the victorious quadriga on the *reverse*, do not at all accord with the usual notions of Greek art before 400 B.C.

A very magnificent kind of signet was also much used in Magna Graecia during the 4th century B.C. a massive ring with a large flat bezel, all of gold, engraved like a gem with designs of great beauty.

Gold signets.

A splendid example in the British Museum has, engraved in the gold, a copy of the quadriga on the silver decadrachms of Syracuse. Examples of these gold signets signed with the artist's name are mentioned below, see page 73.

The gem-room of the British Museum also contains two extremely beautiful engraved signet-rings of gold, from tombs in Magna Graecia (Castellani Collection).

One of these has a bezel of pointed oval form, on which is cut a very beautiful female head of about 400 B.C. Another has a figure of a youth on horseback, riding at full speed, a marvel of spirited design and minute workmanship, cut with as much sharpness of touch as if the material had been a hard stone instead of soft, pure gold.

Engraving on gold.

According to Pliny *Hist. Nat.* XXXII. 23 the use of signet-rings made wholly of gold originated in Samothrace. He says that they were not uncommon among the Romans of his own time, but his statement that they were first used in the reign of Claudius is obviously incorrect. In fact rings wholly of gold are among the earliest known examples of signets; as, for example, the ring of "Cheops (Chufu)," who built the great pyramid, dating about 3730 B.C., and those found in the tombs of Mycenae, described at page 17.

Gold signet of Cheops.

The lists cut every five years on marble *stelae*, as inventories of the sacred treasure of Athene, which was preserved in the Parthenon at Athens, give some interesting examples of gifts of gems, rings and other jewellery about the time of the Peloponnesian war.

Parthenon treasure.

The wife of an Athenian called Kimon and a lady named Dexilla dedicated many articles of jewellery; among them

Votive gifts.

were various gold and plated rings set with *onyx, jasper* and coloured *paste*. The inscription runs thus—Ἐγ κιβωτίῳ ποικίλῳ, ὃ Κλειτὼ ᾽Αριστο...ίου, Κίμωνος γυνὴ ἀνέθηκεν... [σφρ]αγὶς χρυσοῦν δακτύλιον ἔχουσα· Δέξιλλα ἀνέθηκεν... σφραγῖδε ὑα[λίνα ποι]κίλα...ὄνυξ σφραγὶς χρυσοῦν δακτύλιον ἔχων, σφραγὶς ἴασπις χρυσοῦν δακτύλιον ἔχουσα, σφραγὶς ἴασπις περικεχρυσωμένη, σφραγὶς ὑαλίνη περ[ικεχρυσ]ωμένη χρυσοῦν δακτύλ[ιον ἔχου]σα, σφραγῖδες δύο ἀργυ[ροῦς δακτυλ]- ίους ἔχουσαι, σφραγῖδες ὑάλιναι ⌐||, σφραγὶς περίχρυσος, κ.τ.λ.[1] "In a many-coloured (enamelled?) casket, Kleito the daughter of Aristo..., the wife of Kimon dedicated (the following)...A seal-ring of gold,...Dexilla dedicated...two signets with paste gems of various colours [probably imitations of onyx], an engraved onyx set in a gold ring, an engraved jasper in a gold ring, an engraved jasper set in gold [or set in metal plated with gold], an engraved gem made of paste set in gold and mounted in a gold ring, two signets in silver rings [probably the device was cut on a silver bezel], seven engraved gems of paste, a signet plated with gold, &c."

Gems and rings.

In similar lists of other years the following gems and rings occur—ὄνυξ μέγας τραγελάφου πριαπίζοντος, σταθμὸν ΔΔΔ⊢⊢, "a large onyx engraved with an ithyphallic antelope, weighing 32 drachms," its great weight suggests that it was possibly an oriental cylinder; δακτύλιοι σιδηροῖ ⌐|||, "eight iron rings;" σφραγῖδες λίθιναι χρυσοῦς δακτυλίους ἔχουσαι ⌐||, ἄνευ δακτυλίων ⌐, "seven signets of stone in gold rings, five without rings;" χρυσῷ σφραγῖδε ||, "two gold signets," meaning rings in which both hoop and bezel were of gold. In the Parthenon inventories the word σφραγὶς is used for an *engraved* gem, the plain jewel being called λίθος[2], or else mentioned simply as "a jasper," "an onyx."

Votive gem.

In the Greek *Anthologia* (v. 205) we read of the Sorceress Nico's gem being dedicated in the temple of Aphrodite. It is described as an amethyst (ἐξ ἀμεθύστου γλυπτή) strung on a cord made of purple wool, and set in a golden stand. The

---

[1] See Böckh, *Die Staatshaushaltung der Athener*, Berlin, 1851, Vol. II. p. 263.

[2] In Greek of the best literary period the feminine ἡ λίθος seems frequently a poetic form : in later times it was more uniformly used to denote a *precious* stone.

device on it was the magic wheel, ἴυγξ[1]. It was probably a large scarabaeoid or perhaps even an Oriental engraved cylinder.

In later times, from the reign of Alexander downwards, large collections of engraved gems (δακτυλιοθῆκαι) were made by wealthy Greeks, such as Attalus II. King of Pergamus, 159—138 B.C., and enormous prices were sometimes paid for the work of a celebrated engraver. *Collection of gems*

The wearing of costly gems seems to have been very common in certain Hellenic districts. Aelian (*Var. Hist.* XII. c. 30) tells us that in the Greek colony of Cyrene in Northern Africa, even the poorest person wore a gem of the value of 10 minae (about £40 to £50) and that "the gem-engravers there were a marvel," though whether for their number or their skill he does not explain. *Gems in Cyrene.*

The writer of the Apocryphal *Book of Ecclesiasticus* (xxxviii. 27) who was probably a Jew of Palestine, mentions, among the craftsmen without whom "cannot a city be inhabited," the makers of signets—"they that cut and grave seals, and are diligent to make great variety," an interesting testimony to the importance of this branch of art[2].

In some cases large numbers of rings were worn by ladies of rank. For example when the tomb of a Queen of the Chersonesus, at Nicopol in the Crimea, was opened, no less than ten rings were found upon the fingers of the skeleton— all of them fine Greek work of the 4th century B.C.; see *Comp. Rend. Comm. Arch.* 1864, p. 182, and Pl. V. *Rings from Nicopol.*

The recumbent figure on an Etruscan terra-cotta sarcophagus in the Louvre has four rings on one hand, two of them with very small hoops only reaching to the first joint of

---

[1] One form of the ἴυγξ was a wheel on which a bird of the wryneck tribe was fastened. If spun in one direction it inspired love, but revolved in the other direction it caused hatred to be developed in the heart of the victim of the magical spell; Pindar, *Pyth.* IV. 381 and Pliny, *H. N.* XI. 47, 107. The phrase ἕλκειν ἴυγγα ἐπί τινι meant "to set the wheel in motion in order to produce the magical effect upon some one"; see Xenoph. *Mem.* III. 11, 17.

[2] The high estimation of Greek gems during the later period of art is borne witness to by the number of epigrams on engraved gems which occur among the collection of poems in the Greek *Anthologia*.

the fingers. This explains the very small size of some ancient rings both of Greek and Roman workmanship.

With regard to the names used for the various parts of a signet-ring, it may be noted that, owing to the manner in which the gold wire of a swivel ring frequently encloses and frames its scarab, the name σφενδόνη, Latin *funda*, was given to that part of the ring which borders the gem, on account of its resemblance to the stone in a sling: see Eur. *Hippol.* 876, and Pliny, *Hist. Nat.* XXXVII. 116 and 126.

Funda.

The gem itself is ψῆφος, δακτυλικὴ ψῆφος, σφραγὶς or ἡ λίθος; in Latin, *gemma*. In modern English the part of the ring which bears the device, whether on metal or on a stone, is called the *bezel:* the rest of the ring being the *hoop*, and its thickened part near the bezel the *shoulders*.

Bezel.

In French the *chaton* is the whole bezel, while the word *collet* is popularly, but not technically, used for the *funda* or metal border which frames the gem.

Chaton.

With regard to the Greek use of signets, Professor Jebb has kindly pointed out to me and explained the following interesting passage in Isocrates, *Or.* XVII. § 33, 34, where two different classes of sealing appear to be referred to.

The Voting-urns (ὑδρίαι), containing the names of the Athenians who were eligible for the office of Judge in the dramatic contests at the city Dionysia, were placed under the charge of the ταμίαι τῶν ἱερῶν χρημάτων or Temple-wardens for safe keeping on the Acropolis of Athens, most probably in the treasure-chamber of the Parthenon.

Voting-urns sealed.

For the sake of security each urn was sealed both by the Prytanes and by the Choregi—σεσημασμέναι μὲν ἦσαν ὑπὸ τῶν πρυτάνεων, κατεσφραγισμέναι δ' ὑπὸ τῶν χορηγῶν, meaning, Professor Jebb suggests, that the urns were not only sealed up by the Prytanes, perhaps with a sort of corporate or common seal, but were also *countersealed* by each of the Choregi with his own private signet (σφραγίς).

Counter-seal.

In a similar way, during mediaeval times, it was usual for an official, such as a bishop or an abbot, to sign important documents with his great seal of office and also with his *secretum* or personal signet.

CHAPTER III.

LATER GREEK GEMS AND ETRUSCAN SCARABS.

THOUGH the Greeks highly appreciated the beauty of engraved gems, and, at least from the time of Alexander, gave large prices for the works of celebrated engravers, yet it was among the Romans of the Imperial period that the passion for collecting ancient gems, like that of buying other costly works of art, rose to the highest pitch of extravagance.

Collectors of gems

Many of the wealthy Romans formed cabinets of engraved gems, containing examples both of antique and contemporary workmanship, but in either case the gems which were thought worthy of the *dactyliotheca* were probably the work of Greek not Roman artists.

Pliny (*Hist. Nat.* XXXVII. 4) mentions the dedication by the Emperor Augustus in the Temple of Concord in the Roman Forum of a gold horn containing a sardonyx, popularly supposed to be the original gem which Polycrates Tyrant of Samos, in vain threw into the sea to appease his Nemesis: older records however tell us that this celebrated stone, engraved by Theodorus of Samos, was an emerald; see Herod. III. 39 seq.[1]

Ring of Polycrates.

Moreover the gem of Theodorus was engraved with a device, which according to Clemens Alexandrinus was a lyre —the ring being the royal signet of Polycrates and therefore necessarily having an engraved device; while Pliny tells us (*H. N.* XXXVII. 8) that the sardonyx of Augustus was plain— "intacta inlibataque est." The Temple of Concord contained

[1] See below, page 69, for a further account of the gem-engraver Theodorus.

3—2

an important collection of gems, among which the so-called "ring of Polycrates" made, Pliny tells us, but a poor figure.

Gems of Scaurus.

The earliest gem collector, Pliny says (*Hist. Nat.* XXXVII. 11), was M. Aemilius Scaurus, the stepson of Sulla; a man of enormous wealth, whose temporary theatre, built during his aedileship in 58 B.C., was one of the costliest and largest buildings in Rome[1].

Gems of Pompey.

The next collection of Greek gems in Rome was that which had belonged to Mithradates, and was dedicated in the Temple of Capitoline Jupiter by Pompey the Great, whose victory and its consequent spoils created, Pliny says, the taste for gem-collecting in Rome (*Hist. Nat.* XXXVII. 12)[2].

Caesar's gems.

Pliny mentions that Julius Caesar gave a collection of ring gems (*dactyliotheca*) to the Temple of Venus Genitrix, which he built in the centre of his new Forum Julium. Suetonius also tells us (*J. Caes.* 47) that Julius Caesar was always ready to give high prices for gems which were the work of any of the famous old Greek engravers.

Gems in the Temple of Apollo.

Marcellus, the favourite nephew of Augustus, dedicated another collection of gems in the Temple of Apollo on the Palatine Hill—the most magnificent of the many public buildings with which Augustus enriched the city of Rome; see Pliny, *Hist. Nat.* XXXVII. 11.

Seals used as locks.

It was not, however, till comparatively late times that engraved gems were regarded as objects to place in a collection of works of art or even to set in jewellery as personal ornaments. Their real use was for long the purely practical one, that of signets, either to give authority to a document, or else, instead of a lock, to secure doors, box-lids and the like, so that they could not be opened without the knowledge of the owner who had affixed his seal; see page 34.

Aristophanes (*Thesmo.* 424—428) has an amusing passage referring to the custom of securing doors with a seal—

[1] The splendours of the Theatre of Scaurus are described by Pliny in many different passages; see *Hist. Nat.* XXXIV. 36, XXXVI. 50, 113 and 189.

[2] In the same way, according to Pliny (*loc. cit.*) the rage for pictures was the result of the capture of Corinth by L. Mummius (146 B.C.), and the taste for other luxuries, such as embossed silver plate, cloth of gold and bronze couches, was brought about by the conquests of L. Scipio and Cn. Manlius.

Πρὸτοῦ μὲν οὖν ἦν ἀλλ' ὑποῖξαι τὴν θύραν, *Aristoph.*
ποιησαμέναισι δακτύλιον τριωβόλου· *Thesmo.*
νῦν δ' οὗτος αὐτοὺς ᾠκότριψ Εὐριπίδης 424 428.
ἐδίδαξε θριπήδεστ' ἔχειν σφραγίδια
ἐξαψαμένους·

The θριπήδεστα σφραγίδια appear to have been worm-eaten bits of wood used as rude seals, because no two would be exactly alike and the pattern made by the worms was too complicated to allow of imitation. *Wood seals.*

An analogous contrivance was adopted by some of the early Ottoman Sultans of Turkey, who both signed and sealed their edicts by the single act of pressing the inked palm of the hand on the document, so that the lines of the skin printed off on the parchment or paper, forming a device which no forger could possibly copy. The elaborate device on modern Turkish coins is derived from the old hand-printed signature of the mediaeval Sultans, though it has since been partly modified into a sort of complicated monogram of the Sultan's name. *Hand sealing.*

Votive offerings dedicated in temples were in some cases sealed with an impression of a signet in clay. During Mr Flinders Petrie's recent excavations in Upper Egypt examples of this were discovered; as, e.g. a bronze votive adze tied round with thread, the knot of which was sealed with a clay impression of a scarab. *Sealed offerings.*

The scarabs of Egypt and the signet-gems of the Greeks and Romans were also commonly employed to seal the plaster stoppers of amphorae full of wine. Many examples of these with the seal unbroken have been found in the Delta and elsewhere in Egypt. *Sealed wine-jars.*

With regard to the use of signets in the wine-cellar, Horace mentions as the test of a good-tempered house-master—"Signo fracto non insanire lagenae," that he did not go wild with passion even if he found that the seal of a wine-jar had been broken. Pliny, in his treatise on finger-rings (*Hist. Nat.* XXXIII. 26), refers to the same custom when he says "nunc cibi quoque ac potus *anulo* vindicantur a rapina"

Work on ugly stones.

This practical use as signets explains why in so many cases among ancient Greek gems very beautiful work is engraved upon an ugly stone, the markings of which interfere with and obscure the design. The main object was that the *impression* from the gem, rather than the *stone* itself, should be beautiful. This is notably the case with the celebrated head of Medusa from the Strozzi collection, now in the British Museum, which is cut on a very opaque and much mottled chalcedony,—a fact which is evidence in favour of the antiquity of this beautiful gem, in spite of its style, which certainly suggests the hand of an artist of the Renaissance, rather than one of any classical period.

Scarab form.

As has been already mentioned, until about the middle of the 4th century B.C. Greek gems were usually cut in the scarab or scarabaeoid form; the latter were frequently of large size, especially when made of chalcedony, in which case the old method of wearing the signet strung on a cord round the neck still survived. After that, from the time of Alexander downwards, the custom came in of having gems engraved on a thinner slice of stone; and the brilliant varieties of sard or carnelian became the favourite gem to work upon. For the sard the thinner body of stone was an advantage, making it more transparent and effective, whereas the older scarabaeoid shape was best suited for the pale bluish or milky chalcedony, which looks poor if cut very thin. This rule is not without many exceptions; thin sard gems occur of date much anterior to Alexander's time, and the use of chalcedony was never given up either by Greek or Roman gem-engravers.

Thinner form of gem.

Convex gems.

Another common variety of shape, used mainly by the Romans, was to have the side of the gem, on which the design was cut, convex; the plain back being flat. This form is very common among Roman gems of Imperial times, and it was often used for stones the colour of which requires an extra thickness of body to bring out the full richness of tint, as in the case of carbuncles and reddish sards. A less common shape, largely used for mediaeval and modern gems, was the reverse of the last, namely a convex back, with a flat face. Either of these forms is especially suited to the carbuncle, which looks glassy and poor in colour if not convex on one side[1].

The modern name for this rounded form is *en cabochon*: it is now only used for a few stones, such as opal, turquoise and carbuncle; transparent gems being almost always cut with many facets.

Gems en cabochon.

The *cabochon* shape was used for all gems throughout the middle ages, and it was not till the 16th century that the faceted form was much used. In many cases the old rounded form gives much greater beauty to a gem, especially to one in which the chief beauty is colour rather than brilliance or "fire." The diamond, on the other hand, if not cut in facets, has little more beauty and effect than rock crystal.

Gems in facets.

Stones, such as the amethyst and the garnet, which often look poor and tawdry when faceted, have great decorative beauty when cut in the older fashion, and the modern system is applied, with great want of taste on the part of jewellers, to many stones which are quite spoilt by it.

Old and modern methods.

Another advantage of the old system of cutting is that flaws, which are destructive of the beauty of a faceted gem, in many cases do little, if any, injury to a stone cut in the *cabochon* form.

In Oriental countries the old method of shaping gems still survives, and modern Indian jewellery of very great beauty and decorative effect is often made with gems, which, in the hands of a European jeweller, would be almost valueless.

Oriental gems.

The only antique examples of faceting were those gems in which the natural crystalline form was preserved, namely the diamond which was too hard to cut, and the beryl which in some cases had its natural hexagonal crystals polished; Pliny, *H. N.* XXXVII. 76. The emerald also was often used in its natural crystalline form.

Beryl and diamond.

[1] 'Carbuncle' and 'garnet' are different names for the same gem according to the shape in which they are cut—the "carbuncle" being the stone *en cabochon*, and the "garnet" cut with facets. 'Cabochon' is derived from the Portuguese 'cabo,' a head.

Emerald bought by Ismenias.

Period of Alexander.

Graeco-Roman gems.

Portraits on gems.

With regard to the prices paid by the Greeks for fine gems, we have little or no information.

Pliny (*Hist. Nat.* XXXVII. 6) tells a story of how the flute-player Ismenias[1], who lived in the time of Alexander the Great, sent six gold staters to buy an emerald engraved with a figure of the sea-nymph Amymone, and was disgusted to have two staters returned to him with the gem, on the ground that an insult had been offered to the emerald through its price being beaten down. In this case however, as Mr King remarks (*Handbook of Gems*, p. 196), the stone itself may have been worth the greater part of the money, so that we have no indication of what the value of the work on it may have been.

According to Pliny, Greek musicians were specially given to the extravagance of collecting and wearing many gems.

During the Alexandrine period and later the character of Greek gems, like that of other works of art, changes very much; the type of figure becomes softer and more feminine in beauty, Homeric scenes are no longer represented, and deities such as Aphrodite or Dionysus, with subjects relating to the theatre or musical contests, become the favourite motives for representation.

Greek gems of this later period and good Graeco-Roman work of the time of the early Roman Empire are usually almost indistinguishable, either in workmanship or in subject. This is frequently the case even with large sculpture in marble[2], and with work so minute as that of the gem-engraver it is harder still to arrive at any certainty.

With the time of Alexander portraits appear for the first time on gems: a little earlier, that is, than the introduction of coin-portraits, which commence with the Diadochi, Seleucus I. King of Syria, and Ptolemy I. of Egypt. Lysimachus

---

[1] Ismenias was the author of a work on precious stones.

[2] A striking example of this is to be seen in the reliefs on the throne of the High Priest of Dionysus in the great theatre of Athens. The figures of Eros with fighting cocks on the arms of the throne and the two Fauns on the back look like the best Greek work of the 4th century B.C., and it is only the feeble archaism of the pseudo-Assyrian relief on the front of the seat which betrays the later origin of the whole.

of Thrace used on his coins, instead of his own portrait, a magnificent head of the deified Alexander, an idealized portrait of the noblest type.   *Portrait of Alexander.*

Though Alexander never committed the impiety of placing his own head in the place of that of a deity on his coins, he employed the celebrated Pyrgoteles to engrave it upon gems —using for that purpose an emerald, according to Pliny, *Hist. Nat.* XXXVII. 8; see below, page 71.

The British Museum possesses two very fine portrait-gems (Nos. 1526 and 1529) copied respectively from tetradrachms of Demetrius Poliorcetes and of a King of Pergamus. Fig. 19 shows the latter, probably a portrait of Eumenes I., 263—241 B.C.   *Pergamene portrait.*

FIG. 19. Very noble example of a Greek portrait gem of the 3rd century B.C., cut on mottled chalcedony, very similar in style to the finest silver tetradrachms of Pergamus; *real size*.

No. 1530 in the same collection is a copy in paste of the coin-portrait on tetradrachms of the great Mithradates, c. 90 B.C.; which, again, seems to have been taken from a large group of sculpture in bronze, probably a quadriga driven by Mithradates; hence the eager expression of the face and the hair blown back by the wind.   *Coin portrait.*

In Roman Imperial times portraits were very frequently cut on gems, especially that of the reigning Emperor, which was commonly worn by his courtiers as a compliment to him.   *Portraits of the Emperor.*

Portrait heads of Greek philosophers were also very largely worn by the Romans in their rings: Cicero (*De Fin.* v. 1) ridicules the Epicureans for their habit of using their master's head as a signet. Heads of Socrates are specially common on gems; see No. 65 in the Fitzwilliam catalogue.   *Philosophers.*

Courtiers' rings.

Pliny (*Hist. Nat.* XXXIII. 41) tells us that a portrait of Claudius in a gold ring was worn as a sort of entrance ticket by those privileged persons who had the right of access to the Imperial presence.

The later Greek and Graeco-Roman gems are in many cases of exceptional value and interest from the fact that their device represents some important work of Greek sculpture—in some cases one which can be identified by descriptions as being some celebrated, but now lost statue or group. Thus, for example, a gem in the British Museum (No. 720) appears to be copied from the famous bronze statue of Apollo holding a stag by its fore-legs at Branchidae by the sculptor Kanachos of Sicyon, who worked in the early part of the 5th century B.C.; see *Proceed. Soc. Ant.* 2nd series, Vol. XI. p. 253[1].

Apollo of Kanachos.

Another gem (Brit. Mus. No. 722) has a representation of the Apollo Sauroctonos of Praxiteles, of which several ancient copies exist both in bronze and marble; and No. 790, a badly cut gem of late Roman date, is interesting for its group of Aphrodite and Ares with Eros at their feet—a noble Greek design of probably the 3rd century B.C., of which more than one Roman copy in marble still exists[2].

Mars and Venus.

Valuable evidence with regard to an important work of art is given by the impression in wax from an ancient gem, which was used as the private signet of Thomas Colyns, Prior of Tywardreth in Cornwall from 1507 to 1539. A document still exists sealed by the Prior with his signet-gem on which was engraved a copy of the celebrated Laocoon group, now in the Vatican.

Laocoon group.

The true position of the lost arms of Laocoon himself and one of the sons is shown on this seal; though the group itself has been restored differently, in a way which very much

---

[1] The finest extant representation of this celebrated statue is on an engraved paste gem in the collection of Mr A. J. Evans at Oxford.

[2] This is the motive of the group to which the Aphrodite of Melos is supposed by some writers to have belonged. The Capitoline Museum possesses a rather ludicrous copy, in which the heads of Ares and Aphrodite are replaced by those of Hadrian and his wife Sabina.

injures the general lines of the composition[1]; see *Arch. Journ.* XXIV. p. 45. It is, of course, possible that Prior Colyns' signet was copied from the then recently discovered Laocoon group during the early part of the 16th century, but on the whole it appears more probable that it was an antique gem.

A great many other instances might be quoted of antique gems which are of value for their record of important works of Greek art, now lost.

The same sort of evidence is frequently given by the *reverse* types of coins; but unfortunately the greater number of coins which illustrate ancient sculpture belong to a late period of decadence, and are too coarsely executed to give an accurate notion of the statues they represent; a large number of examples are given in a valuable work by Professor Gardner and Dr Imhoof-Blumer, *Numismatic Commentary on Pausanias;* first published in the *Journal of Hellenic Studies,* 1885 to 1887.

The importance of antique gems as giving us the designs of lost statues is eloquently pointed out by Professor Story-Maskelyne in his preface to the *Catalogue of the Marlborough Gems,* 1870, p. xxiv.—" if we could but assemble in one collection the still extant gem-signets of the different ages and families of man from the days of Urukh to those of the latest Sasanian kings, we should have a more complete representation of the objects that stirred the minds and ruled the hearts of men through all those many ages and changes of circumstance, than would be afforded by any other single form of their arts—indeed we may perhaps with justice say, than by all the other forms of these that remain to us combined."

It should, however, be observed that gems which bear designs copied from important works of sculpture are in most cases productions of the Roman Imperial period, when the decay of good taste and judgment allowed designs to be cut on gems which were quite unsuited for such a purpose.

The reasons for this unsuitability are obvious; in the first

---

[1] The carefully devised pyramidical scheme of composition in the Laocoon group is spoilt by the position of the restored arms, which straggle, as it were, outside the proper bounding line of the composition.

Requisites of a gem design.

place a design of high merit must be specially suited to the scale on which it is meant to be executed, and therefore no design could be greatly enlarged or diminished without a serious loss of beauty and fitness.

Again, a gem design, being a variety of bas-relief, should be most strictly kept to one plane, quite unlike the natural composition of a piece of sculpture in the round; and, last of all, in copying a statue it was usually impossible to make the design occupy the field of the gem in that complete way which was thought so desirable by the engravers during the best period of Greek art.

GEMS FROM ETRUSCAN TOMBS.

Etruscan scarabs.

This is a very large class and embraces gems of many different kinds, extending over a long period, but the greater number fall between the 6th and the 3rd century B.C.

Foreign imports.

Among the earlier gems a large number are foreign imports, either of Phoenician or Greek workmanship. The demand for engraved gems, mostly in the form of sard or carnelian scarabs, must have been very great among the wealthy and luxurious people of Etruria, whose gold jewellery is of extraordinary beauty and magnificence.

Scarabs used as ornaments.

These engraved scarabs were not used by the Etruscans merely as signets, but were also employed in large numbers as personal ornaments.

Almost all have some form of the "cable" border, and the majority are cut in the scarab shape, perforated, with the head and wing-cases of the beetle carefully shaped. In some cases the original beetle form has been sliced off[1], for convenience of setting, occasionally leaving traces of the horizontal perforation, found in all true scarabs.

Jewelled necklaces.

Many of these sard scarabs from the tombs of Etruria are strung in rows on necklaces, or used as pendants for bracelets and ear-rings, in combination with the most exquisitely delicate gold work.

---

[1] The gem shown in fig. 22, page 107, is an example of this form, which is commonly called the "cut scarab".

In addition to these imported Phoenician and Greek scarabs, a certain number are evidently the work of the Etruscans themselves, who appear to have been the most skilful of craftsmen in all the arts, but endowed like the Romans, with very little power of original design. *Native Etruscan scarabs.*

Scarabs with Etruscan subjects very rarely occur; in almost all cases, not only in style but in subject also, they are copied from Greek gems; favourite subjects being Homeric scenes, heroes in council or battle, and single figures of legendary Greeks of the heroic age, or occasionally athletes of contemporary times; sirens, harpies, centaurs and other Greek mythical subjects are not uncommon. *Subjects on scarabs.*

Not unfrequently these scarabs bear inscriptions in Etruscan characters, most commonly names to explain the subject or person represented, as on the Greek vases of the 6th century B.C. In some cases these names have been added by the Etruscans on imported gems of Greek workmanship[1]. *Inscriptions.*

No class of gem has been so extensively forged as these Etruscan scarabs, especially during the present century, and their manufacture still goes on with much skill in Rome and other places in Italy.

There is an interesting treatise on these gems by Köhler, *Abhandlung über Käfer-gemmen und Etruskische Kunst*, in which Etruscan scarabs are divided into three classes. *Köhler on scarabs.*

I. From the 7th to the middle of the 5th century B.C. gems of good style engraved on sards and other stones of very fine quality, with heroic subjects, frequently taken from the mythical stories of the Trojan and Theban wars. On this class inscriptions are common, usually names to explain the person or the scene which is represented.

II. From the middle of the 5th century to c. 280 B.C.

---

[1] In the same way we see Etruscan and Latin inscriptions rudely cut on the beautiful engraved bronze *cistae* of purely Hellenic workmanship.

The whole subject of Etruscan art has (more recently) been treated in a very learned manner by Dr Helbig in various numbers of the *Ann. dell' Inst. Cor. Arch. Roma*, see 1863, p. 336 and 1870, p. 5; cf. Brunn, *Annali* 1866, p. 442. A large number of Etruscan scarabs are published in the *Bull. Inst. Cor. Arch.* 1831, p. 105, 1834, p. 116; 1839, p. 99.

scarabs with similar subjects, cut on less fine stones, and without inscriptions.

Late scarabs.
III. Period of decadence, c. 280 B.C. to the time of Julius Caesar, rudely cut figures, some almost wholly executed with the drill[1], and cut on stones of poor quality.

This classification is not wholly satisfactory, and Köhler does not sufficiently distinguish between imported gems and those executed by native Etruscan artists.

[1] To this class Köhler would assign the drill-cut scarab shown in fig. 22, page 107.

CHAPTER IV.

ROMAN GEMS.

As is the case with the other arts, the best "Roman gems" are Greek either in design or workmanship, if not in both. The finest gems under the Empire were produced by Greek engravers, in some cases probably slaves or freedmen, or else by Romans who were Greeks by training.

Greek artists in Rome.

There are however a very large number of gems of inferior style which can be called Roman in a fuller sense of the word. Under the Republic the use of engraved gems by the Romans seems to have been comparatively limited—partly, no doubt, on account of sumptuary laws, written and unwritten, like those which so strictly limited the *jus annuli aurei* during the early days of Rome.

A very characteristic example of a Roman gem is that in a signet-ring (formerly in Lord Beverley's collection[1]) which can be dated about the year 300 B.C. owing to its having been found in the great *peperino* sarcophagus (now in the Vatican) of Lucius Cornelius Scipio Barbatus who was consul in 298 B.C. This is a gold ring set with a sard on which is cut, in a dry, wiry manner, a standing figure of Victory, winged and holding a palm-branch. The same figure treated in a similar way occurs on a very large number of Roman gems: No. 31 in the Fitzwilliam collection, engraved on chalcedony, is a good typical example of the design, and of the style of the early Roman gem-engravers generally.

The ring of Scipio.

Plate II.

[1] This historical ring was inherited, with the rest of Lord Beverley's gems, by Mr Heber Percy, and has since been purchased by the Duke of Northumberland; it is preserved, with the rest of the Percy collection, at Alnwick Castle.

Deities on gems.

Plate II.

Greek types.

Latin deities.

Portrait gems.

The most frequently recurring subjects on Roman gems of this class are figures of Jupiter enthroned (see Nos. 26 and 27, Fitzwilliam catalogue) Minerva, Juno and other deities such as the Dioscuri, who were specially worshipped in Rome and are represented on the earliest of the Roman denarii[1]. Another very favourite subject is the goddess Roma, enthroned—a type which was adapted from certain Greek representations of Athene, as, for example, that on the tetradrachms of Lysimachus with the head of the deified Alexander on the *obverse*.

Most of the Roman deities are represented in forms taken from Greek art—Jupiter, Juno and Minerva, the great triad of early Latin worship, have the dress and the symbols of Zeus, Hera and Athene: and it only rarely happens that any deities are represented in a more native and un-Hellenic fashion. One of these exceptional cases of a native Italian deity, who sometimes occurs upon gems and coins of the Republican period[2], is Juno Sospita with a serpent by her side, wearing a head-dress made of goat's skin—the special cultus-deity of Lanuvium.

Under the Roman empire, gems of all kinds, cut on a great variety of stones, and with every degree of excellence of workmanship, were extremely common.

Apart from the Graeco-Roman gems, which had little or nothing about them that was really Roman, the finest class is on the whole that with portrait heads either of the Emperor or some member of the Imperial family, or else that of the private owner of the gem; a large number of this latter class must have been engraved for wealthy Romans, judging from the frequent occurrence of well executed portraits, which cannot now be identified. Even these portraits of Romans are in many cases evidently the work of Greek artists, as their noble and refined treatment clearly shows.

---

[1] No. 33, with a standing figure of Minerva, and No. 49, with a bust of Victory, both in the Fitzwilliam collection, are good examples of Roman gems of the Republican period; they are illustrated on Plate II.

[2] For example the head of Juno Sospita or Sispita is a common *obverse* type on denarii struck by *monetarii* of the Papia and Roscia families.

One of the finest that now exists is the portrait of Julia, Titus' daughter, by the engraver Euodos; see below, page 74.

Among the recently acquired Carlisle gems in the British Museum there is a magnificent intaglio on *chalcedony* with the portrait head of an elderly, close-shaven Roman, with closely cropped hair, somewhat similar in style to the so-called head of Sextus Pompey, signed by Agathopous, in the Florentine collection. This wonderful example of iconic art, though noble and dignified in style, is treated with much minuteness of detail and vivid realism Even a pimple on the chin is represented; suggesting that the sturdy Roman, whose portrait the gem shows us, had similar views to those held by Oliver Cromwell with regard to the desirability of realistic truth in portraiture. The Carlisle gem, like all the finest Roman portraits, is thoroughly Greek in style, and is probably the work of a Greek engraver of the first century B.C.

Carlisle portrait gem.

It may however be earlier than that, as the work both in design and execution is quite equal to the finest portrait heads on the coins of the Seleucid and Attalid Kings struck between about 300 and 150 B.C.

In addition to the Roman taste for gems simply as works of art, their old importance as signets still survived. Pliny records (*Hist. Nat.* XXXVII. 10) that the Emperor Augustus used for his signet the figure of a Sphinx; mainly on account of the accident of his having inherited from his mother two exactly similar gems with this device. Thus when Augustus was abroad he could intrust the duplicate signet to his friends, and so give them authority to issue any necessary edicts in the Emperor's name. The Sphinx, cut in a very gem-like manner, occurs on the *reverse* of a silver coin of the *cistophorus* standard struck in Asia by Augustus; and this coin very probably shows us what his signet-gem was like.

Gem as signet.

Sphinx of Augustus.

The British Museum possesses a fine gem with the Sphinx device (No. 476 in the Catalogue), which seems to have been derived from the early coins of Chios. After a time, owing, Pliny says (*Hist. Nat.* XXXVII. 10), to jokes made on the Sphinx-like obscurity of Augustus' edicts sealed with the Sphinx signet, the Emperor changed the device of his seal,

and used instead a head of Alexander the Great, probably a contemporary portrait by the famous Pyrgoteles.

Imperial signets.

Suetonius (*Aug.* 50) says that Augustus used, at different times, three different signets, first the Sphinx, secondly the head of Alexander, and lastly his own portrait engraved by Dioscorides. This last signet was used after the death of Augustus by subsequent Emperors, down to the time of Pliny's writing his *Historia Naturalis*, with the one exception of Galba, who preferred to seal with his own signet, on which was cut his family device—a dog standing on the prow of a ship; see Dio Cass. LI. 3.

Frog signet.

Maecenas used as his official seal a gem engraved with a frog, a device which was, as Pliny says, well known and much dreaded on account of its association with edicts for the imposition of taxes.

This device of a frog occurs on more than one of the scarabs which have been found in Etruscan tombs. A good example is in the British Museum, No. 474.

Pliny on rings.

A very interesting account of Roman signet-rings[1] is given by Pliny (*Hist. Nat.* XXXIII. 8 to 36). He repeats the legend about the earliest ring being that which Prometheus wore after his liberation by Zeus, with a bit of the rock to which he had been chained, set in a ring made of iron from his fetters, thus saving Zeus from perjury, who had sworn that Prometheus should remain for ever bound upon Mt Caucasus; see Catull. LXIV. 295—298.

Jus annuli aurei.

In early times (Pliny thinks) rings were but little worn by the Romans; among the statues of the kings on the Capitoline Hill, those of Numa and Servius Tullius were the only ones which had rings. The right of wearing *gold* rings was very sparingly granted: at first only to Ambassadors while abroad on state affairs, to whom a gold signet was given at the public expense; on his return to Rome the Ambassador surrendered his gold signet and again wore the usual iron ring of a Roman citizen.

By degrees the *jus annuli aurei* was granted to one official

---

[1] On ancient rings, see the very learned treatise by Kirchmann, *De Anulis*, Sleswick, 1657.

after another; Senators and Consuls being the first to enjoy the privilege. It then became the mark of the Equestrian Order[1], and finally, under the later Roman Empire, the gold ring became the mark of any man of free birth, a silver ring being the badge of a freedman, and an iron ring that of a slave.

Pliny remarks (*Hist. Nat.* XXXIII. 23) that in his time the iron rings of slaves were sometimes plated with gold, "ferrum auro cingunt": a form of signet of which a good many examples have been found, owing to the protection against rust which is afforded by the gold: otherwise iron rings have usually perished from oxydization[2].

With regard to the Roman names for rings, in addition to *annulus*, Pliny says (*Hist Nat* XXXIII. 10) that the δακτύλιος of the Greeks was called in Old Latin *ungulus*, and in later times *symbolum*; the latter word (σύμβολον) referring more strictly to the device on the signet; see Plaut. *Pseud.* II. ii. 53 and IV. ii. 44. Another early Latin word was *condalium*, from κόνδυλος meaning the same as δακτύλιος; see Plautus, *Trinummus*, IV. 3. 7, where the word is not used as meaning specially a slave's ring, since it was probably his master's ring that the slave in the Play lost. A Comedy of Plautus entitled *Condalium* was so named in imitation of Menander's Drama called Δακτύλιος.

The clay or wax impression from the signet was called *sigillum* as well as *symbolum*: e.g. Cicero (*Acad.* II. 26, 85) uses the phrase "sigilla annulo imprimere." The word *signare* is used for the act of sealing, e.g. Ovid, *Metam.* IX. 566,

"Protinus impressa signat sua crimina gemma."

Many ancient gold rings, both Greek and Roman, are made thin and hollow, so as to make the most show at the least cost: they are unfortunately very liable to be crushed. This is the kind of ring which the Roman Flamen Dialis

---

[1] Hence the *modius* of gold rings sent to Carthage by Hannibal after the battle of Cannae, in 216 B.C., or according to other writers three *modii*; see Livy, XXIII. 12.

[2] The use of iron without any gem for betrothal rings still survived in Pliny's time; *Hist. Nat.* XXXIII. 12.

The Flamen's ring.

was obliged to wear, in accordance with the curious and mysterious list of restrictions and duties which are recorded by the celebrated mural painter and historian of Republican Rome, Fabius Pictor (quoted by Aul. Gellius X. 15, § 5). He says—"Item annulo uti, nisi pervio cassoque, fas non est." These light rings of beaten, not cast gold are mentioned by Ovid (*A. A.* III. 221)—

"Annulus ut fiat primo colliditur aurum."

Poison rings.

The cavity in the ring was sometimes filled with poison, so that the wearer could at any moment commit suicide: a method adopted by Hannibal (Juv. *Sat.* X. 164),

"Cannarum vindex et tanti sanguinis ultor
Annulus."

In calling the ring "Cannarum vindex" Juvenal is probably alluding to the *modius* of gold rings, which Hannibal collected from the slain equites at Cannae.

Pliny records (*Hist. Nat.* XXXIII. 14 and 15) that the guardian (*aedituus*) of the Temple of Capitoline Jupiter killed himself with his poison-ring, to avoid being tortured, when the public store of gold, 2000 pounds in weight, was stolen from its secret depository inside the throne of Jupiter. This happened during the third consulship of Cn. Pompeius Magnus, whose colleague M. Licinius Crassus is supposed to have been the robber. See also *Hist. Nat.* XXXIII. 25, where Demosthenes is said to have killed himself with a similar ring.

Theft of gold.

In the same passage Pliny says that some people preferred to have a valuable gem set in a light, hollow ring, so that it might be less liable to injury from a chance fall.

Heavy gold rings.

Others, whose wealth was of recent date, prided themselves on the massive gold of their rings. Martial (XI. 47) ridicules an upstart, who wore on his finger a sardonyx set in a ring which contained a pound weight of gold; cf. Mart. XIV. 123.

Subjects on gems.

As a rule subjects from contemporary history were seldom used for Roman gems, even during the later Republican period, when such subjects were common on the *reverses* of the denarii. Pliny, however, tells us (*Hist. Nat.* XXXVII. 8) that Sulla used as his signet a gem engraved with the surrender in 106 B.C. of the Numidian King Jugurtha. Sulla also, according to Dion Cassius, used a gem with three trophies in allusion to his triple victories: this device also occurs on the *reverse* of one of his denarii.

Sulla' signet.

The same signet device of three trophies was cut on the ring of Pompey the Great, which Julius Caesar showed to the incredulous Roman Senate as a proof of Pompey's defeat and death; see Dion Cass. XLII. 18.

Pompey signet.

Another design, according to Plutarch, was sometimes used by Pompey, namely a lion holding a sword (λέων ξιφήρης). It is interesting to note that the reverse of a rare gold coin struck by Marc Antony about 39 B.C. bears the same subject—a lion holding in its upraised paw a short sword or dagger, possibly copied from the famous signet of Pompeius Magnus[1], who was one of the earliest Roman collectors of engraved gems.

The Roman Emperors seem to have had special curators of their gem cabinets. In the Columbarium of the Imperial freedmen, outside the Porta Capena, a sepulchral inscription was found over the ashes of "Julius Philargyrus libertus a dactyliotheca Caesaris." Another official was the keeper of the Imperial Signet, *custos annuli*, an office which was held in the time of J. Caesar by the father of Trogus Pompeius (Justin, XLIII. 5): "annuli curam habuisse" is the phrase used by Trogus.

Curators of gems.

Keeper of the Seal.

According to Capitolinus, the whole collection of gems formed by Hadrian was sold by Marcus Aurelius, together with other valuable works of art, by public auction in the Forum of Trajan, to pay the expenses of the war with the Marcomanni.

Imperial collections.

One of the most interesting collections of ancient rings is that formed by the celebrated naturalist Waterton, the greater part of which is now in the South Kensington Museum. Among them are some magnificent examples of signets with

S. Kens. Mus. rings.

---

[1] This curious coin is illustrated by Stevenson, *Dictionary of Roman Coins*, London, 1889, p. 58.

Waterton rings.

the bezel in gold, engraved with fine designs of Egyptian, Greek and Etruscan workmanship.

The following are among the most remarkable; a large Egyptian gold ring of Ptolemaic date, which has a *vesica*-shaped bezel with a minutely cut, seated figure of Isis suckling the infant Horus.

A Greek ring of the finest period of art, 5th century B.C., all of gold, has a very beautiful female head with no distinguishing attribute—possibly representing Hera, most exquisitely cut on the gold bezel.

Another Greek ring of c. 400 B.C., which is wholly of bronze, is remarkable for its fine *patina* and perfect state of preservation. On the bezel is cut a seated female figure with most gracefully designed drapery.

Variety of materials.

Among the Roman rings are examples in a great variety of materials, gold, silver, bronze, lead, iron, amber, stone, such as rock crystal or chalcedony, glass, ivory and even enamelled pottery.

One curious ring is cut out of a piece of amber; in it is fixed a fine yellow paste *intaglio* with a head of Jupiter Ammon. In many cases the bronze and iron rings have their gem backed with bright metallic foil, in order that the dark metal might not diminish the brilliance of the stone: cf. Pliny, *Hist. Nat.* XXXVII. 106. Several of the rings are of very small size, being intended only to reach to the first joint of the finger: such rings have often wrongly been taken for the rings of children. It is unfortunately very rare to find a really fine gem in its original setting, most ancient rings which now exist have engraved gems of rather poor design and workmanship.

Cheap gems.

Under the Empire, as the old restrictions with regard to wearing rings gradually passed away, an enormous quantity of cheap gems seem to have been engraved. Among the commonest subjects are single figures of the various deified abstractions, which the Romans invented very freely, and also adapted from the Greeks.

Figures of *Salus* with her serpent, *Fortuna* with cornucopiae and rudder, *Abundantia, Indulgentia, Felicitas, Bonus*

Eventus and many others are constantly repeated on the inferior Roman gems, in exactly the same forms as on the *reverses* of the Imperial denarii and aurei. The older deities, such as Jupiter, Juno, Minerva, Roma and others are no less common, and have the same close relation to the *reverse* types of coins.

Another favourite Roman device for signet-gems is some form of what is usually called a *gryllus*, a composite monster made up with much ingenuity by joining together masks and various animals: see No. 90 in the *Fitzwilliam Catalogue*.

According to Pliny (*Hist. Nat.* XXXV. 114) the famous Graeco-Egyptian painter Antiphilos, who executed a number of fine pictures which were brought to Rome to adorn the *Porticus* of Philip and that of Pompey in the Campus Martius, also painted a ludicrous figure known as the *Gryllus*. Hence, Pliny says, the name *grylli* was given to pictures of that comic class. The word also means a grasshopper or a cricket. It is still used in modern Italian for fanciful and grotesque figures.

In the first century A.D., Pliny says (*Hist. Nat.* XXXIII. 41), the fashion came in to Rome of wearing gems engraved with a figure of Harpocrates or some other Egyptian deity. Among the many new sects which flourished under the Roman Empire, that of the worship of Isis and Serapis was the most popular; and even as early as the time of Augustus it was an important cult in Rome. A large number of Romano-Egyptian gems now exist: see Nos. 104 and 105 in the *Fitzwilliam Catalogue*. Figures of Horus or Harpocrates, the god of Silence, of which No. 20 in the same collection is a good example, were much used for signets, probably as a hint for discretion and silence with regard to the contents of the letter or other document that it was used to seal[1].

Astrological gems, engraved with a lucky horoscope, were also very largely used under the Roman Empire, when superstitions of all kinds were specially rife.

In the second and third centuries A.D. Mithraic and Gnostic

---

[1] A mediaeval analogy is the common type of seal engraved with the words "lecta lege: lecta lege."

Talismans.

types were very common; especially gems engraved with the mystic sun-god *Abraxas* and the Demiurgus *Cnoubis:* see No. 106, *Fitz. Mus. Cat.*

These and many other devices were highly valued throughout the Imperial period as having talismanic or magical powers of protection and good luck;—the power of the talisman depending partly on the device, partly on the stone it was cut upon, and lastly on the season or planetary hour when the gem was engraved. Such gems were called by the Greeks τετελεσμένοι or φαρμακῖται, and *amuleta* by the Romans; see Pliny, *Hist. Nat.* XXXVII. 118.

Metallic amulets.

In some cases metal signets of this class have a little dot or pin of gold or silver let into the field; the union of two metals giving an additional talismanic virtue to the device. This may possibly have originated in the accidental discovery of the mysterious galvanic effect which is produced when two adjacent metals are touched by the tongue. This would naturally be noticed in those not uncommon rings which have the bezel made of one metal and the hoop of another.

Styles of gem engraving.

With regard to the style of Roman gems, the finest, both in intaglio and in cameo, were produced under Greek influence, if not by Greek artists, during the Augustan age. It is noticeable, as has been already remarked, that in many cases fine gems of the Roman Imperial period are engraved with copies of statues, whereas during the best Greek time the designs on gems were specially devised for glyptic purposes. During the Flavian period the work was, as a rule, inferior in style and coarser in execution[1]; but a few years later, in the time of Hadrian, there was a remarkable revival both of good taste and of technical skill, which came to a rather sudden end about the close of the second century A.D. in the reign of Septimius Severus.

Coins set in rings.

After that, the decadence of gem engraving, like that of the other arts, continued without intermission. Hence arose, in the third or fourth century, the not uncommon fashion of wearing in rings and other ornaments fine gold coins

---

[1] The portrait of Julia the daughter of Titus by Euodos, in the Paris Bibliothèque, is a remarkable exception to this rule.

(*aurei*) of the earlier Emperors, instead of a badly engraved contemporary gem, a custom which was imitated by people of Celtic and Teutonic race in much later times.

This however did not bring the engraving of gems to an end: the art still was largely practised, though the old skill was lost, both in technique and design.

By the time of Constantine, at the beginning of the 4th century, gem engraving in Rome had, like all the other arts, sunk to its lowest ebb; and the craftsmen of Byzantium skilful as they were in enamelling and working in the precious metals, seem not to have very largely developed the glyptic art, even during the wonderful outburst of technical skill and artistic excellence which took place in the time of Justinian, in the early part of the 6th century A.D.

Christian gems of the Roman period are, as a rule, of very poor workmanship.

The commonest subjects are Christ the good Shepherd, represented after the old pagan types of Hermes Psychopompos or Orpheus playing to the listening beasts—subjects which frequently occur among the early Catacomb paintings. The Christian monogram ☧, the dove and olive branch, and other symbols of this kind were very often cut on gems of the 4th and 5th century.

A very fine Christian gem worked with exceptional delicacy has a standing figure of a winged Victory[1] holding a tall cross, a design copied from a not uncommon *reverse* on a gold *solidus* of Honorius, c. 412 A.D. This gem is in Dr Drury Fortnum's collection, one of the finest in the world for its Christian gems and rings[2].

---

[1] It is interesting to note that the usual mediaeval representation of an angel appears to have been derived, through many stages, from the winged Victory of the Greeks.

[2] Dr Fortnum has written at various times many valuable papers on the subject of Christian gems and rings, especially in the *Archaeological Journal*; see Vol. XXVI. p. 137; XXVIII. p. 266; XXIX. p. 305; XXXIII. p. 111, and XLII. p. 159.

SASANIAN GEMS.

Sasanian Dynasty.

During the lowest period of artistic decadence in Rome, a great many large but feebly cut gems were executed in Persia under the successors of the Achaemenidae, from the third century A.D. down to the Moslem conquest of Persia in 632. The finest of these have portrait busts of the King, frequently a Shapur or a Hormizd, or of the Queen, with name and titles in Pehlevi characters. The name *Sasanian* is derived from a man called *Sasan*, a supposed ancestor of Ardashir, the first king of this dynasty, who began to reign about 212 A.D.

Origin of name.

The Persian gems of this period are frequently large and decorative in style, though poor in the details of the design and coarsely cut. A great part of their beauty depends on the fact that usually they are cut on carnelian, rock crystal, amethyst or carbuncle of very fine and brilliant quality. In most cases the gems are convex, either in front or at the back.

Materials and forms of gems.

The conical and the scarabaeoid forms were used occasionally in Persia, even at this late period, especially when the material employed was chalcedony; No. 24 in the *Fitzwilliam Catalogue* is an example of this, as it is also of a favourite Sasanian class of subject—that of hunting scenes, the king on horseback attacking lions, boars, stags and other animals. Some large Sasanian intaglios are cut on unusual materials, such as *turquoise* and *lapis lazuli*. Both these magnificently coloured stones of very fine quality are largely found in Persia. Persian lapis lazuli is the finest in the world.

Moslem gems.

In the year 632 A.D. the fanatical disciples of Mohammed conquered the degenerate successors of the warlike Achaemenidae, and thenceforth the signet-gems of the Persians have been mostly engraved with names or pious sentences, owing to the precept of the Koran which again introduced the old Mosaic law forbidding the likeness of any living thing to be represented. In later times the Persians adopted a modified form of the Moslem Faith, and, to a large extent, have ignored this prohibition—much to the horror of the orthodox Sunni sects.

CHAPTER V

CAMEO GEMS.

IN addition to the usual signet-gem with its device sunk (*intaglio di cavo*), there were, especially under the Roman Empire, a certain number of gems cut in relief, which were intended, not for impressing seals, but for use as ornaments. This is what is meant by the modern word *cameo*[1], a name which is probably of Arabic origin. Such works in relief were included by the Greeks under the name τύποι ἐγγεγλυμμένοι, and were called by the Romans *ectypae*—words, which, however, were applied to reliefs in metal and other materials as well as to cameo gems. *Gems cut in relief.* *Ectypae.*

Pliny (*Hist. Nat.* XXXVII. 173) describes certain stones as being especially suited for cameo cutting—"Gemmae quae ad ectypas sculpturas aptantur." One of the earliest examples of the mention of a ring-cameo by a classical author is in a passage of Seneca (*De Beneficiis*, III. 26), who speaks of a man wearing a cameo portrait of the Emperor—"Tiberii Caesaris imaginem ectypam atque eminente gemma."

The oldest existing examples of cameos (not including Egyptian work) are some curious gems of the 6th century B.C., with a Gorgon's mask or other figure cut in very slight relief, frequently on the back of a scarab instead of the usual beetle form[2]. An example of this rare class of gems is mentioned below at page 88, as being signed by its engraver. *Earliest cameos.*

---

[1] In mediaeval documents spelt also *camahutum*, *chamah*, *camaut*, *camahieu* and in many other ways.

[2] Two characteristic examples of early cameos are illustrated in the *Journ. Hell. Stud.* vol. VI. p. 285; see also *Brit. Mus. Cat.* p. 58.

Greek cameos.

Some very fine cameos of this kind were found in the tombs at Kertch, dating about 400 B.C. or rather earlier: for example a gold swivel-ring with a scarab-shaped carnelian, but having the back cut in relief, into the form of a sleeping lion: the flat side has a running lion, in intaglio.

Another similar scarabaeoid, with a lion cameo on the back, has on the reverse a trophy of arms: see *Ant. du Bosph. Cimmérien au Musée de l'Ermitage*, Pl. XVII. Nos. 8 and 11. Another ring from a Kertch tomb is set with a cameo head of Athene cut in deep red carnelian. It was found on the skeleton hand of a lady who wore eight rings.

Cameos in sard.

These early cameos are mostly cut in sard, carnelian or some other stone of homogeneous colour, but the later cameos of Roman date are mostly cut on some stratified stone, such as the onyx or sardonyx, in order that the design might be cut in one stratum, and be set off by having its background of another colour.

Phalerae cameos.

One of the most important classes among the Roman cameos are large, full-faced heads of Medusa or Jupiter, carved in a thick piece of onyx or sardonyx, and used to ornament the *phalerae* in the middle of the bronze cuirass of an emperor or general of an army. The Medusa's head was often inlaid in the *aegis* which formed a principal ornament on the Imperial cuirass. A very beautiful example of this was dredged up in the Tiber in Rome in 1886, and is now in the possession of Dr John Evans, P.S.A.; see *Proceed. Soc. Ant.*, vol. XI. 1887, p. 396. It is cut in bold relief on a very thick piece of onyx, which measures about $3\frac{1}{4}$ inches across. The British Museum possesses a very fine Gorgon's head cut in high relief in a brilliant amethyst, which was probably a similar ornament.

Large cameos.

A few Roman cameos exist of very great size, some as much as from 10 to 12 inches square. The most famous are the "Coronation of Augustus" at Vienna[1], and the "Apotheosis of Augustus" in the Paris Bibliothèque. Both are elaborate

---

[1] The Vienna collection is specially rich in Roman cameos of great size: a large circular cameo of an eagle is specially magnificent, measuring about 9 inches in diameter, and very noble in design.

compositions, with many figures in two or three tiers, evidently designed and executed by some very skilful Graeco-Roman artist.

Vienna cameo.

The Vienna cameo was bought by Rudolf II. for a sum equal to £10,000 in modern money.

The *Apotheosis of Augustus* was, according to a probably correct tradition, given to the Treasury of the Sainte Chapelle in Paris by Louis IX. shortly before the middle of the 13th century.

"Cameo of France."

In a Latin inventory of the precious objects in this treasury dated 1341 it is described thus:—"Item. Unum pulcherrimum *camaut* in cujus circuitu sunt plures reliquiae." In later inventories it is called "le grand camahieu de France." In 1343 Philip VI. lent it to the Pope, but in 1379 Charles V. restored it to the Sainte Chapelle. This magnificent cameo had been mounted in an elaborate frame of gold and enamelled work of Byzantine style, containing cavities, closed with plates of rock-crystal, in which various relics were preserved; but unfortunately this beautiful frame-work was lost in 1804, when a party of burglars broke into the Bibliothèque and carried off many of its most precious objects, including a priceless collection of large Roman medallions both in gold and silver.

The cameo itself was recovered, but its setting and the other objects in the precious metals perished in the melting pot; see *Revue Archéo.* V. 1848, p. 186.

Another historical cameo in the Bibliothèque is the so-called "Apotheosis of Germanicus", with a figure crowned by a Victory and borne up to Heaven on the back of an eagle, the usual Roman way of representing the Apotheosis of an Emperor or Prince. This large sardonyx gem was for many centuries in the possession of the Abbey of Saint-Èvre; but in 1684 the monks sold it to Louis XIV. for his collection of gems, which he was then transporting from Versailles to the Palace of the Louvre.

Cameo of Germanicus.

The King gave the monks the enormous sum of 7,000 gold écus for this cameo—equal in modern value to more than double the number of pounds sterling.

Cameo Jupiter.

A third cameo in the same collection in Paris also has considerable historical interest[1]. It was given to the Cathedral of Chartres in 1357 by King Charles V., as is recorded in one of the inscriptions on the gold enamelled frame which still surrounds the gem. This cameo, which is cut in sardonyx, has a standing figure of Jupiter holding a sceptre and thunder-bolt; at his feet is an eagle, on account of which the cameo was venerated in mediaeval times as representing St John, the eagle being taken for the Evangelist's symbol.

Till the Revolution in 1789 the cameo remained in the Cathedral treasury at Chartres.

Cameo cup.

The so-called "cup of the Ptolemies" is also now in the Paris collection. This is a large two-handled *cantharus*, cut out of one immense nodule of sardonyx, and covered on the outside with cameo reliefs of various Dionysiac figures and symbols, of rich decorative effect, though not designed with very good taste. It is a purely Roman design of the first or second century A.D.

This very remarkable cup was given in the 9th century by one of the Carlovingian Kings to the Abbey of St Denis, where it was occasionally used as a chalice at Mass.

At the coronation of the Kings and Queens of France it was an ancient custom for the Queen to take the "housel-sip" of consecrated wine from this cup[2].

Like the "Apotheosis of Augustus," this cameo-encrusted *cantharus* was stolen in 1804, and then lost its elaborate gold foot, though the cup itself was restored to the Bibliothèque, when the burglars were arrested in Holland, whither they had escaped with the non-meltable portion of their spoil.

Naples patera.

On the whole the finest Graeco-Roman cameo in the world is in the form of a large circular *patera* of translucent agate, 8 inches in diameter, in the Museum of Naples. It has

[1] See Chabouillet, *Cat. des camées et pierres gravées de la Bibliothèque Impériale*, Paris, 1858, page 1, no. 4.

[2] Long after the consecrated wine was, as a rule, withheld from the laity, the sovereigns of France at their Coronation-Mass continued to receive the sacrament in both kinds, an interesting survival of very primitive times when the offices of King and Priest were held by the same man.

a cameo relief on both sides; one is a magnificent head of Medusa, and on the reverse side is an allegorical subject representing the Nile as the source of the fertility of Egypt. Both in design and execution it is a work of remarkable beauty, far superior in treatment to the more famous cameos of Paris and Vienna.

Cameo of the Nile.

It has unfortunately been damaged by having a hole clumsily drilled through its centre; otherwise it is perfect.

The British Museum possesses a very noble portrait-bust of Augustus in profile (No. 1560) illustrated as frontispiece to Mr A. H. Smith's *Catalogue*.

Head of Augustus.

It is cut boldly, in a very good style, but without much minuteness of detail, in a sardonyx of three layers measuring 5 inches in height. On the breast an *aegis* is represented with central *phalerae* with the Medusa's head, like that in Dr Evans' collection.

The most beautiful Roman cameos, which are usually of much smaller size, are portrait-heads of Emperors, Empresses and other members of the Imperial family.

One of the finest in the British Museum is a profile bust of Julia, the daughter of Titus (No. 1607 *Brit. Mus. Cat.*), apparently copied from the celebrated intaglio signed by Euodos.

Cameo of Julia.

This cameo may, however, be the work of one of the very skilful gem-engravers of the last century.

No. 43 in the Fitzwilliam Collection is a well designed, but somewhat coarsely cut bust of Juno in onyx, dating probably from the early period of the Roman Empire.

A few gems exist, caprices of the Roman engravers, which combine *intaglio* and cameo; as, for example, one in the British Museum from the Blacas collection (No. 1568) which has an *intaglio* portrait head of the Empress Livia in the character of Ceres, surrounded by a border with the symbols of the other chief deities cut in relief.

Besides the use of large cameo heads for the *phalerae* of Imperial armour, they were also made to ornament the massive *fibula* or brooch which fastened the Emperor's cloak (*paludamentum*) on one shoulder. They were also used in a lavish and often tasteless way for many other ornamental

Brooch cameos.

Cameos on armour.

purposes by the purse-proud Romans. Tomb reliefs of the 3rd and 4th century A.D. sometimes show the cuirass studded with five or six big cameos; as, for example, the monument of M. Caelius in the Museum at Bonn. A few of these large cameos have additional life and transparency given to certain parts of the relief by having a cavity cut out at the back, so as to partially reduce the thickness of the translucent gem.

This is the case with the Medusa head in chalcedony in the *Marlborough Collection*, No. 100, one of the finest *phalerae* gems known.

Method of cameo cutting.

On the whole the Roman love for cameos cut out of stratified gems had a degrading influence on the glyptic art. It was rather a tricky sort of ingenuity that was fostered by the wish to have gems with the design worked out of three or four layers of different colours, the background being one colour, the flesh of the head another, the hair a third, and perhaps a wreath round the head in a fourth, the uppermost stratum. Great skill is often shown by the way in which the artist has designed his subject to suit the successive layers of varied colour, but he was usually seriously hampered by the exigencies of the thin strata; and work of this elaborate kind has an awkward flatness of modelling, and necessarily a complete want of graceful modulation in passing from one plane to another of the relief. However, cameos such as these are showy and highly decorative at a distance, and that is what Roman taste seems to have preferred in all branches of art.

Cameos of glass.

PASTE CAMEOS: remarkable skill was shown by the Roman glass-workers in their copies of large and elaborate onyx cameos, executed in pastes of different colours fused together so as to resemble the various strata of the onyx and sardonyx. The difficulty of securely fusing the relief in opaque white paste on to a ground of differently coloured glass must have been very great. The finest of these paste cameos have usually received, after the glass was cold, a good deal of finishing work, executed with the various tools which were used in cutting real onyx. Without these final touches the relief was liable to be blunt and spiritless in effect.

Final tooling.

A large number of cheap paste cameos, executed without

any final tool-work, seem to have been made under the later
Roman Empire, with glass of two or more colours to imitate
the stratified gems such as onyx and sardonyx.

Several antique examples of these paste cameos were used, *Cameos in mediaeval shrine*
about the year 1300, to decorate that magnificent painted and
enamelled retable, which was made for the high altar of
Westminster Abbey, and is still preserved in the south
ambulatory of the choir.

This mediaeval use of antique pastes and also of real
stones was very common, especially for retables, reliquaries,
and even rings. Many fine cameos *(camahutai)*, some of great
size, were among the numerous antique gems which Henry III. *Westminster Abbey*
used to decorate the magnificent gold shrine of Edward the
Confessor, and many other gems were hung round the shrine
as votive offerings.

Almost every mediaeval shrine or reliquary of any importance was more or less enriched with antique gems, both
in cameo and intaglio.

One of the most important cameos in paste is in the
Vienna collection—a fine head of Augustus in blue glass,
with the signature of Herophilus the son of Dioskourides,
incised on the field[1].

The British Museum possesses a large fragment of a paste
cameo (from the Townley collection) of quite a different class
—not a copy of an engraved gem, but rather of the nature of *Cameo tablet.*
a relief for mural decoration. This magnificent slab or tablet
has in high relief a nude figure of a youth, representing Bonus
Eventus, which must have been (when complete) seven or
eight inches in height.

It is Greek in style, modelled with great skill and taste,
and is formed, not in a stratified material with differently
coloured layers, but in fine blue paste, speckled to imitate
lapis lazuli. It has first been formed in a mould, and has
afterwards been worked with the ordinary gem-engraver's
tools, exactly in the same way as if it had been a real piece of
lapis lazuli. In beauty of colour and in excellence of finish
it is quite as fine as if it were a real stone cameo.

[1] This cameo is described below at page 76.

M.

CHAPTER VI.

INSCRIPTIONS ON GEMS.

1. THE OWNER'S NAME: Egyptian scarabs, Assyrian cylinders and a certain class of Phoenician gems very commonly have on them the name of their owner, in the first case in hieroglyphs, in the second in cuneiform characters, and in the last in the early characters, prototypes of the Greek and Latin Alphabet, which were used in common by various Semitic races, such as the Jews, the Phoenicians and the people of Moab. One of the earliest of existing Semitic inscriptions (shown on fig. 20) is the name *Haggai ben Shebaniah*, cut in two lines on a small gem found near Samaria by the Palestine Exploration Society. The date

Jewish signet.

FIG. 20. Signet of Semitic type, with no device except the owner's name in Phoenician or Hebrew characters of the earliest form, dating from a time when the same alphabet was used in common by the Jews, the Phoenicians and other neighbouring Semitic races. The cut is nearly *double the real size*.

of this interesting signet is about the 9th or 8th century B.C. The owner was probably a Jew[1]. Many Phoenician gems

---

[1] The description of Aaron's breast-plate in the Book of *Exodus* (xxviii. 17 to 21), specially records that its gems were engraved with the name of each tribe "like the engravings of a signet," but these stones were, most probably, of Phoenician workmanship, as was the whole Temple of Solomon with all its decorations and fittings.

with the owner's name have been found in various far distant places: one was even discovered a few years ago on the south coast of Ireland.

Owners' names.

Owners' names rarely occur on Greek gems of the best period; and the earliest Greek gems—those of lenticular form—date from before the introduction of writing among the Greeks, and therefore have no sort of inscription. An early example of a gem with the name of its Greek owner is No. 4 in the *Fitzwilliam Catalogue*, the *agate* scarab of Phoenician type which is mentioned above at page 14; in the field is cut, in characters of the early part of the 5th century B.C., KPEONTIΔA EMI, "I am the badge (or signet) of Kreontidas," the word σῆμα (or σφραγίς) being understood.

Plate I

Scarab of Semon.

In the Berlin Museum is a fine scarab in black *jasper*, with a kneeling figure of a nude girl holding a *hydria* under the jet of water which issues from the lion's head spout of a fountain. On it is cut the owner's name "Semon," ΣΗΜΟΝΟΣ, in characters of Ionian style. This very fine example of archaic work was found in the Troad; its date is probably a little earlier than the gem of Kreontidas, about the end of the 6th century B.C.; see *Jahrbuch Arch. Inst.* 1888, p. 116, and Plate 3, No. 6.

Scarab of Thersis.

An earlier example of this class of inscriptions is on a very remarkable little scarab of the 6th century B.C. which is published in an interesting paper on early Greek gems by Rossbach, *Archaeol. Zeit.* 1883, p. 311 seq. and Plate 16, No. 19. On the underside of the scarab is the following inscription, which occupies nearly the whole of the *field*, ΘEPSIOS EMI SAMA ME ME ΑΝΟΙΓΕ for Θέρσιός εἰμι σᾶμα· μή με ἄνοιγε, "I am the device of Thersis; do not open me." At the end of the inscription is the 'device'—a very small dolphin.

Stater of Phanes.

With these inscribed gems it is interesting to compare that very curious electrum stater probably struck by a Persian Satrap named Phanes, c. 600 B.C., with, on the *obverse*, a stag feeding and the *legend* in coarsely cut retrograde characters ΦΑΝΝΟΣ EMI SΘMA—meaning (according to Prof. Gardner) "I am the device or badge of Phanes[1]."

[1] Professor Gardner is inclined to attribute this remarkable stater to a Satrap

Names on tombs.

A similar phrase occurs on many Greek sepulchral inscriptions, as, for example, some found in Cyprus with the name of the dead person in the genitive followed by τὸ σᾶμα ἠμί, written in the peculiar Cypriote syllabic characters: see *Jour. Hell. Stud.* Vol. XI., 1890, p. 67.

Plate I.

On Greek gems of the 4th century B.C. and later the owner's name is rarely inscribed. The very fine 4th century scarabaeoid by Dexamenos (No. 11, *Fitzwilliam Catalogue*) bears the name ΜΙΚΗΣ, possibly the name of the lady who owned the gem[1]; see above, page 28.

Names on Roman gems.

On Roman gems both of the Republican and of the Imperial period owners' names are very common.

Not unfrequently the Roman name is cut in Greek letters, as in the case of the celebrated Diomede with the Palladium by *Felix*, described below at page 75. The nominative and possessive cases are both used for the owner's name on Greek as well as on Roman gems.

Except the gem of Thersis, which has the word σᾶμα, no word for 'gem' or 'signet' is added after the owner's name. A head of Athene on a *sard* in the Barberini collection in Rome has the inscription ΑΠΟΛΛΟΔΟΤΟΥ ΛΙΘΟ[Σ], "the

---

of Halicarnassus (where the coin was found) named Phanes, who in 525 B.C. revolted against the Persian king Cambyses and joined the army of the Egyptian king Amasis; see Herod. III. 4.

The form of the letters of the inscription is, however, clearly earlier in date than 525 B.C., and the type—a stag—would suggest that the coin was struck at Ephesus; see Head, *Hist. Num.*, page 526. The only known example of this stater is in the British Museum.

[1] It is possible that this is a memorial gem, judging from the sepulchral character of its design, in which case Mike may be the name of the deceased lady who is represented on it.

This unusual female name *Mike* or *Mika* occurs on a votive relief, now in the Central Museum of Athens, which represents the goddess Cybele, "the mother of the gods," seated in a throne. At the sides of the relief are small figures of a male and a female worshipper; and above them is the following dedicatory inscription—ΜΑΝΗΣ ΜΗΤΡΙ | ΚΑΙ ΜΙΚΑ ΜΗΤΡΙ ΘΕΩΝ, cut in letters of about the middle of the fourth century B.C. or rather earlier; probably the same date, that is, as the lady represented on the scarabaeoid of Dexamenos in the Fitzwilliam Museum,

The relief is illustrated by Miss Harrison in her valuable work, *the Mythology and Myths of Athens*, London, 1890, page 45.

gem of Apollodotos," but this gem is of very doubtful authenticity.

In some cases, when the name is in very small characters, it is uncertain whether it is that of the engraver of the gem or of the owner: the latter is, as a rule, not only in larger letters than that of the artist, but is also placed in a more conspicuous position.

2. THE ARTIST'S NAME. To decide which are genuine among the many so-called artists' signatures on ancient gems is a very difficult problem, and one which has been discussed by various writers with very different conclusions.

Artists' names.

In the first place it will be well to consider what record we have in classical writers of the names of gem-engravers, (δακτυλιογλέφος or λιθογλυφος, Lat. *gemmarum sculptor*).

The list is a short one. First comes the celebrated *Theodorus of Samos*, one of the most distinguished architects and sculptors in bronze and the precious metals of about the middle of the 6th century B.C., who is frequently mentioned as working in partnership with Rhoecus, or with Telecles, who were also Samians, and probably near blood-relations of Theodorus, though in what precise degree is very doubtful.

Theodorus of Samos.

Theodorus appears to have been specially skilful in metal work, and is mentioned as the inventor or improver of various processes in the manipulation both of bronze and iron: see Pausanias, VIII. 14 § 5; X. 38 § 3; III. 12 § 8.

According to Pliny (*Hist. Nat.* VII. 57), Theodorus was the inventor of various tools for working in wood, namely the *norma* (set-square), *libella* (level), *tornus* (lathe), and *clavis* (perhaps a vice); all of which tools were certainly in use long before the time of Theodorus; see also Pliny, *Hist. Nat.* XXXV. 152[1].

As a gem-engraver the fame of Theodorus rests chiefly upon the celebrated engraved *emerald*, set in a gold ring (σφρηγὶς χρυσόδετος), which was one of the most valued possessions of Polycrates, tyrant of Samos, who was crucified in 522 B.C. The whole story of the ring of Polycrates is told

Ring of Polycrates.

---

[1] Pliny's statements as to the inventors of processes in the arts must always be received with caution. In most cases they are obviously erroneous.

at length by Herodotus, III. 38 seq.; and is mentioned by Pliny (*Hist. Nat.* XXXVII. 3 and 4) with reference to an uncut sardonyx in the Temple of Concord in Rome, which was popularly supposed to be the gem of this dramatic story: see above, page 35. In another place (*Hist. Nat.* XXXIV. 83) Pliny describes a bronze portrait statue by Theodorus of himself, holding in one hand a file or scraper (*lima*) the symbol of his craft, and in the other "a quadriga and driver, so minute that they were covered by the wings of a fly."

Scarab of Theodorus.

The real meaning of this impossible statement was pointed out by Dr Benndorf (*Zeitschrift für Oesterreich. Gymnasien,* 1873, p. 401 sq.), namely, that it was simply a scarab-gem engraved with a quadriga that the artist's statue held.

Most of Pliny's information comes at second or third hand, and the blunder would easily be made[1].

This story, rightly read, tends to show that Theodorus regarded gem-engraving as an important branch of his art[2], since he represented himself holding a scarab-gem, as a specimen of his skill. Most probably there was more than one distinguished Samian artist called Theodorus, so that the various inventions which are attributed to this name should be referred in part at least to an earlier Theodorus than the contemporary of Polycrates, possibly a grandfather of the later artist, as the common Greek custom was to name a son, not after his father, but after his grandfather—a very fruitful source of confusion in the literary records of artists.

Mnesarchus.

Another Samian gem-engraver of the first half of the 6th century, about whom almost nothing is known, was *Mnesarchus* the father of the celebrated philosopher Pythagoras; see Herod. IV. 95; and Aristotle quoted by Diog. Laertius, VIII. 1.

Pyrgoteles.

The only gem-engravers mentioned by Pliny (see *Hist. Nat.* XXXVII. 8) are these—*Pyrgoteles*, who worked for Alexander the Great, and was (according to the above passage) the only engraver who was allowed to cut the

---

[1] Pliny mentions (*Hist. Nat.* XXXVI. 43) another Quadriga covered by a fly's wings, the work of Myrmecides—possibly a similarly distorted statement.

[2] The art of gem-engraving was called δακτυλιογλυφία; see Plato, *Alc.* 1. 128 C.

portrait of Alexander on an emerald—"vetuit in hac gemma (zmaragdo) ab alio se scalpi quam a Pyrgotele."

In an earlier passage (*Hist. Nat.* VII. 125) Pliny seems to say that Pyrgoteles was the only artist who was permitted to make a marble statue of Alexander—"Idem hic Imperator (Alexander) edixit, ne quis ipsum alius, quam Apelles, pingeret; quam Pyrgoteles, sculperet; quam Lysippus, ex aere duceret." cf. Hor. *Ep.* II. i. 239.

Apuleius (*Florid.* lib. 1) tells us that Alexander's edict was that "solus Pyrgoteles caelamine excuderet:" a phrase that could not apply to gem-engraving, but must mean hammered, repoussé work of some kind, probably in the precious metals.

With these conflicting statements all we can gather with any degree of certainty is that Pyrgoteles was a gem-engraver, and that he had the monopoly of executing portraits of Alexander in some form or material.

In the same passage (*H. N.* XXXVI. 8) Pliny names three other distinguished gem-engravers as being subsequent in date to Pyrgoteles—*Apollonides*[1] and *Cronius*, about whom he tells us nothing, and *Dioscurides*, who engraved the portrait of Augustus, which subsequent emperors used as a signet.

Pliny states (*Hist. Nat.* XXXV. 156) that the celebrated sculptor *Pasiteles*, in the first century B.C., also practised the art of *scalptura*, meaning probably gem-engraving.

The names of two other gem-engravers are known only from epigrams preserved in the Greek *Anthologia*. *Satyreius* who engraved a portrait of Arsinoe of Egypt on *crystal*; *Anth.* IX. 776; and *Tryphon*, who cut on *beryl* a swimming figure of Gallene; *Anth.* IX. 544.

The number of existing gems which have what profess to be artists' signatures is very large, but the great majority of

---

[1] In the Devonshire collection there is a fragmentary *intaglio* on *sard* engraved with a cow lying down, under which (in the *exergue*) is the signature ΑΠΟΛΛΩ-ΝΙΔΟΥ, in incised letters. It has been wrongly described by Dr Brunn and others, as a *cameo* on onyx.

The inscription is not above suspicion, more especially as the Duke of Devonshire bought it from the notorious Baron Stosch, to whom he paid the enormous sum of 1000 guineas, for the sake of the signature of the famous Apollonides.

these are certainly not genuine. In many cases both the gem itself and the signature are forgeries, but a great many genuine gems exist on which a signature has been added by a modern hand.

Ever since the revival of interest in antique gems and their engravers about the time of Lorenzo de' Medici (1449—1492), the value of a genuine stone has been enormously increased by its possessing an artist's signature, and therefore unscrupulous dealers ever since the 15th century have been in the habit of adding the name of some real or supposed glyptic artist on to the gems they wished to sell, whether they were genuine antiques or modern forgeries.

Forged Artists' names.

This rage for artists' names on gems was specially prevalent during the eighteenth and the first half of the present century.

In many cases the signature has been forged with great skill, and owing to the mechanical process by which it is cut and its minute scale, it is very frequently quite impossible to decide whether a signature is genuine or not.

The most diversely different conclusions have been arrived at by many archaeologists, such as Köhler, Stephani, Brunn, Benndorf, Clarac, Chabouillet and Furtwängler, who have written on the subject of signed gems[1]. Any absolute certainty on this matter is practically unattainable, and almost the only signed gems, about which there can be no doubt, are those which have been found by some trustworthy explorer and have never passed through the hands of a dealer, such gems, for example, as the two cranes of *Dexamenos*, found at Kertch, the ancient Panticapaeum, and now in the Hermitage

Gems of Dexamenos.

---

[1] A long list of gem-engravers, real and imaginary, is given by Clarac, *Catalogue des artistes de l'antiquité*, Paris, 1849; see also Brunn, *Geschichte der Griechischen Künstler*, 1859, vol. II. pp. 444—637, and C. W. King, *Antique Gems*, 1866, pp. 211 to 238; and his *Handbook of Engraved Gems*, 1866, pp. 246 to 339, where he gives the gist of Köhler's, Stephani's, and Brunn's treatises on the subject.

The best recent treatise on signed gems is Furtwängler's *Gemmen mit Künstlerinschriften* in the "Jahrbuch des Kaiserlich Deutschen Archäologischen Instituts," 1888, pp. 105 to 139, 193 to 224, and 297 to 325, Plates 3, 8, 10 and 11, and 1889, p. 46.

Museum at St Petersburg[1]. See page vii in the Appendix, where the gems of *Dexamenos* are described.

Another signet found in a sarcophagus in one of the Kertch tombs has what is probably an engraver's signature. This is a ring wholly of gold, on the bezel of which is cut a figure of a Scythian noble clad in a tunic and close fitting trousers with a Phrygian *mitra* on his head; he is seated on a chair, and holds an arrow in his hand. Like most of the other Greek objects from Kertch it is fine work of the 4th century B.C. In the field, in minute letters, is the name *Athenades* [A]ΘΗΝΑΔΗΣ. *Gold signets.*

Signet of Athenade

It is now in the Hermitage collection at St Petersburg: see *Antiqu. du Bosp. Cimm.* Pl. 32, 14, and *Compte Rendu.* 1861, Pl. VI. 11.

The Museum in Naples contains a gold ring which was found on the site of the ancient Capua. Like the last mentioned ring, it is wholly of metal, and has a large bezel of mixed metal inlaid in the gold and engraved with a very noble portrait head of a clean-shaven Roman of middle age, of fine Greek workmanship of the Augustan period.

In the field behind the head, in very small characters, is the signature of the engraver, *Herakleidas*, [HP]ΑΚΛΕΙΔΑC ΕΠΟΕΙ: see *Bull. Inst.* 1855, Pl. XXXI f. It has been suggested that the head is a portrait of M. J. Brutus. *Signet of Herakleidas.*

Apart from the evidence of an ascertained *provenance*, signets which have the engraving on a metal bezel can be trusted far more safely than any engraving on stone[2]; unless indeed the latter is set in a ring which is evidently antique.

Even this test is not infallible, since in some cases gems set in ancient rings have been recut, as is mentioned at page

---

[1] Panticapaeum was a Greek colony in the Tauric Chersonesus (modern Crimea): the population was partly Scythian and partly Hellenic by race. Its tombs have been most remarkable for their rich stores of objects of all kinds of the finest Greek workmanship.

[2] The reason of this is that the softer metal more readily shows signs of age, and, except in the case of gold, usually takes a surface *patina* from oxydization which a forger can hardly imitate. A hard stone, on the other hand, remains unchanged by time, and may be free from all signs of wear.

101, and ancient rings with plain gold bezels have had a modern device cut upon them.

Again we may safely trust those signed gems which are known to have existed in some royal or ecclesiastical treasury from a period earlier than the date when forged inscriptions began to be cut, earlier, that is, than the latter years of the 15th century.

Gem by Euodos.

One of the most notable examples of this is the celebrated portrait of Julia the daughter of Titus on a large and brilliant *beryl* or *aquamarine*, one of the noblest glyptic portraits in the world. It is signed behind the head with the artist's name Euodos, ΕΥΟΔΟC ΕΠΟΙΕΙ, reversed on the gem.

The history of this magnificent gem can be traced back for more than a thousand years. It was once in the possession of Charlemagne, and was given by Charles the Bald to the Abbey of St Denis, where it remained till the French Revolution, among the many gems which were attached as ornaments to enrich a gold reliquary. It is now in the Bibliothèque Nationale at Paris, No. 2089; see page 270 in Chabouillet's *Catalogue*.

Another signed portrait of Julia, of rather coarse workmanship, very inferior to that by Euodos, exists in the Marlborough collection (No. 447).

It is cut on a splendid *hyacinthine sard* of which the upper portion is broken away.

Nikander.

Behind the neck is the signature of *Nikander*, ΝΙΚΑΝΔΡΟC ΕΠΟΕΙ, of almost undoubted genuineness, though the gem lacks the confirmation of so satisfactory a pedigree as that of the work of Euodos.

Another signed gem in the Marlborough collection[1] (No. 341) certainly appears to be genuine, though its pedigree does not go back further than the reign of Charles I., when it formed part of the Earl of Arundel's collection.

It is a large dark *sard*, engraved with a seated figure of Diomede holding the Palladium, and, on the right, is Ulysses pointing to the prostrate body of the Trojan priestess. On

[1] In 1875 the whole Marlborough collection of gems was sold for 35,000 guineas to Mr Bromielow of Battlesden Park in Bedfordshire.

the square *cippus* on which Diomede sits is the signature of the artist *Felix*, in Greek letters ΦΗΛΙΞ ΕΠΟΙΕΙ; and in the field, over Diomede's head, is the name of the owner Calpurnius Severus, in the genitive case, thus—ΚΑΛΠΟΥΡΝΙΟΥ ϹΕΟΥΗΡΟΥ.

Gem by Felix.

There are a great many *replicas* or copies of this gem more or less varied; either with the whole or part of the design, and with various, probably in most cases, forged artists' names, such as Solon and Gnaios.

Furtwängler however accepts as genuine a *carnelian* replica of this design which is signed ΔΙΟϹΚΟΥΡΙΔΟΥ, in the Devonshire collection, first mentioned by Dandelot in 1716. This has only the figure of Diomede seated on a cubical *cippus* with a sword in one hand and the Palladium in the other. In front of him is a statuette on a tall *stele*. The signature is in minute letters in the *exergue*, see *Jahrbuch Arch. Inst.* 1888, p. 220 and Pl. 8, No. 26.

Dioskourides.

By far the most beautiful of all the *replicas* of this noble figure, ancient or modern, is one from the collection of Lorenzo the Magnificent, with LAVR. MED. on the cubical *cippus* on which Diomede sits.

Diomede of Lorenzo.

It has a very wide margin all round, unlike the ancient fashion of filling up the field as much as possible, and is clearly a work of Lorenzo's own time by some unknown artist of extraordinary skill : see page 125.

A variety of this design with Diomede rising from his seat is known from *paste* copies only, the original now being lost or out of sight; in the *exergue* is the signature of Solon, ϹΟΛΩΝ ΕΠΟΙΕΙ, which may possibly be genuine.

The name ΣΟΛΩΝΟϹ on the celebrated *chalcedony* with Medusa's head from the Strozzi collection, now in the British Museum (No. 1256), is certainly not a genuine artist's signature. The same may be said of the head of Maecenas, with a similar inscription, which was published by Fulvio Orsini in 1580 as a portrait of the Athenian Solon. On the last two gems the name, if not a modern addition, is probably that of the owner.

Strozzi Medusa.

Few gems have such a good pedigree as one which is signed by *Eutyches* of Aegaeae, the son of Dioskourides. It

Eutyches.

Athene by Eutyches.

is a very noble full-faced bust of Athene, deeply cut on a large *amethyst*, evidently of the first century A.D., and copied from a statue. In three vertical lines is inscribed in minute characters—

ΕΥΤΥΧΗC
ΔΙΟCΚΟΥΡΙΔΟΥ
ΑΙΓΕΑΙΟC ΕΠ[ΟΙΕΙ].

"Eutyches of Aegaeae the son of Dioskourides made (this)." Apart from internal evidence there is documentary proof of the genuineness of this gem. The Comm. de' Rossi discovered in the Vatican library, among the MS. writings of Cyriac of Ancona, a description of this very gem written in 1445, with the inscription given in full and a Latin translation of it; see *Bull. Inst.* 1878, p. 40; and King, *Handbook of Gems*, p. 284.

A gem exactly answering to this description exists among the Marlborough collection (see *Marl. Gems*, Vol. II. No. 12), and is probably the one mentioned by Cyriac: it has unfortunately lost the last four letters by re-polishing and re-setting; see N. Story-Maskelyne, *Marl. Cat.* 1870, No. 81.

Cameo by Herophilus.

A large cameo in *blue paste* with a very fine laureated head of Augustus in very high relief, in the Vienna collection, is signed by *Herophilus*, another son of Dioskourides,

ΗΡΟΦΙΛΟC
ΔΙΟCΚΟΡΙΔ[ΟΥ].

This gem also appears to have a good pedigree: it is in a mediaeval setting, and is said to have belonged to a Church in Germany many centuries ago. Father Wilhelm in his *Luxemburgum Romanum*, written in the 17th century, describes this cameo as being then in the treasury of the Church of Echternach. Drs Brunn and Furtwängler consider the signature to be genuine, in spite of the unusual spelling of "Dioskorides."

Hyllus.

The name of a third son of Dioskourides called *Hyllus* occurs on some antique gems.

A *sardonyx* cameo in the Berlin Museum with a finely executed head of a young Faun has the signature thus—

ΥΛΛΟC ΔΙΟCΚΟΥΡΙΔΟΥ ΕΠΟΙΕ. In most cases this name is a modern forgery. Among the genuine examples may be ranked a *sard* in the St Petersburg Museum with an intaglio head of Apollo; in the *field* is the name ΥΛΛΟΥ.

Hyllus.

This gem was formerly in the collection of Lorenzo de' Medici, and bears his name LAVR. MED. cut in the usual conspicuous fashion.

The Bibliothèque at Paris contains a very finely executed intaglio on *chalcedony*, a bull advancing with lowered horns, and decked out in Dionysiac ornaments. Above it, in the field, is the name ΥΛΛΟΥ, which may possibly be a genuine artist's signature.

One or two other gems signed by Dioskourides have a pedigree reaching sufficiently far back to, at least diminish the chance of either the engraved figure or the name being a forgery.

Dioskourides.

The celebrated portrait on an *amethyst* of Maecenas (or Solon as it has been called) in the Paris Bibliothèque, No 2077, was known as far back as 1605.

It is a very nobly cut head, with the name ΔΙΟCΚΟΥΡΙΔΟΥ placed vertically behind it: see Chabouillet's *Catalogue*, p. 269.

Furtwängler, however, doubts whether this gem is the identical one which was known in 1605, and suspects it of being modern.

In the Marlborough collection there is a very fine front-faced standing figure of Mercury wearing the chlamys and petasus, cut on an orange *sard*, with the signature ΔΙΟCΚΟΥΡΙ-ΔΟΥ in rather large but lightly cut letters. This gem was described in 1589 by Montjosieu in his *Gallus Romae Hospes*.

Blenheim Hermes.

It is also mentioned by Spon as having previously belonged to Fulvio Orsini, the well known Roman archaeologist. The design on this gem is obviously copied from a statue not unlike the so called Phocion of the Vatican.

It has, as Dr Story-Maskelyne remarks in his *Catalogue of the Marlborough gems*, No. 167, been unfortunately ruined by repolishing the 'field.' A copy by Pichler is in the British Museum, No. 2299.

Another gem which was once in Fulvio Orsini's collection,

Apollonios. and was described in 1589 by Montjosieu (*op. cit.*) is signed by Apollonios ΑΠΟΛΛΩΝΙΟΥ. It is a very beautiful figure of Artemis standing, in profile, wearing a short chiton and resting her hand on a *cippus*. It is evidently copied from a very fine marble statue of Praxitelean type. Köhler supposes it to be from the colossal Artemis of Anticyra by Praxiteles, but the coin *reverses* of Anticyra, which probably show this statue, represent a figure of different design; see Gardner and Imhoof-Blumer, *Numismatic Commentary on Pausanias*, Plate Y, No. XVII. and page 124.

Dioskourides. Another gem, the design on which is evidently copied from a statue, bears the signature of Dioskourides. It is a very fine *sard* with a standing figure of Mercury wearing a chlamys, seen in profile, except the head which is turned to the front. In one hand Mercury holds a dish containing a ram's head, and in the other a caduceus. Behind, in small letters, placed vertically, is the name ΔΙΟϹΚΟΥΡΙΔΟΥ.

Carlisle Mercury. This gem was for long in Lord Carlisle's collection; but has, in the present year 1890, been purchased, with the rest of the Carlisle gems, by the British Museum. Neither the engraving nor the signature have a very genuine look; it is a suspicious circumstance that it once belonged to Baron Stosch, to whom the production of many forgeries is due.

The same design, but without the questionable signature, occurs on another gem in the British Museum, No. 705 in Mr Smith's *Catalogue*, which may possibly be a genuine antique in spite of the unusual material it is engraved upon, a soft stone of an opaque green colour. The Carlisle gem may perhaps be a copy of this, executed (with the addition of Dioskourides' name) for Baron Stosch; it is cut on a brilliant sard of fine golden tint, a kind of stone which was frequently used by the engravers of the last century for their best works. However, even if the Carlisle Mercury be a modern production, it is certainly a very beautiful gem and is the work of a most skilful artist.

Among the other gems which bear the name of Dioskourides the most genuine appears to be one which was found in 1756 on the estate of the Duke of Bracciano near Rome.

It is a *sard* engraved with a beautiful full-faced head of a female with long flowing ringlets and small horns over the forehead—possibly representing Io. The signature ΔIOC-KOYPIΔOY is cut vertically in microscopic characters, in the field at the side of the head; see *Jahrbuch Arch. Inst.* 1888, p. 222 and Plate 8, No. 25.

The British Museum possesses two gems of very minute workmanship with a similar front-faced head of Julius Caesar, one from the Riccardi collection on *sard*, and another on *jacinth* from the Blacas collection. Both have what professes to be the signature of Dioskourides.

The Blacas gem is certainly a modern work: the modelling of the face is exaggerated and too minute in style, and the name is wrongly spelt in two places ΔIOCKOPIΔOΣ and has the square sigma Σ instead of the rounded form C used by Dioskourides. On the Riccardi gem the name is cut in the right way ΔIOCKOYPIΔOY; see Brunn, *Griech. Kunstler*, II. p. 497; *Jahrbuch Arch. Inst.* 1888, p. 301, and Plate 11, Nos 13 and 14; and *Brit. Mus. Cat.* Nos. 1557 and 1558[1].

In addition to those already mentioned the following are among the most important gems with artists' signatures, but they are not in all cases free from suspicion.

Pamphilos; on an *amethyst* in the Paris Bibliothèque engraved with a seated figure of Achilles playing on a lyre, with his arms placed around him, very pictorial in style.

By the lyre is cut vertically the name ΠΑΜΦΙΛΟΥ; see Chabouillet, *Catalogue*, No. 1815, p. 243.

A slightly modified *replica* of this, with the same inscription is in the Devonshire collection; and another, probably a copy of the Paris gem, is in the British Museum (No. 2305). This copy has been engraved on a genuine ancient gem, on the back of which is cut the sacred Gnostic word IAω.

[1] Another artist called Dioskourides from Samos, and of about the same date, was a worker in mosaic.

A very minutely executed theatrical scene, with musicians playing and dancing, worked in glass *tesserae* was found in Pompeii, with the inscription ΔΙΟΣΚΟΥΡΙΔΗΣ ΣΑΜΙΟΣ ΕΠΟΙΗΣΕ at the top of the picture; see *Real Museo Borbonico*, Vol. IV. 1827, Plate 34. It is now in the Museum at Naples.

Pamphilos.

The Paris *amethyst* was given to Louis XIV. by Professor Fesch of Basle, so it cannot be a quite modern forgery. It is possible that the inscription meant that the design was copied from a painting by the famous Greek artist Pamphilus, as is suggested by its picture-like style.

Agathopus.

Agathopus; a fine *beryl* or *aquamarine* in the Florence collection (Uffizi gallery) is engraved with a very noble head of a Roman, supposed to be Sextus Pompey, in the style of the best Greek iconic heads, such as those on the tetradrachms of Eumenes of Pergamus. Behind the head, in two horizontal lines, is the signature ΑΓΑΘΟΠΟΥC ΕΠΟΕΙ.

This magnificent gem was known in the 16th century, and in 1707 it was published by Maffei in his *Gemme Antiche*: it is said to have been found near Rome, set in a massive gold ring. The British Museum possesses a *replica* or copy on sard of this portrait, with the signature and in addition the letter **L**, which is supposed to be a mark of its having once belonged to Lorenzo the Magnificent; there is hardly sufficient space in the field for Lorenzo's usual mark, LAVR. MED. See *Museum Florentinum*, Vol. II. Pl. I., fig. 2; and *Brit. Mus. Cat.*, No. 1552; cf. also Köhler and Stephani, *Gesammelte Schriften*, 1850—3, p. 338.

Onesas.

Onesas; in the Florentine collection is a very fine laureated head of the youthful Herakles on *sard*, with the lion's skin over his shoulder: the upper part of the head is broken away. In a horizontal line is the signature ΟΝΗCΑC.

The hypercritical Köhler calls this a modern gem, but it has all the appearance of being genuine.

As much cannot be said of another gem in the Florentine museum with the inscription ΟΝΗCΑC ΕΠΟΙΕΙ, a standing figure of a Muse playing on a lyre, on *paste*.

Its wide margin and general style suggest that it is a work of some early Renaissance artist.

It was known in the 17th century, and cannot therefore be a quite modern forgery.

Philemon.

Philemon; in the Vienna collection is a fine *sardonyx* gem engraved with a nude figure of a hero with a club, standing in front of an archway, in which the corpse of the Minotaur is lying, representing Theseus at the door of the Cretan labyrinth.

Behind Theseus is cut, in a vertical line, the inscription ΦΙΛΗΜΟΝΟC.

Philemon

Both Kohler and Stephani consider this a modern gem, not without reason: it is very pictorial in style.

A *paste* in the Strozzi collection with the head of an ivy-wreathed Faun has the inscription ΦΙΛΗΜΩΝ ΕΠΟΙ[ΕΙ], but this also is of doubtful genuineness.

Anteros; another gem, about the authenticity of which very different opinions have been expressed, is an *aquamarine* in the Devonshire collection, with, in the *exergue*, the inscription ΑΝΤΕΡΩΤΟC.

Antero.

The design represents Herakles staggering under the weight of the slain Marathonian bull.

It is a very noble and beautiful work, certainly not of quite modern date, but most probably copied from some ancient terra cotta or marble relief by one of the ablest gem engravers of the 16th century.

The same name occurs on the fragment of a very beautiful *onyx* cameo now in the British Museum, among the Carlisle collection. This fragment consists only of the upper part of a subject which may possibly have been the Judgment of Paris. Little more remains than the head of Paris wearing a Phrygian cap and holding a veil away from his face in a very feminine manner, and, on the other side, the head of a female figure. The top of the cameo is occupied by the overhanging branches of a tree, from which a quiver is suspended. At the right hand side is the inscription in minute incised letters ΑΝΤΕ...ΕΓ... probably for ΑΝΤΕΡΩC ΕΠΟΙΕΙ.

Cameo by Anteros.

The comparatively small portion which is, unfortunately, all that now exists of this remarkable cameo is of extraordinarily beautiful and minute workmanship, and the signature appears to be perfectly genuine.

Teukros; of rather similar style, and possibly of the same date as the Herakles and the bull, is an *amethyst* in the Florentine collection with Omphale (or Iole) standing in front of Herakles who is seated on a rock.

Teukros.

M. 6

Teukros.   The name ΤΕΥΚΡΟΥ is cut vertically in very minute characters, quite unlike the bold style in which an owner's name was usually engraved on a signet. A great many copies of this or a similar design exist. The sensuous softness of the modelling of the nude forms is more like the production of an artist of the Renaissance period than that of an ancient engraver, even of the late Greek or Graeco-Roman school.

Though they can hardly be accepted as genuine, the two last mentioned gems are among the most skilful examples of the glyptic art that any age has ever produced.

Moreover they are not slavish copies, but bear the impress of real original power on the part of their engravers.

Aulus.   *Aulus;* probably no other artist's name, real or forged, occurs on gems as frequently as the name of Aulus. It is introduced on a large number of the Poniatowski forgeries, e.g. on one in the Fitzwilliam collection, see page xxv, No. 11.

In many cases the name is clearly that of the owner, not of the engraver, as for example, on a magnificent fragment of a *sard* in the British Museum with a head of Asklepios. In front of it, on a tablet, is the name ΑΥΛΟΥ in large characters[1]. In fact, putting aside those gems on which the name is a forgery, and those on which it stands for the owner, it is very doubtful whether any would be left to prove that there was a gem-engraver named Aulus.

Hellen.   *Hellen;* the name ΕΛΛΗΝ or ΕΛΛΗΝΟC occurs on various gems of doubtful authenticity. Mr King has suggested that this is one of the ways in which the celebrated gem-engraver
Il Greco.   Alessandro Cesati, known as *il Greco,* used to sign his works. Alessandro was by birth a Cypriote and was one of the most famous gem-cutters of the 16th century; see below, page 127.

It is also probable that the inscription ΑΛΕΞΑΝΔΡΟC or ΑΛΕΞΑ more or less contracted are other forms of the same artist's signature. So also, perhaps, the name ΚΟΙΝΤΟΣ ΑΛΕΞΑ, Quintus Alexander.

For example an *onyx* cameo in the Florentine museum

---

[1] This is the view taken by Stephani; *Gesam. Schrift.* III. p. 342; but Köhler in his usual fashion rejects the gem altogether, quite without reason; see *ib.* p. 179.

with a lion, Cupid and two female figures, signed ΑΛΕΞΑΝΔ. E. *Cesati.*
is known to have been engraved by Cesati. It is probably
the cameo mentioned by Vasari as one of Alessandro Cesati's
finest works.

In any case there is no real reason for including either of
the last two names among those which can fairly be assumed
to be signatures of artists.

Epitynchanus; this name, which occurs on several important *Epityn-*
gems, may possibly be a genuine artist's signature, at least in *chanus.*
some cases. Gems so inscribed are mostly portrait-heads,
such as Marcellus and Germanicus. A very beautiful *sardonyx* cameo in the British Museum with a head of a youthful
Roman, supposed to be Germanicus (No. 1589), has the
incised inscription ΕΠΙΤΥΓΧΑ.

No. 1575 in the same collection is a fine *amethyst* intaglio
with a front face of a Roman lady, supposed to be Livia, the
wife of Augustus, in the character of Ceres. In the field is
the contracted name ΕΠΙΤ.

What is possibly the same name, contracted to ΕΠΙ, occurs
on a fine *carnelian* in the Paris Bibliothèque, engraved with a
figure of Bellerophon mounted on Pegasus. As possessing
an artist's signature this gem is very doubtful, but the device
itself appears to be genuine, and the gem had been known
for a long time before 1854 when it passed into the Paris
collection[1].

[1] See M. Hase's Edition of Léon Diacre, published in Paris in 1819.

CHAPTER VII.

INSCRIPTIONS ON GEMS (*continued*).

Signed cameos.

CAMEOS WITH ARTISTS' NAMES: in judging of these, if the name, like the rest of the design, is in relief we have the advantage of knowing that it must have been cut by the original engraver of the whole design, and cannot have been added by a later hand; so we are at least spared the double difficulty of deciding, first whether the gem itself is genuine, and secondly whether the name may not be a subsequent addition by some forger.

Cameo of Athenion.

In many cases the signatures on cameos are not in relief, but are incised, like the name on an *intaglio;* all such signatures must be regarded with some suspicion.

Among the most authentic signed cameos is a large *sardonyx* in the Museum at Naples, with Zeus holding a thunderbolt and driving a quadriga over the prostrate forms of the conquered earth-born Giants. In the *exergue* is the name ΑΘΗΝΙΩΝ in relief, in minute letters. The whole design is clearly the work of a talented artist of the Augustan period; and even the sceptical Köhler throws no doubt upon its genuineness. That the name *Athenion* is that of the engraver rather than of the owner of the cameo is suggested by the minuteness of the characters. Moreover an owner's name, which was a natural addition to an intaglio-signet, would certainly be a less frequent addition in the case of cameo gems. The same name (Athenion) occurs also on a large fragment of a cameo in *blue paste* in the Berlin collection, with a standing figure of a Roman General, supposed to be Drusus the elder, in a triumphal quadriga. The name

Paste cameo.

ΑΘΗΝΙΩΝ, in exactly similar letters to those on the Naples cameo, is placed in the *exergue* of the Berlin paste, which is, no doubt, an ancient copy of a work of the same engraver who cut the Destruction of the Titans by the thunderbolts of Zeus.

In the Florentine collection there is a very good cameo in *sardonyx* with Cupid riding on a lion and playing a lyre. In the *exergue* is the signature in relief ΠΡΩΤΑΡΧΟΣ ΕΠΟΕΙ, which even Köhler admits to be genuine, placing it among the five examples of signed gems which are the only ones he accepts as ancient gem signatures. *Cameo of Protarchos.*

Another very fine signed cameo was in the collection of Lord Beverley, and is now in the possession of the Duke of Northumberland at Alnwick Castle. It is a *sardonyx* with a nude figure of Philoctetes in Lemnos, seated on the ground; in his right hand he holds a bird's wing, using it to fan his wounded foot, which is bound round with bandages. *Cameo of Boethos.*

In the upper part of the field is the name *Boethos*, ΒΟΗΘΟΥ, cut in relief.

The design of this cameo is very skilfully contrived to fill up the surface of the gem in the most complete way, and the details are cut with great minuteness and naturalistic truth, especially noticeable in the head and in the modelling of the chest and ribs.

In spite of Stephani's opinion to the contrary, this cameo bears all the marks of being a genuine antique work of the Augustan age: see *Annali Inst.* 1881, p. 266.

Mr King has however suggested that the name *Boethos* is not that of the engraver of the cameo, but that the gem was copied from an embossed relief in silver by the celebrated sculptor and *caelator* named *Boethos*, who is mentioned by Pliny (*Hist. Nat.* XXXIII. 155) as being one of the principal Greek workers in the precious metals, and (*H. N.* XXXIV. 84) as being the sculptor of the boy struggling with a goose, of which ancient *replicas* are now in the Vatican Museum and elsewhere. However this may be, the motive of this cameo is an early one. *The Caelator Boethos.*

It occurs on an intaglio of the scarab type, within a cable

border, in the British Museum; see *Brit. Mus. Cat.* No. 455; and *Annali Inst.* 1857, Pl. II., fig. 6[1].

Incised names.

Although, as is remarked above, cameos on which the engraver's signature is *incised* must be viewed with suspicion, it cannot be said that in all cases such incised names are modern forgeries.

More than one is accepted as genuine by Dr Brunn[2], as, for example, the *paste* head of Augustus signed by Herophilos, mentioned above at page 76. The cameo of Anteros (p. 81) is also an example of undoubted genuineness.

In the Berlin Museum there is a magnificent *sardonyx* cameo with a figure of Hercules dragging Cerberus by his chain, a most exquisitely modelled and minutely finished work, with, in the *exergue*, the name ΔΙΟCΚΟΥΡΙΔΟΥ.

Dioskourides.

This cameo certainly was known in the 16th century: part of the *field* is broken away and is now replaced in plain gold.

With regard to the *motive* of this cameo, an interesting passage occurs in the *Autobiography* of the Florentine artist Benvenuto Cellini, lib. I. cap. 27. Cellini tells us that during his first stay in Rome (from 1524 to 1527) he was in the habit of buying from the peasants large numbers of ancient gems, which they found while digging in the vineyards in and around Rome. Among these was the *emerald* with the dolphin's head, mentioned below at page 135, and a magnificent head of Minerva on a large *topaz*. The finest of them all was, Cellini says, a cameo with figures of Hercules subduing Cerberus, which he showed to Michelangelo, who remarked that it was the most wonderful piece of work he had ever seen.

Cellini.

It is not impossible that the cameo described by Cellini is the one now in the Berlin collection[3].

---

[1] Both the cameo and the British Museum intaglio are described by Milani, *Mito di Filotete*, p. 86, and Pl. II.

[2] In his *Gesch. der Griech. Künstler*, 1859, Vol. II. Dr Brunn discusses and modifies the conclusions arrived at by Köhler and Stephani, *Gesammelte Schriften*, 1850-3, in which work almost all gem signatures are taken to be forgeries.

[3] It need hardly be said that Köhler refuses to accept this gem as a genuine

In the Museum at Naples there is a very fine *sardonyx* cameo engraved with a figure of Victory driving a *biga*, over which is incised the inscription ϹΩϹΤΡΑΤΟΥ. The gem once belonged to Lorenzo de' Medici and has LAVR. MED. engraved under the horses of the *biga*.

Cameos of Sostratos.

Among the gems of the Carlisle collection, recently purchased for the British Museum, is a fine onyx cameo with Cupid leading a chariot drawn by two panthers. In the *exergue* the name ϹΩϹΤΡΑΤΟΥ is incised in minute letters. The same name occurs on a small, delicately cut intaglio in the same collection, with a figure of a winged Victory sacrificing a bull, on which she rests one knee. The name ϹΩϹΤΡΑΤΟΥ is cut in the *exergue* in very small characters[1]. Both these appear to be undoubtedly genuine examples of an artist's signature.

If the truth could be known it would probably be found that a large proportion of so-called artists' signatures on gems of all sorts really are names of owners, more especially in the case of signet gems, intaglios. Artists were much more likely to introduce their own names on cameos for the reasons which are indicated at pages 92—93.

Owners' names.

If however the same name is found to be repeated on several gems of similar date and style, as is the case with the above-mentioned name Sostratos, we may fairly assume that it is the genuine signature of an engraver.

Gem signatures, unlike artists' names on coins, are rarely cut on part of the engraved device; usually they are placed in the field. There are however one or two possible exceptions to this rule, as, for example, the full faced head of the dog Sirius, with a collar round his neck. Several *replicas* and copies of this exist[2]: one of the finest is No. 270 in the Marlborough collection, engraved on a very beautiful oriental *carbuncle*: it has ΓΑΙΟϹ ΕΠΟΙΕΙ on the collar[3].

Sirius gem.

antique: in fact he denies the authenticity of all the signatures of Dioskourides: see *Gesamm. Schrift.* III. p. 287.

[1] This gem is published by Tassie, Plate XLV. No. 7760.

[2] One in the Berlin Museum, cut on *rock crystal* by Lorenzo Massini for Baron Stosch, has the modern signature ΜΑϹΙΝΟϹ (Masini) ΕΠΟΙΕΙ.

[3] The signature on the Sirius gem in the Marlborough collection, and even

88   ARTISTS' NAMES ON   [CHAP. VII.

The two similar gems in the British Museum, from the Payne Knight and the Blacas collections (Nos. 1115 and 1116), are without the signature.

Victory of Onatas.
A very beautiful and large *chalcedony* gem in the British Museum (*Brit. Mus. Cat.* No. 1161), engraved with a figure of Victory erecting a trophy, a somewhat similar design to that on a Syracusan tetradrachm of Agathocles, has, on the ribbon-like folds of a long flag attached to a spear, in characters of somewhat indistinct form, what is possibly the artist's name ONATA[Σ][1].

The genuineness of this noble gem has been questioned, but Furtwängler and other good authorities accept it as a genuine Greek work of the early part of the 4th century B.C.

Dates of signed gems.
With regard to the dates when engraved gems most frequently received the signature of the artist, it may be remarked that this was very rarely done before the 4th century B.C. In fact signed gems were very exceptional throughout the whole of the autonomous Greek period; by far the majority of those which now exist are the work of Greek engravers during the time of the Roman Empire, especially the Augustan period.

There is however in the British Museum (No. 479 in Mr A. H. Smith's *Catalogue*) one very remarkable signed gem which apparently is not later than the middle or latter part of the 6th century B.C.

Gem of Syrias.
It is one of those curious scarabaeoids which have on the curved back a design carved in delicate relief—in this case a Satyr's head—the earliest form of cameo, mentioned above at page 59.

The device sunk on the flat or signet side of the scarabaeoid is a standing figure of a bearded harp-player, and round the edge of the *field* is the inscription which Mr A. H. Smith gives as ϚVPIAϚ ΕΠΟΙΕϚΕ[2].

the gem itself is by no means above the suspicion of being the work of Natter, the name is probably a blunder for ΓΝΑΙΟC.

[1] Furtwängler is inclined to read the inscription ΟΝΑΙΑ; see *Jahrbuch Arch. Inst.* 1888, p. 204.

[2] Others read the name of the artist, not as *Surias*, but as *Dories*, ΔΟΡΙΕϚ; see Furtwängler, *Jahrbuch Arch. Inst.* 1888, p. 196, and Pl. 8, No. 1.

This is a quite exceptional gem: almost no others occur with an artist's signature till the 4th century B.C., to which period the various signed gems found at Kertch evidently belong; see page 73.

In the case of Greek *coins*, artists' signatures were not uncommon during the latter part of the 5th century B.C., but the greater number belong to the first half of the 4th century.

On Roman coins artists' signatures are unknown.

On *Greek vases* painters' names were most common during the 6th and 5th centuries B.C., and till about the middle of the 4th century. *Signed vases.*

After the time of Alexander artists' names on pottery soon totally disappear.

ARTISTS' NAMES ON COINS.

As some guide to forming a judgment with regard to signatures on gems it may be well to consider the somewhat analogous case of coins which bear the artist's signature.

With very few exceptions, the coins on which artists' names occur are those of Sicily and Magna Graecia during the 5th and 4th centuries B.C., especially coins of Syracuse, Catana, Metapontum, Tarentum, Heraklaea, Velia, Thurium, Camarina and a few others. The great decadrachms of Syracuse, signed by *Kimon* and *Euainetos*, are among the chief glories of numismatic art. *Signed coins.*

The name is usually in the nominative, the word ΕΠΟΙΕΙ being understood, though in some cases the genitive is used, as if before ΕΡΓΟΝ; and it is cut in very small characters—sometimes of microscopic minuteness. As a rule the artist inserts it in a way that makes it as little conspicuous as possible, so as not to rival the importance of the type *legend*. For this reason it is frequently introduced on some detail of the design; thus, for example, *Kimon* signs on a dolphin under the main head on the *obverse*, or on the band which binds the hair of Persephone.

Eukleidas.

The name ΕΥΚΛΕΙΔΑΣ occurs among the ornaments of Athene's helmet on a Syracusan tetradrachm: and in many other cases the signature escapes all but the most minute examination. In some examples the name is more conspicuous, though cut in microscopic characters, as on some Syracusan *reverses*, which have a tablet inscribed ΕΥΑΙΝΕΤΟ held by a flying Victory—possibly a sort of pattern or trial-piece by this wonderful engraver.

Mr Evans on signed coins.

Mr A. J. Evans, in his *Horsemen of Tarentum*, 1888, page 120, was the first to point out that, very frequently, when a coin has the same name repeated twice, the signature in the one case was, probably, introduced as that of the engraver of the coin-die, and, in the other case, as that of the same person, not in his quality of artist, but as the ἀργυροκόπος, or actual striker of the coin, as a guarantee for its being of the requisite weight and purity of metal.

This very ingenious suggestion satisfactorily explains what was previously a very puzzling problem. It may yet be possible to discover some definite reason for these names being sometimes in the nominative and sometimes in the possessive case.

On many coins the artist's name is not given in full, as it usually is on gems, but in a contracted form or with an initial only. As Mr Evans has pointed out, the same coin-engraver seems often to have worked for more than one city; coins of different colonies both in Magna Graecia and Sicily occurring with the same signature.

A very interesting paper on the signed coins of Sicily and Magna Graecia was recently read by Mr Evans before the Numismatic Society in London, and will shortly be printed in the *Num. Chron.*, Vol. for 1890. Several examples of hitherto unpublished coins with artists' names, in the possession of the writer, were described in this paper; among them were the following—a tetradrachm of Himera with the usual *reverse*, the nymph Himera sacrificing at an altar; on the cornice of the altar, in letters of microscopic minuteness, is the signature ΚΙΜΟΝ. The remarkable thing about this unique coin is that its style shows it to be not later

Kimon the elder.

than about 470 to 465 B.C., and therefore it supplies an example of a signed coin nearly half a century earlier than any which had previously been known.

The artist who signs himself ΚΙΜΩΝ may possibly be the grandfather of the later ΚΙΜΩΝ, whose name occurs on a dolphin under the head of Persephone on one of the celebrated Syracusan decadrachms which were struck towards the close of the 5th century, and also on other coins of the same city. *Kimon the younger.*

Another signed coin, hitherto unpublished, was a Syracusan tetradrachm with the artist's name ΕΥΑΡΧΙΔΑΣ, a die-engraver who worked in conjunction with the Syracusan *Phrygillos*, who is mentioned below. *Euarchidas.*

A new signature of ΕΞΑΚΕΣΤΙΔΑΣ occurs on a tetradrachm of Kamarina, not cut on the *exergual* line, but on a double *pinax* or diptych (πτυκτός πίναξ) held by a flying Nike over the victorious quadriga on the *reverse*. *Exakestidas.*

As a commentary on the gem-like style of the coins of Sicily and Magna Graecia during the 5th and 4th centuries B.C., it is worth while to notice that one very beautiful gem, with a seated figure of Eros playing with *astragali*, has an apparently authentic artist's signature ΦΡΥΓΙΛΛΟΣ ; and that the same artist's name occurs on several very beautiful coins, as, for example, on the *obverse* of a Syracusan tetradrachm of a little before 400 B.C. with a head of Persephone. The *reverse* type, a quadriga, has the signature of another artist, who signs himself ΕΥΘ, perhaps for Εὔθυμος. *Phrygillos.*

It is quite possible that the gem with the figure of Eros may be the work of the same Phrygillos who engraved the Syracusan coin *obverse;* Raoul Rochette and (more recently) Furtwängler and Mr A. J. Evans have accepted this theory[1]. *Eros of Phrygillos.*

The very few artists' names that occur on coins outside of Sicily and Magna Graecia are sometimes treated in a different

---

[1] See Furtwängler's *Gemmen mit Kunstlerinschriften*, "*Jahrbuch des Kais. Deuts. Instit.*" 1888, Band III. p. 197, Pl. 8, No. 4. I have not been able to ascertain who is now the possessor of the Eros of Phrygillos.

On Sicilian coins with artists' names, see Rudolf Weil, *Die Künstlerinschriften der Sicilischen Münzen;* Berlin, 1884.

way, being cut in larger, more conspicuous characters, and having, in two cases, the word ΕΠΟΕΙ (sic) after them.

Theodotos. A beautiful tetradrachm of Clazomene in Ionia (near Smyrna) has a full-faced head of Apollo on the *obverse*, and by it, in the field, in two straight lines, the signature

ΘΕΟΔΟΤΟΣ
ΕΠΟΕΙ.

The position of the head on the die is arranged so as to give ample room for this inscription, which is by no means hidden away, like most of the former class of signatures.

Neuantos. A similar inscription occurs on a much less beautiful tetradrachm of Cydonia in Crete, which has on the *obverse* a profile head of Ariadne, and in the field the signature ΝΕΥΑΝΤΟΣ ΕΠΟΕΙ.

Both these remarkable coins are of about the middle of the 4th century B.C.

Pythodoros. A third Cretan coin, of the city of Aptera, near Cydonia, has the signature ΠΥΘΟΔΩ[ΡΟΣ] in large letters, but without the word ἐποίει, which only occurs on the two last mentioned coins.

Coins struck in the mainland of Greece very rarely bear an artist's signature. The most notable examples are the fine silver *staters* issued about the middle of the 4th century
Coins of Arcadia. B.C. by the Arcadian Federation. On the *obverse* is a noble head of Zeus Lycaeos, and, on the *reverse*, a figure of Pan seated on a rock, with the *pedum* or shepherd's crook in his hand. On the rock, in minute characters, is the engraver's signature ΟΛΥΜ. or more rarely ΧΑΡΙ.; see Head, *Hist. Num.* page 373.

Signed vases. It may at first seem strange that artists' names should be so rare on gems and coins, and so common upon Greek vases —which belong to an inferior grade in the rank of the lesser arts. The reason is probably this, the coin-type was a thing of public importance and had a distinctly sacred character, so it may usually have been thought presumptuous for an artist to introduce his name in such a place[1]. Again,

[1] The sacred character of the types on coins was the reason why portraits of

the gem was meant for personal use as a signet, and most *Use of* men probably would have objected to another name than their *gems.* own being set on their seals; unless the engraver were an artist of such fame that his signature materially added to the value of the gem, as appears to have sometimes been the case in the Roman Imperial period. With painted pottery the *Vases.* case was different: a maker's or painter's name could offend nobody, and was proportionally, of quite insignificant size, in no way interfering with the painted pictures on the vase. If however the gem were large and not intended for use as a signet, such as the Julia of *Euodos*, or still more if it were a cameo, there would be less reason to object to an artist's name being inscribed upon it.

In all cases where the name on a gem is cut in large *Owners'* letters, and is in the genitive, it may (if not a modern ad- *names.* dition) be considered to be the name of the owner. Owners' names in the nominative also occur, but not usually in minute characters such as engravers used. A certain number of gems exist which have the name of some distinguished *Sculptors'* sculptor, such as *Pheidias* or *Scopas*: in most cases these are *names.* obviously modern forgeries, but there may possibly be some antique Roman examples in which a gem has a copy of some piece of sculpture together with the name, not of the engraver of the gem, but of the sculptor of the original statue.

3. EXPLANATORY WORDS: on many Oriental cylinders, in addition to the owner's name, an inscription explains who are the gods or heroes engraved upon it.

So also Greek scarabs and scarabaeoids of the 6th and 5th *Words on* century B.C. have in some cases names cut by the side of the *scarabs.* figures on them to explain the subject, a very common practice on the painted vases of the same period.

This is specially the case with the scarabs found in Etruscan tombs, both those which are imports of Hellenic workmanship and those which are native Etruscan imitations of Greek designs; see above, page 14.

Again, on Graeco-Roman and Roman gems which re-

living persons were not introduced till comparatively late times, after the death of Alexander the Great.

present some god or goddess the inscribed name of the deity is frequently added.

Words of explanation.
This was specially necessary with the crowd of deified abstractions which appear so often on coins and gems of the Empire; since in many cases it would be impossible to know what subject was intended without a word of explanation, such as *Concordia, Munificentia, Felicitas, Indulgentia*, or the like, the symbols and attributes used by the Roman artists being not sufficiently numerous and varied to indicate, without ambiguity, so large a collection of abstractions.

On the finest gems both of the Greek and the Graeco-Roman period inscriptions of this class rarely occur—the device being intended to tell its own story, and the artist having sufficient skill to do so in a sufficiently intelligible manner.

Magic words.
4. TALISMANIC INSCRIPTIONS occur frequently on the later Roman gems used by the Mithraic, Gnostic and other mystic sects. The magical word *Abraxas*[1], and the names of the three Gnostic Aeons, ΙΑΩ, ΟΛΟΜΟΝ, ϹΑΒΑΩ are of specially common occurrence.

A great number of other mysterious combinations of letters were cut on these talismanic stones. The Paris Bibliothèque contains a large and varied collection; see Chabouillet's *Catalogue*, p. 282 seq.[2]

A profession of the Divine Unity (like that of a modern Moslem) is of frequent occurrence on gems of the second century A.D.—ΕΙϹ ΘΕΟϹ ϹΑΡΑΠΙϹ, and other similar phrases: see Nos. 20 and 105, *Fitzwilliam Catalogue*.

In several places (*H. N.* XXXVII. 124 &c.) Pliny expresses his contempt for the superstitious belief in the magical power of gems, but nevertheless these mystic devices were very popular under the late Empire, especially when one of the favourite Roman cults arose out of a combination of the

---

[1] The meaning of the word Abraxas is explained in the Appendix; *Cat. of Fitz. Gems*, No. 20.

[2] For information on this curious subject see Matter, *Histoire du gnosticisme*, Paris, 1850; and C. W. King, *The Gnostics and their remains*, 2nd ed. London, 1887.

Gnostic philosophy of Alexandria with the mystical Mithraic worship of Persia.

5. WORDS OF GREETING *and the like:* these are common on gems of the Roman Imperial period, usually written in Greek: as, for example, XAIPE, EYTYXI, MNHMONEYE (see No. 110, *Fitz. Cat.*), ΦΙΛΕΙ ΜΕ, ΖΗϹΑΙϹ ΠΟΛΛΟΙϹ ΕΤΕϹΙΝ and the like.

Words of greeting.

A curious onyx cameo in the Marlborough collection (No. 643) appears to have been a love gift from a lady. It is engraved with a hand pinching an ear and the inscription

ΜΝΗΜΟΝΕΥΕ ΜΟΥ ΤΗϹ ΚΑΛΗϹ ΨΥΧΗϹ
ΕΥΤΥΧΙ ϹΩΦΡΟΝΙ

"Remember me, your pretty love.
Good luck to you, Sophronios."

Inscriptions such as this are frequently cut in cameo, and occupy the whole field of the stone; they usually have the letters cut in relief in the white stratum of an *onyx*, on a dark ground.

Proverbial phrases sometimes occur on late Roman gems; the following Philosophical maxim is specially common

Proverbs.

Λέγουσιν ἃ θέλουσιν
Λεγέτωσαν
Οὐ μέλει μοι.

A free translation of this phrase is inscribed over the doors of various houses in Scotland, built in the 16th and 17th centuries;

They haif said.
Quhat say they?
Lat thame say.

An example in the Paris Bibliothèque has the following addition at the end of this phrase

ϹΥΦΙΛΕΜΕ
ϹΥΜΦΕΡΙϹΟΙ

meaning "Love me: it is for your advantage (to do so)."

Votive gifts.

6. DEDICATORY INSCRIPTIONS on gems are rare. An example is in the Marlborough collection, No. 256—a very large *nicolo*, with Astarte on a lion and the Dioscuri. In the *exergue* is cut ΑΜΜΩΝΙΟΣ ΑΝΕΘΗΚΕ ΕΠ' ΑΓΑΘΩ, "Ammonios dedicated this for a blessing." It is a gem of the late Empire, probably of North African workmanship.

A *sardonyx* cameo of the Roman Imperial period, with a male and female portrait head facing each other, in the Hermitage Museum at St Petersburg, has, between the two faces, the names ΑΛΦΗΟC CYN ΑΡΗΘѠΝΙ, in incised letters. This is probably a votive inscription, the cameo having been dedicated in some temple, perhaps by a husband and wife[1].

The Virgin's ring.

In the middle ages this gem was preserved in the treasury of the Abbey of St Germain-des-Prés, where it was revered as having been the betrothal ring of St Joseph and the Virgin Mary; it is worn smooth with the kisses of thousands of pilgrims.

When the Abbey was sacked, during the French Revolution, this venerated cameo was carried off and sold to a Russian General, who presented it to the collection of the Emperor of Russia.

---

[1] Some archaeologists explain this inscription as being the signature of two joint gem-engravers, but the inscription seems to be later than the cameo itself, and is larger and more conspicuous than is usually the case with artists' signatures on gems.

CHAPTER VIII.

THE CHARACTERISTICS OF ANCIENT GEMS.

FINE Greek or Graeco-Roman engraved gems are among the most beautiful works of art that exist. They combine noble design and exquisite, but not too minute, finish with the greatest beauty of material, such as the rich, brilliantly coloured *sard* or the *sapphirine chalcedony* with its exquisitely soft, milky lustre. *Beauty of gems.*

The more brilliant varieties of *sard* glow with a sort of internal lustre when held up to the light, and the device engraved upon them comes out at once soft in effect, and clear in outline, with a sort of beauty which hardly can be rivalled in any other branch of art.

Small as gems are in scale, the Greek artist possessed the rare secret of giving grandeur of effect without the aid of great size; and some of the most minute gem engravings seem to have all the dignity of a large group or bust in marble or bronze[1]. *Grandeur of style.*

As a rule the general design or composition of an antique gem is very skilfully contrived to occupy as fully as possible the "field" or flat surface of the stone, leaving the least possible quantity of empty margin. In the gems of the 6th century B.C. this principle is sometimes carried almost too far, and the figures are occasionally bent into somewhat strained

[1] This grandeur of effect produced by work on the smallest scale is well exemplified by the wonderful "Siris bronzes" in the British Museum, and by the still more beautiful heroic figure from the Lago di Bracciano, which is exhibited in the same case; see A. S. Murray, *Hist. of Greek Sculpture*, 2nd ed. 1890, II., page 346, where the latter statuette is illustrated under the title "Bronze from Tarentum."

attitudes in order to bring them within and yet close up to the curved limits of the "field." An example of this is illustrated in fig. 16 at page 25.

Skilful composition. But in the best work of the 5th and 4th centuries B.C. the highest amount of skill and taste is shown in designing the composition so as to fall easily and gracefully within the necessary limits[1]: see fig. 17 at page 26. Thus we find that in the best class of gems with a *guilloche* border the most projecting portion of the composition is often allowed to *Borders.* encroach slightly upon the border, thus giving a look of freedom to the whole, and making the border an essential part, not a mere frame, to the design. In the finest gems with a border in the Fitzwilliam collection this is the case: see Nos. 5, 10 and 11 on Plate I.

In the early Greek painted vases of what is called the Oriental style the same dislike to unoccupied spaces is to be seen—the so-called *horror vacui*, which leads the painter to fill up his ground by a semé pattern of rosettes, crosses and other ornaments.

One of the most obvious differences between antique and modern gems is this absence of margin or unoccupied space in the former class.

Modern style. Thus the exquisite Diomede with the Palladium from Lorenzo de' Medici's collection, though in some respects very Greek in style, being copied from an antique, is very unlike an ancient gem in the wide extent of margin all round the figure.

The Poniatowski forgeries have the same modern peculiarity; see, for example, *Modern Gems*, No. 11 in the catalogue of the Fitzwilliam gems in the Appendix.

Roman style. In the case of Roman gems this rule does not apply; the device by no means invariably fills up the whole field. Far less skill and taste are shown in adapting the design to the shape and size of the gem. The same remark may be made with regard to Roman coins, especially the *reverses* of aurei

---

[1] In Greek coins of the best style we see the same fully occupied field, and the same wonderful skill in suiting the design to the space. On Roman coins these points are much less attended to by the die-cutters.

and denarii of the Imperial period, with a single standing figure of some deity or deified abstraction, the scale of which is frequently small in comparison to the whole circular field of the coin, leaving a large proportion of unoccupied space on each side of the figure.

Roman coins.

Another noticeable point is that, while many modern gems are *pictorial* in style, those of the ancients are rather of a *sculpturesque* character—simple in composition, with very few figures, seldom more than three during the best periods; and the whole design is treated strictly on one plane, like the relief-sculpture of all good artists. The skilful treatment of the 'relief'[1] with a certain monotony of surface, avoiding excessive projection, is one of the chief characteristics of good Greek work.

Simplicity of treatment.

In gems of the Roman period the 'relief' is often much exaggerated, with an excessive roundness of form, very unlike the flat relief of the 5th century B.C. In many cases this excessive amount of projection suggests that the design is a copy of some piece of sculpture in the round.

Apart from the details of the treatment, the whole design of some gems of Imperial date shows that the gem-engraver has copied some statue of large scale, regardless of the fact that the design was quite unsuited for reproduction on a minute scale[2]. On fine Greek gems, on the contrary, the design is exactly suited to the very stone it is cut upon, seldom looking like a reduced copy of some larger work, and still less like a reproduction of a statue.

Copies of statues.

All these rules are however quite useless for distinguishing between ancient and modern gems when the work of a clever forger is in question, a man who has carefully studied and copied the characteristics of genuine antique gems.

Tests for gems.

The fact is that in no other class of art is it so difficult to distinguish the genuine from the false; partly because age makes no alteration, gives no *patina* to a hard polished gem; and secondly, because, owing to the hardness of the material

---

[1] 'Relief' is here used as referring, not to the intaglio itself, but to the impression from it.

[2] For examples of this, see page 78.

and the laborious method of working it, there is necessarily something mechanical in the process of engraving a gem, which diminishes the prominence of the artist's personal peculiarities and touch.

Copies of antique gems.

Moreover many of the cleverest forgeries are copies of some antique gem or paste, so there is nothing in the design to betray a modern origin. Copies made by the most skilful engravers of the last century, such as Natter, Pichler and Burch, are often quite indistinguishable from antiques, especially when we remember that a highly polished, fresh-looking surface is not always a proof that the gem is modern.

Field re-polished.

A large number of genuine antique gems have had their flat field repolished in modern times, much, of course, to the injury of the work. This unfortunate habit was specially prevalent in the 17th and 18th centuries: many of the best gems of the Marlborough and Devonshire collections have been sadly spoilt by this reckless treatment. And again, many gems, which have rested undisturbed in a tomb, still have their original polish as fresh and brilliant as when the stone was first cut.

Original polish.

The skilful forger is careful to use only such tools as were in use among the ancients, and there are often no means of deciding whether a wheel cut or a drill cavity in a hard gem was made yesterday or more than two thousand years ago.

Tests for forgeries.

A great number of different tests have been suggested for the recognition of genuine and forged gems; but the imitation of none of these criteria presents any real difficulty to a skilful and intelligent forger. Proofs of antiquity have been said to be these—extensive use of the "diamond-point," complete internal polish of the details of the design; and again internal polish which, though once complete, has been slightly dulled, as if clouded by the human breath.

With a little extra trouble any modern engraver can polish the whole of his design; and a drawing-stump with some diamond or emery powder will readily take off the apparent freshness of the polish, and give the requisite clouded look to the work.

A still better method of clouding the original polish has been recently adopted by the Roman forgers. A shower of diamond dust is blown out of a small tube against the sunk part of the intaglio; a method which was suggested by the "sand-blast" which is sometimes used on a large scale to drill or carve stone for building purposes.

Tricks of forgers.

The more obvious signs of age, such as a worn surface, covered with fine scratches, are given to modern gems in many different ways. The most deceptive appearance of long wear is produced by cramming the newly cut gem down a turkey's throat, and leaving it for a few days to be shaken up with the bits of stone and gravel which are contained in the turkey's craw.

Freshly cut cameos readily take the marks of age, first by the use of the ordinary rubbing and scratching processes, and secondly by the use of a mixture of iron filings in acid, which rapidly gives to the white layer of an onyx the dead, glossless look which is frequently the result of great age.

Even the fact that a gem is seen to be in its original antique ring-setting is no absolute security against fraud. The present writer has seen in the work-shop of a Roman *intagliatore* a skilful engraver at work on an antique gem which had been found set in a massive gold signet-ring on the skeleton hand of the occupant of an Etruscan tomb. Without removing the gem from its setting the engraver rapidly drilled out the very slight and shallow original design, and produced another much more imposing *intaglio*, with a very beautiful head, carefully copied from a Syracusan coin: the subsequent treatment of the gem with emery and diamond powder entirely removed its obvious look of freshness, and the original setting remained as a false witness to the antiquity of the work.

Set gems result.

The result of all this is that in many cases no archaeologist, however learned, can attain to real certainty about the age of a gem—a quite trustworthy criterion has yet to be discovered.

Fortunately in most cases imitations of antique gems are not the work of a forger who combines sufficient knowledge with the requisite skill, and a careful study of ancient gems will save the student or collector from being deceived by any except forgeries of the most skilful kind.

Gems re-cut.

Among the most difficult cases to distinguish are those gems, which, though originally antique, have been partially or wholly re-cut by a modern hand.

In the last century, and even more recently, this was a very common trick of the Italian dealers, especially in the case of cameos.

Pistrucci.

A very large cameo on a magnificent *sardonyx*, now in the St Petersburg collection, was wholly reworked early in this century by Benvenuto Pistrucci, who (without any fraudulent intention) executed much work of this kind for the Roman dealers, when he was a young man working in Rome, about the year 1804. The St Petersburg cameo represents a Roman Emperor standing and being crowned by a female personification of some city. The gem was originally very late Roman work of the rudest execution. It is now well-cut work, which appears to be of the style of the early empire.

Cameo Flora.

Pistrucci, who was born in 1784, was the last of the really distinguished gem-engravers of modern times. He was the artist of the famous cameo head of Flora, a work of purely modern design on a fragmentary onyx, which he executed for a small sum for some unscrupulous dealer, who sold it for £500 to Payne Knight as an antique Greek gem[1]. Pistrucci wrote a very interesting autobiography, in which he gives an instructive account of how this and others of his early gems were passed off by the Roman dealers as antiques; see p. 147 of Dr Billing's *Science of Gems*, 1867, in which extracts from this autobiography are published. Pistrucci was employed as a die-cutter in London under George IV. and William IV.

St George and the dragon.

He is the author of the fine group of St George and the dragon which is still used on the English sovereigns and crowns—a very happy contrast to the dies produced by more recent artists.

[1] Payne Knight's taste and knowledge are exemplified by the fact that he tried hard to prevent the purchase for a comparatively trifling sum of the Elgin marbles on the ground that they were inferior works of art, and of Roman Imperial date!

CHAPTER IX.

THE TECHNIQUE OF GEM-ENGRAVING (δακτυλιογλυφία or λιθουργική).

THE tools used by the ancient gem-engravers were mainly of three different sorts, namely the *drill*, the *wheel* and the "*diamond-point*." In using all these the gem itself was firmly fixed in a bed of cement made of pitch and pounded pottery (*testae tunsae*). The tools were held in the engraver's hand, who thus had a greater freedom of touch than a modern gem-engraver, who usually works in the reverse way, having his drills and wheels fixed, and the gem loose in his hand[1]. *Tools for gem-cutting.*

I. THE DRILL (τρύπανον, hence mod. Italian *drepano*)[2] was worked in the old fashion, which still survives in the East: the string of a small bow was wound round the stick of the drill which was made to revolve by moving the bow rapidly backwards and forwards. The butt end of the drill revolved inside a cap or tube, which the engraver held in his hand, and so directed the point to the right place; he could not, of course, hold the drill by its revolving part. *The drill.*

It is only long practice that enables a workman to manage successfully the difficult task of carrying on simultaneously a distinct movement with each hand; so in some cases, especially when working larger sculpture, an assistant worked the

[1] The word γλύφειν is used by the Greeks for the process of engraving gems: hence the modern phrase "glyptic art." In Latin *sculpere* has the same meaning, but it is also used for other processes, such as carving in marble, equivalent, that is, to the word *sculpere;* see Pliny, *H. N.* XXXVI. 15.

[2] The word τόρνος (Latin *tornus*) appears to be used for any revolving tool; thus it means both the *drill* and the *wheel* of the gem-engraver, as well as the *lathe* used in many different crafts.

bow, leaving the engraver free to direct the point of the drill. This is indicated in some of the reliefs found in Egyptian tombs which represent sculptors at work on statues of porphyry or granite, materials of such hardness that they could only be worked by drills and emery.

Sculptor's drill.

A Roman sarcophagus, published by Blümner, *Technologie*, III. p. 220, has a very interesting relief showing a sculptor at work on a lion's head which is one of the ornaments on a fluted sarcophagus which he is carving. He holds in his hand a pipe-drill which is made to revolve, not by a bow, but by a cord which a boy assistant is pulling backwards and forwards, the τρυπανία of Pollux, X. 146.

Drill bows.

In 1889—90 Mr Flinders Petrie found in tombs in Upper Egypt several examples of the bows used to work small drills. They are of hard wood, about 14 inches long, slightly bent, and have near each end a square hole in which the cord was fastened. Exactly similar bows are commonly used even now for drilling both in the East and elsewhere.

Fire drill, ἀχάλκευτον τρύπανον.

The word τρύπανον also means an instrument used in kindling fire; the primitive method being to get a spark by the friction of a drill of hard wood, worked with the bow so as to bore a hole in a piece of softer wood; cf. Soph. *Frag.* 640.

Many of these "fire-sticks" have been found in Egypt, with rows of drilled holes in them, each charred by the friction of the drill.

The same method of getting fire by friction is still employed by various savage races, who work the drill both with and without the bow.

Gem-cutter's drill, χαλκευτὸν τρύπανον.

In gem-engraving the point of the drill, which cut into the stone, was of soft metal, usually bronze, and varied in size from that of an ordinary pin to a good-sized knitting needle or even larger. The actual cutting of the drill was done, not by the metal, but by the fine emery powder (σμύρις, *Naxium*) which, mixed with oil, was kept constantly smeared upon it. The minute particles of emery, which is a form of *corundum*, stick in the soft metal under the pressure, and so give a steady cutting surface. If hard steel were used the emery powder would not adhere to the drill, and the cutting would go on much slower[1]. Even wood or bone in connection with emery will make an excellent drill. Some of the Hill-tribes of India even now drill quartz-crystal with a piece of bamboo and emery or sand and water, using the bow to make the drill revolve.

Wooden drill.

The drill and bow-string were not tools peculiar to the gem-engraver, but were used in all the arts of carving and sculpture from the ship-wright upwards. Drills on a large scale, such as augers for boring planks, were worked by a cord held by a man at each end, as is described by Homer *Od.* IX. 382—386, in the passage about Odysseus destroying the eye of Polyphemus. A very interesting gem in the British Museum (No. 305) a Greek scarab of the 5th century B.C., has a well executed figure of a workman (shown in fig. 21), probably a gem-engraver, using the bow-drill on some small object fixed upon a table.

Carpenter's drill.

Gem-cutter at work.

FIG. 21. Greek scarab of the 5th century B.C. showing a man working with the bow and drill: *double the real size.*

Pliny (*Hist. Nat.* XXXVI. 54) speaks of the *Naxium*, or emery of the island of Naxos, as being the best for cutting and polishing gems[2].

Emery.

He gives (*Hist. Nat.* XXXVII. 200) an interesting list of the different tools used in gem-engraving. Speaking of the varying hardness of stones, he says, "tanta differentia est ut aliae ferro scalpi non possint, aliae non nisi retunso, omnes

---

[1] It is for this reason that modern diamond-cutters use, not a steel, but a copper wheel for forming the facets when they are cutting a brilliant, rose- or table-diamond.

[2] The Naxian emery at the present day affords to the Greek government a revenue of more than £30,000 a year.

autem adamante: plurimum vero in iis terebrarum proficit fervor."

Pliny on gem-cutting.

His meaning appears to be this—"only the softest signet-stones (such as steatite) can be engraved by the unaided iron graver; some require the (comparatively) blunt point of a metal drill (used with emery). All stones can be cut with the adamas-point, (that is by diamond or sapphire); but the tool which is the most effective of all is the rapidly revolving drill."

Theophrastus on gem-cutting.

Theophrastus makes the following statements with regard to the engraving of gems—γλυπτοὶ γὰρ ἔνιοι, καὶ τορνευτοὶ καὶ πριστοί· τῶν δὲ οὐδὲ ὅλως ἅπτεται σιδήριον· ἐνίων δὲ κακῶς καὶ μόλις. *De lap.* I. In this passage he probably means to say that gems are engraved either with the diamond-point (γλυπτοὶ) or with the wheel (τορνευτοὶ) or are cut with saws (πριστοί); some are not even scratched by iron. Again at § VII. he says ἔνιαι δὲ λίθοι καὶ τὰς τοιαύτας ἔχουσι δυνάμεις, εἰς τὸ μὴ πάσχειν, ὥσπερ εἴπομεν, οἷον τὸ μὴ γλύφεσθαι σιδηρίοις, ἀλλὰ λίθοις ἑτέροις γλύφονται.

"Ὅλως μὲν ἡ κατὰ τὰς ἐργασίας καὶ τῶν μειζόνων[1] λίθων πολλὴ διαφορά. Ἄλλοι πριστοὶ γάρ, οἱ δὲ γλυπτοὶ καθάπερ ἐλέχθη, καὶ τορνευτοὶ τυγχάνουσι, and further on, he adds, οἱ δὲ σιδηρίοις μὲν γλύφονται ἀμβλέσι δέ. This paragraph, which is unfortunately full of *lacunae*, seems to be the one from which Pliny is quoting in the above mentioned passage, *H. N.* XXXVII. 200. It is possible that the text of Theophrastus might be amended and the *lacunae* partly filled up by the help of this translation, which appears to be given by Pliny from a more perfect codex than any which now exists. The phrase "non nisi retunso" is clearly Pliny's rendering of Theophrastus' σιδηρίοις μὲν, ἀμβλέσι δέ. Theophrastus wrote his short treatise on gems about the year 315 B.C.

Pliny on Theophrastus.

In most of the archaic gems, and again in those of the period of Roman decadence, the use of the drill is very conspicuous[2]; short curly hair of men or animals is often

---

[1] In this passage the word μειζόνων is probably corrupt, since the *size* of gems has nothing to do with their relative *hardness*.

[2] The archaic glandular gem in the Fitzwilliam collection shows the use of the drill clearly all over the body of the eagle: see Plate I. No. 2.

CHAP. IX.] GEM-ENGRAVER'S TOOLS. 107

represented by a series of close-set drill holes even in work of a good period.

The general blocking out of the figures seems to have been mainly done with the bow-drill, the final modelling and details being put in afterwards with other tools. Some ancient gems have never been carried further than the initial drill work, and look unfinished.

Mode of using the drill.

There are many of these among the 6th and 5th century scarabs in the British Museum; such as No. 447, a red jasper

FIG. 22. Etruscan gem in red jasper, with three figures rudely blocked out with the blunt drill (the "retunsum" of Pliny). The inscribed names [ΑΓΑ]μεμνων, ΜΕΝελαος and ΠΑΤροκλος are probably a modern addition, the work of some dealer, in order to enhance the selling value of the gem: *real size*.

scarab, which represents a standing hero between two seated figures; see fig. 22.

The same use of the drill can frequently be seen in Greek coins, especially for the hair of men[1], and very commonly in the *legends*, the letters of which were formed by first drilling in the iron die a small hole at the end of each straight stroke, and then lines were cut joining the pairs of drill-holes[2].

Drill work on coins.

The emery drill on a larger scale was a very important masons' and sculptors' tool in ancient Egypt and among the early Greeks, as is mentioned above at page 104.

---

[1] This habit of representing hair of a crisp, curly sort by drill-holes seems to have influenced the Greek vase painters of the best "red-figure" period. The hair of heroes on 5th century pottery is often represented by close set dots or pellets of the fine creamy black enamel, giving a fine effect of texture and gloss by the slight relief of the enamel dots.

[2] For example the *legends* on the later tetradrachms of Athens with Magistrates' names are very obviously formed in this way, the work being coarse in execution. In better work the drilled terminations are less conspicuous.

A pebble with a hole drilled through it, ψῆφος τετρυπημένη, was used by the Athenians at their judicial ballots for a vote of condemnation; the undrilled stone, ψῆφος πλήρης, being the sign of a vote of acquittal: see Aeschin. XI. 34.

108   THE TUBULAR DRILL   [CHAP. IX.

Without it, it would have been impossible to work the intensely hard basalts and granites of Egypt, or the conglomerate of Mycenae and Tiryns.

Tube-drills.

THE TUBULAR DRILL: for work on a larger scale a tubular form of drill was used; that is, a bronze tube, either with loose emery powder, or else with minute crystals of *corundum* set along the working edge of the tube.

This tubular drill was known in Egypt as early as about 4000 B.C. Within recent years its use has been revived for blasting and quarrying hard rocks. If this tool had not been re-invented the Alpine tunnels would have been practically impossible.

Alabasti.

The tubular drill was also used by the Greeks for such purposes as hollowing out their alabaster perfume bottles (ἀλαβάστοι), and for many other similar processes.

Tube-drill used for gems.

For such minute work as gem-engraving the tubular drill was rarely employed, but clear marks of its use are to be seen on some of the archaic Greek lenticular gems, as, for example on one, cut in carnelian, in the British Museum (see fig. 23), which has a pillar-like object, probably a tall fire-altar, between two rampant lions—very much like the relief over the well-known "lion-gate" of the Acropolis of Mycenae.

FIG. 23. Early lenticular gem in carnelian, which shows clearly the use of the wheel and of two kinds of drills—the tubular and the solid drill; *real size*. Cf. gems in Ἐφημερίς, 1888—9, Plate 10.

In this interesting gem (No. 106, *Brit. Mus. Cat.*) the eyes of the lions and the terminations of the pillar are sunk with minute tubular drills. The rest of the work is engraved with the solid drill, and with the little wheel.

Kallimachus.

According to Pausanias (I. 26 *ad fin.*) Kallimachus, the inventor of the Corinthian style, was the first to use the drill for stone—λίθους πρῶτος ἐτρύπησε; but this is, of course, a mistake. Drills were used in Egypt for hard stone nearly 4000 B.C., and in Greece many centuries before the time of Kallimachus, whose golden lamp in the temple of Athene Polias on the Acropolis must have been made after the Persian invasion in 480 B.C.[1]

Another instrument used for straight cutting or slitting was a wire strung on a bow. The spring of the bow kept the wire taut while it was being drawn backwards and forwards with the usual supply of emery and oil, thus cutting like a saw into the gem. On a large scale this sort of wire saw (*serra*) was used by the Romans in cutting the thin slabs of coloured marble (*crustae*) used so much under the Empire for wall decoration. For the softer marbles, sharp sand and water were used instead of emery.

Wire saw.

2. THE WHEEL (τόρνος, *rotula*)[2]: this was a minute disc of bronze which was set on a long, slender shaft of wood or metal and worked with a bow and tube like the drill; emery and oil being applied to it in the same way. The wheel cut, of course, at right angles to the shaft, not in the same direction as the drill did. According to the direction in which the workman moved the little wheel it could cut either a long line or a broad sunk surface[3].

The wheel.

In the early lenticular gems its use is specially visible, and indeed to use the wheel for any other purpose than blocking out the design requires exceptional skill on the part of the operator; otherwise it produces a very coarse and clumsy style of work; see fig. 24, which shows an early lenticular gem cut in rock crystal.

Early wheel-work.

Examples of obvious wheel-work among the Fitzwilliam gems are the wings of the eagle on the glandular gem, Plate I. No. 2; and the scarab of Kreontidas, Plate I. No. 4. The wheel is largely used by modern gem-engravers in Italy, who call it *il rotellino*.

---

[1] For further information about Kallimachus, see Vitruvius, IV. i. 10.
[2] The word *tornus* is also used for a lathe.
[3] This sort of wheel and the drill are both among the most important instruments of the modern dentist; but he uses hard steel, instead of copper and emery, having a less refractory substance to deal with.

Wheel-disc.

Another kind of wheel was used in later times for quite a different purpose, namely for cutting slices of gems, λιθο-πρίστης. This was a very thin disc of metal, several inches

FIG. 24. Rudely worked lenticular gem, which illustrates the use of the wheel, the drill and the adamas- or diamond-point; *real size.* This gem and that shown in fig. 23 date possibly as early as 14 or 15 centuries B.C.

in diameter, which was fixed as it revolved, the stone being pressed against its edge, like the circular saw of the modern timber-merchant. In this case, as with the other wheel, the actual cutting was done, not by the metal of the wheel, but by the emery and oil with which it was kept constantly charged.

Ezechiel on gems.

The Prophet Ezechiel in his lamentation for the doom of the king of Tyre (xxviii. 13) gives a long list of precious stones, followed by the words (translated in the Revised Version) "the workmanship of thy tabrets and of thy pipes";

Pagnini's Version, 1527.

and in one version of the Latin Bible " opera tympanorum tuorum et foraminum tuorum." In his *Numismatique des Satrapies*, p. 71, the Duc de Luynes has made the interesting suggestion that the *tympana* and *foramina* of Ezechiel are really the ordinary tools of the gem-engraver, the "wheel"

Polishing process.

and the "drill." The *tympanum* probably means, not the cutting wheel, but a sort of revolving drum made of wood, which, when covered with powdered haematite or ochre, was used to polish the surfaces of gems, the process called λιθοτριβική by the Greeks.

Stone wheel.

Another, quite different sort of wheel was used, not for engraving the designs on gems, but merely for shaping roughly the stone.

This was a wheel made of fine whetstone, such as the black "Lydian jasper," shaped and fitted and supplied with water exactly like an ordinary grindstone for sharpening knives, but on a much smaller scale. It was probably worked with a treadle, like a lathe, and the gem was pressed against it as it revolved. The flat field of a signet gem and its rounded edges were probably, as a rule, formed with this instrument, the polishing being done afterwards with dry powdered ochre.

3. THE DIAMOND-POINT: this tool was not used with the bow, but was held in the hand like a pencil, or like the "dry-point" of a modern etcher.

It consisted simply of a natural crystal of *adamas*, set in a bronze or iron handle; see *O. T. Jerem.* xvii. 1, "The sin of Judah is written with a pen of iron, with the point of a diamond." Pliny describes this tool in his paragraph on the *adamas* (*Hist. Nat.* XXXVII. 60) under which name is included both the true *diamond* and the white *sapphire*, which comes next to it in hardness.

He says "expetuntur hae (crustae, chips) scalptoribus, ferroque includuntur nullam non duritiam ex facili cavantes."

The truth is that whole crystals, not *crustae*, have the best cutting power, and it is probably these that were mostly used by gem-engravers[1].

Less hard substances than the *adamas* were used sometimes in the same way. Herodotus (VII. 69) speaks of the Aethiopians pointing their arrows with the same sort of hard stone or flint that was used for engraving signets; λίθος ὀξὺς πεποιημένος τῷ καὶ τὰς σφρηγῖδας γλύφουσι. The steatite scarab-signets of Egypt are soft enough to be cut by obsidian or flint. Many arrows tipped with these stones have been found in Upper Egypt, and even in the tombs of Thebes.

Most of the details and all the artistic finish of a well engraved gem was given by the use of the diamond-point, which allowed an amount of freedom of touch in the artist's hand far beyond what could be got with any of the other more mechanical tools. It was however much more laborious

[1] The modern glazier's diamond is always a natural crystal; a splintered or cut bit of diamond will readily scratch glass, but would not make the deep slit which is necessary to divide a sheet of glass neatly.

Use of diamond-point.

to use it, and required great technical skill on the part of the engraver. By working over and over the same place with the point its scratchy lines could be got rid of, but on some of the gems of finest style and period the artist has not troubled to do this completely, and has left some of the original lines in a way that adds to the spirited beauty of the gem, though at a sacrifice of high finish. This is a point in which the mediaeval or modern forger is specially liable to fail; he is usually too careful to leave no trace of the actual tool-work.

Gems in Brit. Mus.

The use of the diamond-point can be clearly traced in one of the most graceful gems in the British Museum (No. 562), which has a figure of a girl dressed in a long chiton, standing and holding a *hydria*.

The lines of the hair, the long straight folds of the drapery, and even the *hydria* in her hand are all executed with the point: thus giving a sort of sketchy look to this very beautiful design, which probably dates from the time of Pheidias[1].

FIG. 25. Greek gem with a head of Zeus, of very noble style, inscribed EE: the use of the diamond-point in working the hair and beard is very distinct.

Head of Zeus.

Another very beautiful gem in the British Museum (No. 464) illustrates the use of the diamond-point; see fig. 25. This is a scarab of green jasper from the Blacas collection, with a head of Zeus of most noble style, within a cable border, dating from the first half of the 5th century B.C. The delicate lines cut with the diamond-point are specially visible in the working of the hair and beard of this head.

[1] Among the Fitzwilliam gems, the use of the point is most visible on Nos. 6, 12 and 19, Plate 1.

See also above, fig. 16 at page 25, in which the hairs of the Satyr's tail are scratched in with the same instrument.

Something very similar to the style and touch of gem engravings is to be seen in some of the finest Greek vase paintings of the late black-figured style, dating from the middle or latter part of the 6th century B.C. *Incised lines on vases.*

The inner markings with incised lines on these black figures are in many cases executed with a gem-like delicacy and minuteness; and it is very probable that the fine lines, sharply and clearly cut through the hard black enamel, were actually executed with the jewel-pointed tool of the glyptic artist. This is specially noticeable in the delicate wavy lines of the hair both of men and animals, and indeed in all the incised lines of such miniature work as that on Mr Malcolm Macmillan's little vase from Thebes, mentioned above at page 24. *Diamond-point.*

Practical experiments on fragments of Greek pottery have convinced the present writer of the great difficulty of producing a perfectly clean line on the hard enamel with any point of metal—even one of hard steel, such as the Greeks did not possess. The diamond-point on the other hand, which was a familiar tool to the ancient Greek, produces the cleanest lines with ease.

4. THE FILE (*lima*). A very useful tool for smoothing level surfaces on gems, such as the flat field of a signet, was made by a mixture of emery and melted resin[1]; when hard this mixture has a very keen cutting power. This is probably the tool that Maecenas alludes to in his letter to Horace— *The file.*

"Nec quos *Thynica lima* perpolivit
Anellos, neque jaspios lapillos." *Anth. Lat.* I. p. 413.

As is mentioned above (see page 70) the *lima* was the tool held by the statue of the bronze sculptor and gem-engraver Theodoros as a symbol of his craft.

One form of *lima*, used for working in metal and also for cutting the softer stones, such as steatite, was probably a file made of iron, not unlike those which are now used. It would

---

[1] The modern method is to mix melted shell-lac and diamond dust.

however be of no use for working the harder stones, such as those of the quartz class, and still less those of more refractory kind; see page 157, where a table of the relative hardness of gem-stones is given.

Ring of Hippias.

Apuleius, in a curious passage near the beginning of the second book of his *Florida*, mentions the use of the *lima* and the *tornus* by the Sophist Hippias, who wore a gold ring set with an engraved gem, entirely the work of his own hands, both stone and setting.

5. THE FINAL POLISH. After the sunk design of an engraved gem was completed, it was necessary, both for the sake of its beauty, and also to prevent the wax or clay of the seal from adhering to it (see Pliny, *H. N.* XXXVII. 104), to polish, as completely as possible, the internal sunk part.

Method of polishing.

This was done in a laborious way by working the finest powder of some metallic oxide such as haematite, or ochreous earth, into all the depressions of the work with a soft point of wood, a bird's quill, or some other yielding and slightly elastic substance. The flat field of a gem was polished with much greater ease by rubbing it on the surface of woollen stuff sprinkled at first with emery and then finally with the finer powdered ochre. The revolving drum (*tympanum*) already mentioned was used for this purpose.

Paste gems.

THE TECHNIQUE OF "PASTE" GEMS. *Paste*, which is only another word for the finest sort of glass, was made with great skill by most classical nations—especially by the Phoenicians, the Greeks and the Romans. In splendour of colour, in luminous texture, in hardness and durability, the ancient pastes are very superior to those made in modern times. One reason is that modern pastes or false jewels are largely composed of oxide of lead, the object being to increase the "fire" or lustre of the paste, though at the expense of its hardness and durability.

In ancient times, before the modern custom of faceting jewels had been invented, fine deep colour was the first requisite, and sparkle or lustre was but little regarded[1].

[1] The materials used in making ancient pastes are mentioned below, see page 153.

In making a paste signet the process was this—a mould *Moulding* was made from an engraved gem by pressing it against a *of pastes.* mixture of clay which had been ground in a mortar, together with a large proportion of finely powdered pottery, till it was a perfectly smooth, plastic and homogeneous mass. The clay mould, with the impression of the original intaglio in relief, was very carefully baked in a potter's kiln, and then a red-hot lump of the glass or paste, in a soft pasty state, was gently pressed upon the mould till it received the complete imprint of the original gem. If done carefully, by a skilful glass-worker, the result was an almost exact facsimile of the original intaglio.

When it had cooled, its ragged edges and the rough back *Wheel* were cut smooth and polished by the lapidary's wheel and *work.* emery powder, till it was ready for setting in a ring.

In the British Museum there is a large colourless paste (No. 1518) with a portrait head of Aristippus, which has never had its edges cut smooth: it is still surrounded by a ragged border, just as it came from the mould[1].

Among the fine collection of terra-cotta objects from *Clay* Tarentum, which were presented by Mr A. J. Evans to the *moulds.* Ashmolean Museum in Oxford, are included a number of clay moulds for making paste gems. These are simply lumps of clay on which, while soft, an engraved gem has been impressed, giving the device in relief: this relief of course would be again reversed when the soft glass was pressed into the clay mould, thus forming a paste *intaglio*.

Among these moulds are two standing figures of Dionysus, two of a winged Victory writing on a shield, and more than one of Eros.

In some cases antique pastes have been made, not by any *Engraved* moulding process, but by using the ordinary tools of the gem- *pastes.* engraver; treating, that is, the paste exactly as if it had been a real jewel. One of the finest examples of this kind of paste

---

[1] An account of the making of paste gems is given by Heraclius in his treatise *De Artibus Romanorum*, written in the 9th century.

A MS. of this work, in the library of Trinity College, Cambridge, was published by Raspe, London, 1783.

Paste of Gnaios.

is No. 621 in the Marlborough collection (Story-Maskelyne's *Catalogue*, 1870) engraved with a standing figure of an athlete of the Diadumenos type, with the name ΓΝΑΙΟΥ, probably that of the owner of the gem, partly obliterated by repolishing. The quality of this paste, which once belonged to Pope Clement VIII., is so fine that it has usually been described as a *jacinth* or *beryl* of exceptional beauty, even by experts such as the gem-engraver Natter.

Occasionally a combination of both processes was used, the paste being first cast and then its device worked over and sharpened by the use of tools—a somewhat analogous process to that employed by Greek and Roman moneyers, who frequently first cast and then struck coins in high relief.

Paste Scarabaeoids.

Many scarabaeoids of colourless paste, too large for rings, have been found within recent years in Cyprus and elsewhere in Greece. Nos. 8 and 9 in the Fitzwilliam collection are examples of these: the combination of moulding in the device, with cutting on the edges and back, is very obvious in these two pastes.

Paste signets (σφραγῖδες ὑάλιναι) seem to have been made in great numbers for the poorer classes, both among the Greeks and the Romans of the Empire. As a rule they were not mounted in gold rings, but in silver, bronze or iron—in many cases the inferior metals were plated with gold[1]. The signets which cost only 3 obols (Aristoph. *Thesm.* 424; see p. 37) were probably paste copies, set in bronze.

Foil backing.

Paste gems very frequently were set with a backing of polished metal foil, which, by reflecting the light through the paste, gave it increased brilliance and depth of colour.

The same method of setting was often adopted for real stones: Pliny (*Hist. Nat.* XXXVII. 106) speaking of one sort of *sard*, says "argenteis bratteis sublinuntur"; while *sards* of a different colour "brattea aurea sublinuntur." At *Hist. Nat.* XXXVII, 126, Pliny describes two methods of setting gems, either with an open bezel, or with a backing of gold-coloured

---

[1] In England and France, during the 14th and 15th centuries, it was usual for the jewellers' guild in each town to have a rule prohibiting its members from setting *paste gems* in real gold, or *real gems* in plated metal.

foil—"hae funda includuntur perspicuae, ceteris subicitur aurichalcum."

A colourless paste or crystal was sometimes made to imitate a carbuncle by backing it with a crimson foil. Many other tricks were known to the ancient jewellers, and Pliny gives various directions how to tell true from false gems by testing their weight, hardness and apparent feeling of coldness, all of which qualities are greater in a real stone than in a paste; see *Hist. Nat.* XXXVII. 98 and 128 and 198. At § 197 Pliny warns his readers against sham *sardonyxes*, made by cementing together three slices of different coloured stones so as to produce the three layers of the natural gem. *False gems.*

In most cases, however, paste gems must have been sold as honest copies; as works of art they frequently have great merit, both from the sharpness of their impression and from the splendour of their colour.

In the tombs of various parts of Cyprus a considerable number of large rings have been found made wholly of glass. The hoop of the ring is usually of colourless glass, and the bezel is filled with a large paste brilliantly coloured green or crimson to imitate an emerald or a carbuncle; they are not engraved with any device, but have a plain convex surface. These false jewels were fixed in the hollow prepared for them with a little fine cement, which in many cases has perished and allowed the coloured paste to fall out. *Rings from Cyprus.*

These rings are very decorative in effect, owing to the magnificent deep colour of their imitation jewels. The collection of glass from Cyprus in the Fitzwilliam Museum contains many fine examples of these rings, especially one with a large paste emerald still in its place.

In Roman times paste cameos were very frequently made; the commoner sort being merely casts, like the signet or *intaglio* paste, but the finest are all worked over and finished with the gem engraver's tools. *Paste Cameos.*

The Portland Vase is the most magnificent example of what may be called a paste cameo on a large scale. In it and similar glass vases there was no moulding: the whole work was done exactly as if the artist had been cutting an

Portland vase.

onyx. That is to say, it was first completed as a deep blue vase, completely covered and the blue surface hidden by an opaque layer of white glass; and then, when it was quite cold, the engraver set to work and cut and drilled away the white upper layer—modelling his figures in the white layer and cutting down to and exposing the blue body of the vase to form the ground of his reliefs[1]. An excellent description of the Portland Vase is given by Mr A. H. Smith in his *Catalogue of the Gems in the British Museum*, p. 225 seq.

Signed glass.

Among the many examples of Greek art of the 4th century B.C. which have been found in the tombs of Kertch are some elaborate glass cups, which are specially notable for their having the artist's name on them, followed by the word ΕΠΟΙΕΙ.

Cameo work on glass vessels, like that on the Portland Vase, was not uncommon in Egypt during the later Ptolemaic period and in Rome under the early Empire; it was usually very beautiful both in design and execution.

It is essentially gem-engraver's work, and in some cases shows almost miraculous skill in the way the workman has undercut his design in the brittle glass.

Feats of skill.

The most wonderful feats of skill in this direction belong to the time of extreme artistic decadence, when the Romans took pleasure in seeing the most lavish waste of an artist's labour, owing to his working in some material which was utterly unsuited to his design. Hence the Roman love for statues in porphyry, or even obsidian and rock crystal with other costly absurdities of that kind.

Late Roman glass.

Amazing examples of this skilful use of the gem-engraver's tools are to be seen in some cups of greenish glass, which have, on the outside, in a ruby red layer, an open net-work of linked rings, all cut out of the solid glass, and under-cut, so that, with the exception of a few slender pins of glass, the inner cup is quite free from its net-work covering. Several cups of this pattern have been found at various places; all of course more or less broken. Usually they have the owner's

---

[1] Martial (XIV. 94) mentions this kind of work, which he calls *toreumata vitri*, that is glass worked with the gem-engraver's tools.

name in large letters along the top—each letter in red glass being under-cut and joined to the pale green cup beneath only by two or three of the slender pin-like supports.

The best preserved of these wonderful cups is in the Strasburg Museum; it bears the name of the Emperor "Maximianus Herculeus Augustus," who was put to death by Constantine's orders at Massilia in 310 A.D. This gives the date of these goblets covered with the wheel and drill-cut net-work.

Cup of Maximian.

Pliny gives (*Hist. Nat.* XXXVI. 190 to 199) a very interesting account of the glass-maker's art.

At § 193 he mentions the three principal methods of working ornamental glass. After the materials were fused together into a "frit," (he says) "ex massis rursus funditur in officinis tinguiturque, et aliud *flatu* figuratur, aliud *torno* teritur, aliud argenti modo *caelatur*," that is, "after remelting in the furnace, and adding the colouring matter, some of the glass is formed by *blowing*, some of it is cut on a *wheel*, and some of it is *worked in relief* like silver plate." Examples of ancient glass shaped with emery on the gem-cutter's wheel or lathe are not uncommon, and the term *caelatura* would naturally be applied to work in relief such as the Portland Vase[1].

Pliny on glass.

Among the gems in the Fitzwilliam collection, No. 37 is a good example of a gem, cast from a well-executed head of Hermes, in paste skilfully coloured to resemble a fine golden *sard*.

Plate II.

METAL SIGNETS (δακτύλιοι ἄψηφοι or ἄλιθοι): those rings which have the device sunk in a *metal* bezel were formed in various ways. The finest have the design *cut* with tools in the same way as if they had been of stone. Examples of these, signed by the artist, are described above at page 73. Others, especially the gold Etruscan rings, have the device

Bezels of metal.

---

[1] One curious class of Roman pottery, usually in the form of bowls of coarse "Samian ware," is ornamented by simple patterns deeply cut with the lapidary's stone wheel on the hard clay, after it had been fired in the kiln. The British Museum (Romano-British department) possesses many examples of these wheel-cut bowls from various British sites; but they are probably of Gaulish workmanship.

stamped from a die on a thin plate of gold, which was then soldered by the goldsmith into its place on the ring.

Cast rings. A third method, used for the cheaper class of bronze rings, was to *cast* the bezel in a relief mould; but this plan left the impression blunt and spiritless, unless afterwards touched up by tooling[1].

---

[1] On the technique of gem-engraving as practised in the first half of the eighteenth century, see Natter, *Traité de la méthode de graver en pierres fines*. On the whole Natter was perhaps the most skilful of all copyists of antique gems. In some cases he certainly forged the names of ancient artists, but not unfrequently, he signed his own work ΥΔΡΟΥ, 'Natter' meaning a 'water-snake' in German.

CHAPTER X.

GEMS IN MEDIAEVAL TIMES.

OWING to the extreme decadence of the glyptic art during the early middle ages many of the French kings and Emperors of the West, from Charlemagne downwards, frequently used antique gems for their royal signets. Charlemagne himself sealed his edicts with a portrait head of Marcus Aurelius. Louis I., on a document of 816 A.D., has imprinted as his seal a head of Antoninus Pius. *French signets.*

The same practice was adopted by various English kings before the Norman Conquest, such as Offa King of Mercia and several others.

The *legend* on these seals is added on the gold border which frames the ancient gem.

In most cases the gem itself is now lost, but we have impressions of them on countless early charters. Some of these impressions are from gems of very fine workmanship, dating from as early as the times of the *Diadochi*, but more frequently they are inferior works of late Roman date. One of the finest of these gems, known from its impression on a charter in the British Museum, was used as the royal signet of Odo or Eudes, who was King of France from 888 to 898 A.D. It is a noble contemporary portrait head of Seleucus IV., King of Syria, who reigned between 187 and 176 B.C.; see *Arch. Journ.* XI. p. 261. *Seals on charters.*

There were however a certain number of large signets and other intaglios engraved on rock crystals by artists of the Byzantino-Rhenish school for the early Emperors of the West. Impressions exist of a signet of Lothaire I. (840— *Crystal signets.*

Signet of Lothaire.

855 A.D.), with a full-faced bust of the Emperor, very rudely cut. Another of the same Emperor's signets still exists, set in the gold foot of an altar-cross in the Cathedral of Aix-la-Chapelle. It has a profile portrait of Lothaire in a helmet, and round the rim of the crystal itself is engraved the inscription ✠ XPE · ADIVVA · HLOTHARIVM · REG., "O Christ help King Lothaire¹." At the same time large intaglios were cut in rock crystal for various decorative purposes; to ornament gold shrines or reliquaries, and for personal jewellery. The British Museum possesses one of the finest examples of this—a large circular intaglio cut in very brilliant crystal, which was worn as a *morse* or cope-brooch by the Abbot of Vézor.

It is minutely engraved with Biblical subjects and is inscribed LOTHARIVS · REX · ME · FIERI · FECIT.

Papal ring.

During the mediaeval period the use of seals or signets was no less important than in classical times. Part of the ceremony during the consecration of a Pope, a cardinal or a bishop consisted in investing him with an official ring. That used at the installation of a Pope has been for many centuries known as "the fisherman's ring," from its device, a figure of St Peter fishing from a boat, cut on the gold bezel. Hence the heading often placed at the beginning of Papal *Briefs* and other documents "Sub Annulo Piscatoris." In many cases, especially during the 10th to the 13th centuries, when the art of gem engraving was almost extinct, episcopal signets were in the form of a gold ring set with an ancient Greek or more commonly a Roman gem.

Bishops' rings.

These were frequently selected with a device to which a fanciful Christian meaning might be given, such as the head of Jupiter which was used by the Benedictine monks of Durham as a portrait of St Oswald; it was set in a gold mount on which was inscribed ✠ CAPVT · SANCTI · OSWALDI · REGIS ·; another example is the three-headed *gryllus* monster used as his signet by Archbishop Roger,

---

¹ It is illustrated in Vol. I. of Cahier et Martin, *Mélanges d'Archéologie:* see also *Arch. Journ.* XVIII. p. 222.

with the *legend* added ✠ CAPVT · NOSTRV · TRINITAS · EST ; see *Vetusta Monumenta*, Vol. I., Pl. 59[1].

For many centuries after the fall of the Western Empire the belief in magical signet-gems survived, and, to some extent, it lasted throughout the Middle Ages. Even the most orthodox Prelates of the Church did not wholly disbelieve in the magic of gems. Many Bishops used for their episcopal ring of office an *Abraxas* gem; as for example Seffrid, Bishop of Chichester from 1125 to 1151, whose gold ring, set with an *Abraxas* jasper, was found in his coffin, and passed into the Waterton collection; see *Arch. Jour.* XX. p. 224–238. In the present year 1890, when the tomb of Hubert Walter, Archbishop of Canterbury from 1193 to 1205, was opened, his gold ring was found set with a *plasma* on which was cut the *Cnoubis* lion-serpent[2], like No. 106 in the Fitzwilliam collection.

Magical gems.

In the 15th century, together with the revival of classical learning, there was a fresh outburst of superstitious belief in the magic efficacy of engraved gems, even among the most enlightened scholars of the age, such as Lorenzo the Magnificent, Pico della Mirandola, Pope Leo X., and many others.

Belief in magic.

Throughout the Middle Ages, as is mentioned above, great numbers of antique gems, and especially cameos, were used to decorate the most costly of the gold reliquaries. The celebrated beryl *intaglio* of Julia by Euodos, mentioned at page 74, was for many centuries one of the many gems which decorated a gold shrine in the Treasury of the Abbey of St Denis, near Paris. This magnificent gem was set face downwards on a backing of brilliant gold foil, and thus presented the appearance of a translucent relief. This method of setting engraved gems was frequently practised by the

Gems on shrines.

---

[1] For further information on this class of signet, see *Arch. Journ.* Vol. xx. p. 224; and *Proceed. Soc. Ant.* Vol. xiii. 2nd Series, 1890, p. 45 : cf. also King, *Antique Gems and Rings*, 1872, p. 386.

[2] The crozier of the same prelate had its knop set round with four antique gems, of late Roman work, coarsely cut. The three which still remain in the crozier are these—1, a seated figure of Ceres on *red jasper*; 2, a hand holding three ears of wheat, on *carnelian*; and 3, a stag, also on *carnelian*.

mediaeval jewellers, and if the stone is a very transparent one the effect is very soft and beautiful.

Several of the numerous antique gems which studded the famous *chasse* of the Three Kings of Cologne were set in this manner on foil, face downwards.

Metal seals.

In spite of the great decadence of technical skill the art of gem-engraving never wholly died out, though for many centuries it was but rarely practised, partly owing to the use of signets made wholly of silver or bronze[1]. If an engraved gem was used, it was usually an ancient Roman one, set in a metal collar on which the necessary inscription was cut.

Mediaeval gems.

There are however a few gems engraved in the 14th century in existence, of very fair workmanship; as, for example the signet of Charles V. of France, a minutely cut full face on a *spinel-ruby*, set in a gold ring, on which is inscribed *Tel il nest*, "there is none such as he." This very signet is described in the royal inventory made in 1379. It is now in the Marlborough collection, No. 583: it is illustrated by King, *Handbook of Gems*, p. 128, No. 2, but is wrongly named in the text. In the same work (at page 122) King quotes Scipio Ammirato (*Hist. Flor.* p. 741) as mentioning the forging of the signet of Carlo di Durazzo in 1378 by a clever engraver of gems—" Peruzzi, il quale era singolare intagliatore di pietre."

Revival of gem engraving.

The great revival of gem-engraving did not, however, begin till the time of Lorenzo de' Medici in the latter part of the 15th century.

So also with regard to collections of ancient gems, although our mediaeval forefathers showed considerable powers of appreciating their beauty, yet it was not till the 15th century that gems were studied or collected with any real enthusiasm.

Donatello.

Vasari tells us that the great Florentine sculptor Donatello, who died in 1466, was an ardent admirer of ancient gems and coins, and that he took antique cameos and coins for his models when he carved that noble series of medallion reliefs which still exists in the Palazzo de' Medici (or Riccardi) in Florence.

---

[1] See Chabouillet, *Glyptique du Moyen Age*, Rev. Arch. 1854, p. 550.

The earliest example we have recorded of a real collection of ancient gems, since classical times, is that of the Venetian Paul II. (Barbo), who was Pope from 1464 to 1471. *Paul II.*

He is said to have paid large sums for Greek and Roman gems of all kinds—cameos and intaglios—both for his cabinet of gems, and also to set in the numerous rings with which he used to load his fingers.

Piero de' Medici, who died in 1469, formed a small collection of gems, which were inherited by his son Lorenzo the Magnificent, who also acquired the collection of Pope Paul II., thus obtaining the nucleus of what afterwards became the large and important *dactyliotheca Mediceana*, which unfortunately was dispersed in the century after Lorenzo's death. *Piero de' Medici.*

When Lorenzo de' Medici himself began to collect gems, soon after 1469 when he became ruler of Florence, he showed a special love for cameos and intaglios of large size, and was eager to buy, not only antique specimens, but also the works of the very able Italian artists of his own time. *Lorenzo de' Medici.*

One of the most beautiful gems that any age has ever produced is the copy, on a large *sard*, in intaglio of the *Diomede with the Palladium* (mentioned at page 75), which was executed for Lorenzo de' Medici; the mark LAVR. MED. is cut on the *cippus* upon which Diomede is seated. *Diomede of Lorenzo.*

This magnificent gem, which is a more perfect work of art than any of the antique examples of this subject, is obviously the work of a 15th century artist, having a wide margin round the figure and other signs of post-classical date.

Whether they were cameos or intaglios, ancient or contemporary, Lorenzo the Magnificent had all his most important gems engraved with his own name in large letters thus, LAVR. MED. *Lorenzo's mark.*

Many gems, especially cameos, with Lorenzo's name exist in various collections: most of these, if not antique, are executed in a classical manner, but one or two fine gems are in the style of contemporary Florentine art, and look as if they were the work of pupils of Donatello, while others resemble the style of Antonio Pollaiuolo.

GEM-ENGRAVERS [CHAP. X.

Delle Carniuole.

One of the ablest engravers who worked for Lorenzo de' Medici was Giovanni, surnamed "delle Carniuole" for his skill in cutting *carnelian* gems.

The fine intaglio portrait of Fra Girolamo Savonarola, now in the Uffizi collection, is one of his most celebrated works, very noble in style, and full of life-like vigour and realistic truth.

Lorenzo's engravers.

Others of Lorenzo's gems were engraved by Francesco Francia the famous Bolognese painter and goldsmith, by Marco Moretti, by Domenico (called) de' Cammei, and by Leonardo da Milano; the last two were both natives of Milan, and were greatly famed for their portrait heads.

Camillo Leonardo, in his *Speculum lapidum*, a work on gems published at Venice in 1502, mentions four artists as being the chief gem-engravers of his time; these were Anichini of Ferrara, Giovanni Maria of Mantua, Tagliacarne of Genoa and Leonardo of Milan, who worked for Lorenzo.

Leo X.

Lorenzo de' Medici's love for gems was inherited by his son Pope Leo X. and also by various other Popes of the 16th century, most of whom were liberal patrons to all skilful *intagliatori*—a very numerous class in Italy at that time.

Vasari.

An interesting chapter in Vasari's *Vite dei pittori &c.* (Part II. Vol. I. page 285 seq. in the edition of 1568) is devoted to the gem-engravers of the Renaissance. Vasari specially praises the works of Piero Maria da Pescia, who engraved both coin-dies and gems for Leo X.[1], Valerio dei Belli (il Vicentino) famed for large crystal intaglios, who lived from 1468 to 1546, Giovanni da Castel Bolognese, 1496—1553, Matteo dal Massaro, who died c. 1548, Alessandro Cesati (il Greco) a native of Cyprus[2], Giov. Antonio de' Rossi and various other engravers who lived and worked in Milan. In

Foppa.

another chapter Vasari mentions Ambrogio Foppa (il Cara-

---

[1] See *Archiv. Stor. Ital.* 3rd Series, Vol. III. Part I. p. 221; and *Fitz. Mus. Cat.* page xxiii, No. 1.

[2] See page 82, for an account of the way in which Alessandro Cesati signed his gems.

For a general account of the gem-engravers of the Renaissance see Mariette, *Pierres Gravées*, Vol. I. p. 114 seq.

dosso), a famous Milanese sculptor and goldsmith, as being also remarkable for his skill in gem engraving. Most of these artists were also cutters of dies for coins and medals, and workers in gold and silver.

The portrait of Pope Paul III. (Farnese), on a medal by Alessandro Cesati, is a very beautiful work; it was enthusiastically admired by Michelangelo. The *reverse* of this medal, with a nude figure of Ganymede pouring water on a lily plant, is a work of extraordinary skill, and strongly classical feeling in the modelling of the nude. In this respect it curiously resembles the figure of Eros on the celebrated gem signed by Phrygillus, especially in the soft, melting contours of the flesh and its delicate grace of pose. *Aless. Cesati.*

Many others of the medals, both cast and struck by Italian artists of this time and during the previous century, are works of the very highest artistic excellence, quite equalling in merit the best productions of the ancient Greek engravers of coin portraits. The earliest and on the whole the greatest of this class of Medallists was the Veronese painter Vittore Pisanello, who died about 1451, but he does not seem to have practised the art of gem-engraving. His medals, like nearly all those of the 15th century, were not struck from dies, but were cast from a wax model by the *cire perdue* process, and he had therefore no need to learn the difficult art of sinking his design in a hard material such as a steel die or a gem. *Medals of Italy.* *Pisano of Verona.* *Wax casting.*

In the 16th century, medals were mostly struck and so came naturally within the scope of the gem-engraver's craft, whereas under the older system the large cast medals could be produced by any sculptor in bronze, or even by a painter such as Pisanello, if he could model his design in wax.

The celebrated Benvenuto Cellini (1500 to 1571) was a skilful engraver of gems and coin-dies as well as a sculptor and a goldsmith. Like most of the Italian gem-engravers of the 16th century he devoted himself to the cutting of cameos rather than intaglios. *Cellini.*

After Cellini's time the art of gem-engraving in Italy shared in the general decadence of all the arts from painting and sculpture downwards.

There still were many engravers who possessed great technical skill, but their designs rapidly deteriorated in point of style or became mere servile imitations of the gems of classical times.

Forged gems.

Thus there gradually grew up a class of clever engravers who, if not intentional forgers of antique gems, yet produced works which were so carefully and skilfully imitated from ancient examples that they were frequently sold for very high prices as being genuine antiques.

Deception of this kind was then easier than it would be now, owing to the low standard of archaeological knowledge and criticism which was then prevalent—a state of things which lasted till the early part of the present century. Thus

Old collections.

it happens that most famous old collections of gems, such as those of the Dukes of Devonshire and Marlborough, which were formed by various wealthy collectors at a great cost during the 17th and 18th centuries, usually contain a large proportion of professedly antique gems which really date from modern times. At present the more advanced state of the science of engraved gems enables collectors to buy with greater judgment and with less risk of being deceived by unscrupulous dealers.

CHAPTER XI.

Materials used for Antique Gems.

Our chief literary sources of knowledge about the precious stones known to the ancients are a treatise by Theophrastus, περὶ λίθων, written about 315 B.C., and the 37th Book of Pliny's *Natural History*, which is mainly a compilation from Theophrastus and various other authors.

Writers on gems.

As a rule antique gems are rarely engraved on really fine and costly stones.

Mr Story-Maskelyne has remarked, in his Catalogue of the Marlborough collection, that if we have to decide which of two gems is the original, and which the copy, it will usually be found that the modern one is on the finer stone of the two.

Quality of stones.

On the whole the *sard* is the most beautiful material which is commonly used for ancient engraved gems, though it is hardly of sufficient value to rank as one of the so-called "precious stones."

A well engraved design on a clear orange or golden-tinted sard combines beauty of nature and beauty of art in a quite unrivalled manner.

The following are the chief stones used in ancient times for engraved gems and other decorative purposes.

First of all in value comes the ADAMAS, Greek ἀδάμας, "unconquered"; it is described by Theophrastus, *Lap.* 19, and by Pliny, *Hist. Nat.* XXXVII. 55 to 60.

Adamas.

Neither the Greeks nor the Romans had any really scientific knowledge of precious stones, and we usually find that more than one kind of gem is classed under the same name.

Adamas.

The word *adamas* is certainly used both for the *diamond* and for the *white sapphire*.

In one place (*H. N.* XXXVII. 56) Pliny seems to describe the double pyramidical shape of the natural crystal of the true diamond when he says the *adamas* is formed "ut si duo turbines latissimis suis partibus jungantur."

Tests for Adamas.

But when he goes on to say (§ 57) that the *adamas* will not break if struck by a hammer on the anvil, and that it will stand the test of fire, he is certainly speaking of another and very different stone.

The diamond is easily broken along planes of cleavage parallel to the natural faces of its crystal, and, being composed of pure carbon, it is the only gem that is combustible.

The mistaken application of these two tests has caused the destruction of a great many newly found diamonds even in the present century[1].

True diamond.

It is fairly certain that in ancient times it was considered impossible to cut or polish the true diamond on account of its excessive hardness. In those rare cases in which a true diamond occurs in an ancient work of art it is in its natural crystalline form, unworked by the lapidary.

Examples of its use are very rare.

Bronze statuette.

The most remarkable case, probably unique in Hellenic art, is a very beautiful bronze statuette in the British Museum, about seven inches high, of the finest archaistic work, probably of the latter part of the 5th century B.C. The motive of this figure is similar to the numerous marble archaic female statues, which have been found on the Acropolis of Athens, among the broken fragments resulting from the Persian sack in 480 B.C.; see Mrs Mitchell, *Ancient Sculpture*, p. 280.

Diamond eyes.

With one hand the lady holds up her long chiton; in the other hand, outstretched, was a bud or flower. Minute natural crystals of diamond are fixed in the pupils of the eyes, giving a wonderful look of life and spirit to this masterpiece of Greek plastic art.

---

[1] Recent examples of newly found diamonds being destroyed in this way in the United States are given by G. F. Kunz, *Gems of North America*, New York, 1890.

The crystals are so minute that without a close inspection they might easily pass unnoticed[1].

Diamond rings.

Perhaps the only other known examples of antique diamonds are those in a few rare Roman rings of a late Imperial period.

The Waterton collection of rings contained one of these, with a diamond octahedral crystal set in a gold ring, surrounded with a border of pierced open work, dating probably from the 4th or 5th century A.D.

It was not till the latter part of the 15th century A.D. that the discovery was made that a diamond could be cut and polished with its own powder. Till that time, throughout the Middle Ages, the natural crystal was used uncut, as it was in classical times.

Medici badge.

The well known badge of the Florentine Medici family is an example of this: it consists of three ostrich feathers passed through a ring in which is set a natural pyramidical crystal of diamond.

The *adamas* of the Vulgate is translated "diamond" in the Authorised Version of the Old Testament *Exodus*, xxxix. 10—13), where the list of the twelve gems on Aaron's breastplate is given.

Aaron's breastplate.

But this stone cannot have been the true diamond, as on it was engraved the name of a Tribe, "like the engraving of a signet," a feat which was quite beyond the power of any ancient engraver, even the skilful Phoenician who probably cut and engraved the gems on the Jewish High Priest's "rational."

Ezechiel's list.

Ezechiel, xxviii. 13, gives the following list of gems (English Version) "sard, topaz, diamond, beryl, onyx, jasper, sapphire, emerald, carbuncle." Here again the word "diamond" is probably wrongly used for some other hard, colourless stone: cf. *Apocalypse of St John*, xxi. 19 to 21.

In most cases, it seems probable, by the word *adamas* is meant the *white sapphire*, a stone which comes next to the diamond in point of hardness.

[1] This wonderful statuette is said to have been found at Verona, but it appears to be of the finest Attic workmanship.

The jewel-set tool mentioned by Pliny (*H. N.* XXXVII. 60) may have been set either with splinters of the true diamond or of the sapphire.

Sapphire.

The modern SAPPHIRE is probably the HYACINTHUS, ὑάκινθος, of classical authors; Pliny, *H. N.* XXXVII. 126. Solinus truly says that only the diamond will scratch it. The *sappirus* is quite a different stone, as is mentioned below.

The true *sapphire* is a pure crystalline form of *corundum*, an oxide of aluminium, Al_4O_3 of a fine blue colour.

It is very rarely used for ancient gems, partly, no doubt, on account of its extreme hardness, which makes it very difficult to engrave. The few really antique examples of work on the sapphire are mostly of the Imperial Roman period; it appears to have been very rarely used by the Greeks, except as an ornament for jewellery.

The Marlborough collection contains one of the most beautiful engraved sapphires in existence, a Medusa head in full face, of the first or second century A.D., finely cut on a pale blue stone; No. 98, *Marl. Cat.*

No. 485 in the same collection is a good contemporary portrait of Caracalla on a large sapphire of good quality.

Star-sapphire.

The *star-sapphire*, when held in a strong light, shows inside it the figure of a six-rayed star, the result of its peculiar crystalline structure.

This is probably the *astrion* of Pliny (*Hist. Nat.* XXXVII. 132), an Indian gem which he describes thus—"huic intus a centro stella lucet fulgore pleno lunae."

A variety of this was the *asteria* (§ 131) found in Carmania and in India: the latter kind, Pliny says, is difficult to cut or engrave.

It is doubtful whether any ancient examples exist of the use of this stone for engraved gems.

Ruby.

The RUBY is chemically the same as the sapphire, only with different colouring matter.

The finest examples have the tint of pigeons' blood. The ruby appears to be one of several precious stones which were included under the name ἄνθραξ and *carbunculus*, a red-hot coal; Pliny, *H. N.* XXXVII. 92 to 98.

Theophrastus speaks of quite a small ἄνθραξ being worth as much as 40 gold staters, so he is probably speaking of the ruby, not of the carbuncle.

At the present day a fine large ruby is worth much more than a diamond of the same size; whereas rubies and diamonds of less than one carat in weight are of about the same value.

In the 16th century, according to Benvenuto Cellini, a ruby of one carat was worth eight times as much as a diamond of the same weight[1].

Antique gems engraved on the ruby are very rare, even more so than engraved sapphires, but it was occasionally used in Roman Imperial times for small cameo heads. In the Devonshire collection there is a very late Roman figure of Venus Victrix cut in intaglio on a ruby of very great beauty, but, with very few exceptions, engraved gems on the true ruby are either of mediaeval or modern date.

Nearly all that Pliny writes under the heading *carbunculus* seems to refer to the *garnet* or *carbuncle*.

Possibly Pliny means to describe the ruby (*H. N.* XXXVII. 99) where he mentions *anthracitis...fossilis carbonibus similis*, like a red-hot coal, the ἄνθραξ of Theophrastus. Pliny's method of classifying gems according to their *colour* makes it specially difficult to be certain what stone he is describing in each case.

The same gem has frequently many different colours; and very different gems have almost the same tint in some cases. Thus, for example, the pure crystalline form of *corundum* may be blue, red, yellow or colourless, giving to the gem the names respectively of *sapphire, ruby, Oriental topaz* and *white sapphire*. Again the *ruby* and the *carbuncle* may be of almost exactly the same tint.

EMERY, σμύρις, *Naxium*, is an impure semi-crystalline variety of *corundum*, of which the ruby and sapphire are the purer crystalline forms. That from the island of Naxos was

---

[1] Cellini in his *Trattato dell' Orificeria*, published in Florence in 1568, cap. i. gives the following value for fine stones of one carat weight; *ruby*, 800 gold scudi; *emerald*, 400; *diamond*, 100; *sapphire*, 10. The gold scudo was then about equal in purchasing value to a modern sovereign.

Naxium.

considered the best, hence the name which Pliny gives it (*H. N.* XXXVI. 54) "signis e marmore poliendis gemmisque etiam scalpendis atque limandis *Naxium* diu placuit ante alia"; see also *H. N.* XXXVII. 109.

Its use for gem-engraving is mentioned above at page 104. Another variety of *corundum* from Cyprus, called *Cyprium*, was used for grinding down and polishing gems—"ita vocantur cotes in Cypro insula genitae"; *Hist. Nat.* XXXVI. 54.

Emerald.

EMERALD, σμάραγδος; Theophrastus, *Lap.* 23; and Pliny *H. N.* XXXVII. 62 to 75.

In point of value Pliny ranks the *emerald* third; the *adamas* coming first, and the *pearl* (*margarita*) second.

Relief to the eyes.

Pliny tells us (§ 63) that the green of the emerald is so refreshing to the eyes that gem-engravers were in the habit of keeping an emerald by them to look at, as a rest for their eyes during the intervals of their trying labour[1]. Pliny also states (§ 64) that the Emperor Nero used an emerald in some way to help him to see the gladiatorial fights—"gladiatorum pugnas spectabat in smaragdo"; but it is difficult to understand what is the precise meaning of Pliny's phrase. Judging from the context the emerald was used, not as a lens to look through, but as a mirror in which the scene was reflected.

Varieties of beryl.

The *emerald* is the bright green variety of the *beryl*, which consists of silicate of aluminium and glucina, crystallised in hexagonal form. The sea-green variety is the *aquamarine* of modern jewellers.

As Pliny mentions (§ 67), the emerald is specially liable to defects in the form of flaws and cloudiness; in fact a large and yet quite flawless emerald is never to be seen.

Pliny mentions a great many varieties of the *smaragdus*, evidently including several different green stones under this name. Quoting Theophrastus (*Lap.* 23) he mentions (§ 74 and § 75) various columns and obelisks of considerable size, which were said to be made of *smaragdus*, but were more probably of green glass; as, for example, the column in the

Large paste emeralds.

---

[1] In a previous passage (XXIX. 38) Pliny says that a green scarabaeus beetle was used by gem-engravers for the same purpose—"gemmarum sealptores contuitu eorum (scarabaeorum) acquiescunt."

Phoenician temple of Baal at Tyre, which is also described by Herodotus, II. 44. Pliny also tells us, on the authority of Apion, that in the great Egyptian labyrinth (in the Fayûm) there was a statue of Serapis made of *smaragdus*, which was about fourteen feet high.

Antique gems on emerald are not common, but some fine examples do exist, dating from the time of the Roman Empire: as a rule, Pliny says, the emerald was worn unengraved, *Hist. Nat.* XXXVII. 64. At § 6, however, he mentions a Greek emerald gem, engraved with a figure of Amymone, which was sold for four gold staters in the 4th century B.C. (see above, page 40); but engraved emeralds of pre-Roman date are now almost, if not quite unknown. One of the finest examples of the use of the emerald is a cameo of Medusa's head in the Devonshire collection, cut on a large stone, probably about the time of Hadrian. *Antique emerald.*

Most of the ancient engraved emeralds which now exist are stones of poor quality, but Benvenuto Cellini tells us of one, dug up near Rome, which he bought from a peasant, which must have been a stone of remarkable beauty: see Cellini's *Autobiog.* lib. I. cap. 27. *Cellini's emerald.*

This emerald was engraved with a dolphin's head, but it was chiefly valuable for the beauty of the stone. When set in a ring it was sold for a very high price, several hundred *scudi*, in modern value equal to as many pounds.

If engraved with an eagle or the scarabaeus beetle, the emerald was supposed to possess certain magical virtues; see Pliny, *H. N.* XXXVII. 124. *Magic virtues.*

Though the emerald was so rarely employed for the engraved gems of the Greeks, yet it was often used, chiefly for pendants, to decorate gold jewellery. Small emeralds frequently occur in the form of necklace beads, mixed with beads of amethyst and rock crystal, forming a most beautiful combination of colour. *Greek jewellery.*

In many cases these emeralds are not cut; the natural hexagonal form of the crystal is preserved, and nothing is done to the gem except that a hole is drilled through its axis for the insertion of the gold wire which holds it.

Greek emeralds.

A very beautiful gold sceptre of the most elaborate workmanship, in the gem-room of the British Museum, has its top formed in the shape of a flower with outer gold petals and a central boss, which consists of a large rounded emerald or perhaps a paste—not fine in quality, but very beautiful and magnificent in effect. Most of the emeralds used by the Greeks are very full of flaws, and would be despised by a tasteless modern jeweller, but, used with the wonderful skill and good taste of an ancient gold-worker, they are as decorative in effect as if they were of the most flawless and costly kind.

Skill of ancient jewellers.

The same remark may be made with regard to all the jewellery of the Greeks, Etruscans and other classical races: the most beautiful results were gained by the old goldsmiths even when they had to use gems which would now be rejected as valueless. A stone pale in colour and full of flaws, which would have little beauty if cut in facets, when cut in the old *cabochon* form and set in the exquisitely delicate pure gold-work of the ancient jewellers becomes a gem of the highest decorative value. No modern art is in a more hopelessly degraded state than that of the jeweller.

Beryl.

The BERYL, βήρυλλος, is, as Pliny rightly states (*Hist. Nat.* XXXVII. 76 to 79), of the same nature as the *emerald*. As a jewel it was, he tells us, sometimes used uncut, the natural hexagonal faces of its crystal being simply polished.

The most valued variety was the *aquamarine*—" qui viriditatem maris puri imitantur"; and next to that the *chrysoberyl, chrysoberulli*, of a brilliant golden tint, and the *chrysoprasus*, golden, but with a tinge of leek green.

Indian beryl.

According to Pliny (§ 78) the *beryl* was a specially favourite gem in India, where it was frequently worn, not set in gold, but perforated and strung upon an elephant's bristle. If the stone were of the finest quality it was not drilled, but was set between two bosses of gold; in which case, we are told, the Indians "preferred *beryls* of cylindrical form, rather than the usual shape used for gems." Like the *emerald*, the *beryl* is usually not free from flaws.

The Indians, Pliny tells us (§ 79), had discovered a way

to imitate various gems and especially the *beryl* by staining rock crystal. This trick is still practised, especially by the German lapidaries, who heat the crystal red hot, and then plunge it into a bath of cold dyeing matter. The sudden change of temperature fills the crystals with minute cracks into which the colouring matter soaks, and so stains even the interior of the crystal, though in an imperfect and uneven way. Many other tricks of the lapidary were practised in ancient times, such as heating the pale yellow topaz and thus changing its tint to pink. *Onyxes* and *agates* are imitated by first boiling *chalcedony* in honey and water, and then treating it with acid or with heat. The honey, which has soaked into the pores of the *chalcedony* to a certain depth, is permanently darkened by the acid; and thus a stone with layers of two different colours is formed. *Sards* can be turned into *sardonyxes* simply by laying the stone on a hot iron, thus forming a whitish opaque layer on the heated surface. *Stained crystal. False agates.*

Various tricks of this kind are mentioned by Pliny (*Hist. Nat.* XXXVII. 79, 98, 195, and 197): in the last passage he describes a different sort of fraud, still commonly used, the manufacture, that is, of a *sardonyx*, with beautifully even layers, by fastening together slices of three different stones. Another clever trick, which is still practised, is the backing a *paste* gem with a thin slice of genuine stone, so that a suspicious purchaser finds the back of the suspected paste will stand the test of a file without being scratched. The paste so treated is sold ready set in a ring, so that the junction of the true stone and the paste is concealed. *Tricks of gem-dealers.*

The *beryl* is not a common stone among ancient engraved gems even during the Roman period, but it is far less rare than the sapphire or emerald. The finest example known is the celebrated portrait of Julia by Euodos, now among the collection in the Bibliothèque of Paris; see page 74. *Ancient beryls.*

In tint this magnificent *beryl* approaches that of the *aquamarine:* it is a stone of special purity and most brilliant lustre, and was one of the most valued gems of the treasury of the Abbey of St Denis.

Beryl. As a rule antique engraved beryls are very pale in tint, often with a faint bluish tinge, but very pure and lustrous, so that the work on them has a specially beautiful effect when the gem is held up to the light, and the design seen by the transmitted rays.

Carbuncle. The CARBUNCLE or GARNET is one of the stones to which Pliny gives the name *carbunculus: Hist. Nat.* XXXVII. 92 to 98[1]. At present the name "carbuncle" is given to the gem when cut *en cabochon* or rounded; if cut in facets it is the "garnet." This fine flame-coloured stone is a silicate of aluminium and calcium together with small quantities of iron, which give its colour; it varies in tint from a deep ruby red to a pale pink.

False carbuncle. Pliny remarks (§ 98) that the *carbuncle* can be very successfully imitated in paste, but the imitations, like paste copies of other gems, can be distinguished by their inferior hardness—"cote deprehenduntur, sicut aliae gemmae, fictis enim mollior materia fragilisque est"; the pastes also are lighter than the real stones, and are less cold to the touch, see *Hist. Nat.* XXXVII. 128.

The carbuncle is not an uncommon stone among the engraved gems of the Roman Imperial period, and it often bears very fine work. When found in its original setting it is frequently backed by gold or silver foil (*brattea aurea vel argentea*) which much increases its beauty[2]. As a rule the surface of the carbuncle, where the design is cut, is convex, and in some cases the back of the gem is hollowed into a concave form, to give greater brilliance and transparency to the stone.

Foiled carbuncle.

Sasanian carbuncles. Gems of the Sasanian class are not uncommonly engraved on large and very fine Oriental carbuncles, probably brought from India.

The carbuncle is also largely used for Greek and Etruscan jewellery. Gold necklaces, bracelets, ear-rings and the like are studded with plain *cabochon*-cut carbuncles backed with

---

[1] The word *carbunculus* is also used to denote a red variety of sand (*arena*); see Vitruv. II. vi. 6.

[2] On the use of foil-backing, see page 116—117.

brilliant gold-foil; the bright yellow of the surrounding gold and the deep red of the gem give a very effective and beautiful contrast of colour. *Greek carbuncles.*

The gem-room of the British Museum contains some of the finest known examples of this elaborate kind of jewellery: many of them, from the Castellani collection, were found in Etruscan tombs, but the most magnificent example came from Olbia in Sardinia[1].

Oriental *carbuncles* are often of very great size. Pliny tells us (*Hist. Nat.* XXXVII. 95) that drinking-cups holding one *sextarius* were sometimes cut out of an Indian carbuncle. Examples of such cups from India still exist: the Hope collection of gems (now dispersed) contained a cup of considerable size hollowed out of a carbuncle of great beauty, and another is preserved in the Mayer collection in Liverpool. *Oriental carbuncles.*

---

[1] Small pieces of garnet cut into thin slices and backed with gold foil are very commonly used in the cloisonné jewellery of Saxon and other Teutonic races.

CHAPTER XII.

MATERIALS USED FOR GEMS (*continued*).

Silicon gems.

Gems of the SILICON *family.*

By far the greater number of antique gems, especially those of pre-Roman times, are engraved on some one of the many forms of *silicon* which exist in great abundance in almost every part of the world. The most familiar examples of this mineral are *rock crystal* or *quartz*, a pure form of *silica* or *oxide of silicon*, and common *flint*, which is the same substance in an amorphous form, coloured by various slight impurities, especially oxide of iron.

These *silicon* stones are specially suited to the gem-engraver on account of their toughness, absence of grain, and sufficient but not excessive hardness, which makes them comparatively easy to work, and at the same time but little liable to injury from wear or fracture.

The *silicon* minerals may be divided into the *three* following classes according to their structure—

Quartz crystal.

I. CRYSTALLINE stones: such as colourless rock or quartz crystal, sometimes known as Brighton or Irish diamonds and other similar names. Slight traces of metallic oxides give various colours to quartz crystal, which is then known by different names, according to its tint: purple crystals are called *amethyst*, pale yellow is *citrine*, orange yellow *Cairngorm* or *Scotch topaz*, leek green is called *prase*: other varieties are called *rose quartz* or *smoky quartz* according to their colour.

Aventurine is quartz crystal filled with minute specks of mica, looking like gold dust.

II. CRYPTO-CRYSTALLINE or AMORPHOUS: the most important varieties of this class are *sard, carnelian, chalcedony, jasper, bloodstone, heliotrope, plasma,* and *opal.*

III. STRATIFIED stones: this class includes all the varieties of *agate, onyx, sardonyx* and *nicolo.*

1. ROCK CRYSTAL is the purest form of *silica*, SiO_2; its Greek name κρύσταλλος means in the first place *ice ;* it is only used by late writers (e.g. Strabo, p. 717) to mean *crystal.* {.sidenote}Rock crystal.

According to Pliny (*Hist. Nat.* XXXVII. 23) rock crystal is simply a form of ice, which has been permanently frozen by excessive cold, and is only found where there is abundance of rain-water and snow; hence, he says, it is abundant in the Alps. Nevertheless Pliny mentions various places, such as Cyprus, where snow and extreme cold are little known, as being among the principal sources of crystal. The largest block of crystal known to Pliny was one weighing about 150 pounds, which was dedicated by Livia Augusta in the temple of Capitoline Jupiter in Rome. In modern times much larger blocks of crystal have been found; one in the Museum at Milan weighs no less than 870 pounds. {.sidenote}Source of crystal.

Cups and other vessels cut out of large blocks of crystal were specially valued by the Romans of the Empire. {.sidenote}Crystal cups.

Pliny mentions (*H. N.* XXXVII. 29) a single bowl for which 150,000 sesterces were paid by a Roman lady; and Nero, in his last moments of despair, shattered to pieces two crystal *cylices*, in order that no one else might possess them.

The coldness of crystal, Pliny tells us (§ 30), made it specially suitable for iced drinks; while cups of *amber* were best for warm drinks, and *murrhine*[1] cups were equally suitable for both. One curious use of crystal is mentioned by Pliny (§ 28): who says that a crystal ball, used as a burning glass, is the best instrument for surgical cautery. {.sidenote}Burning glass.

In some cases, under the later Empire, crystal was used for the nude parts of sculpture on a large scale, such as the face and hands, in spite of its being remarkably unsuited for such a purpose.

[1] *Murrhina* was probably the beautiful purple translucent form of fluor spar, known in Derbyshire, where it is largely found, by the name of "blue John."

Crystal sculpture.

In the gem-room of the British Museum there is a large fragment of a crystal hand from some life-sized statue. The translucent *obsidian*, a natural glass of volcanic origin, was also used in the same way by late Roman sculptors.

Under the Byzantine Emperors crystal vases of great beauty were made, especially wine-jugs, covered externally with decorative foliage and animals in relief[1].

In early times rock crystal was not unfrequently used for signets, especially for the cylinders and cones of Assyria and Babylon.

Crystal gems.

Plate I.

Crystal also occurs among the lenticular so-called "Island gems," and occasionally among gems of the finest period. The Fitzwilliam Museum (*Catalogue*, No. 5) possesses a very fine scarabaeoid gem of about 500 B.C. with a warrior putting on his greaves, cut in the purest and most brilliant crystal.

Among Greek gems of a later period rock crystal is not common, but under the later Roman Empire, especially during the 4th and 5th centuries A.D., it is frequently used for large coarsely cut intaglios, probably intended, not for signets, but for decorative purposes.

It is also sometimes used for the large heads in relief which ornamented the *phalerae* on the cuirass of the Emperor or some high official; see Suet. *Aug.* 25.

Amethyst.

The AMETHYST, a purple variety of rock crystal, is the ἀμέθυστον of Theophrastus, *Lap.* 30 to 31: it is described by Pliny, *Hist. Nat.* XXXVII. 121 to 124. Its name was derived from the supposed power of this gem to enable its wearer to drink freely without the usual consequences (ἀ priv. and μέθυσος), a superstition which Pliny derides (§ 124) as an idle invention of the *Magi*. For Greek gems of the best periods amethyst was very rarely used, but it is not an uncommon stone for gems of the Roman period; it is also sometimes used for Assyrian cylinders, and early scarab gems.

Phalerae.

Phalerae cameo heads of the Imperial period are often cut out of large amethysts, and are very magnificent in effect.

---

[1] Examples of these crystal jugs, almost identical in design, dating probably from the 8th or 9th century A. D., are to be seen in the South Kensington Museum, the Bargello Museum in Florence, and in the Treasury of St Mark at Venice.

Like the carbuncle, its effect is best when the stone is cut in a convex form (*en cabochon*) and is set with a backing of highly polished metallic foil. *Amethyst.*

The amethyst varies very much in depth of colour, ranging from the deepest to the palest tint of purple; antique gems are usually cut on one of the pale varieties. In early jewellery the amethyst is largely used, especially for necklace beads of various forms.

Rock crystal of other colours was sometimes used by the Romans for engraved gems, especially the yellow *citrine*, of which No. 29 among the Fitzwilliam gems is an example. It is probably the *chrysolithus* of Pliny, *H. N.* XXXVII. 126. *Citrine.*

The *prase* is not uncommon, the *prasius* of Pliny (*Hist. Nat.* XXXVII. 113) derived from πράσινος, leek-green: fine specimens are very beautiful in colour, and often bear good work of the Imperial period, especially portrait heads of Emperors and Empresses. *Prase.*

II. Among the second class of *silicon* gems, those which are *crypto-crystalline* in structure, by far the most common as a material for ancient gems is the SARD. *Sard.*

As Pliny says (*Hist. Nat.* XXXVII. 106), "nec fuit alia gemma apud antiquos usu frequentior."

The *sard*, the σάρδιον of Theophrastus, *Lap.* 30 (Latin *sarda*) is described by Pliny, *H. N.* XXXVII. 105 and 106. According to him it was so called from being largely found near Sardes in Lydia; but it is more probable that it is derived from a Persian word meaning 'yellow.'

The *sard* varies in colour from a pale golden yellow to a reddish orange: the name *carnelian* is frequently given to a class of gems identical in chemical composition and closely resembling the sard, but which are less perfectly transparent and of a deeper red in colour. *Carnelian.*

In point of structure the *sard* differs from the *carnelian* in several respects: it is both tougher and harder and its fracture shows a slightly crystalline structure, while the *carnelian* is more completely amorphous and its fractured surface is more smooth and glistening than that of the *sard*, in that respect approaching nearer to *chalcedony*.

Beauty of sard.

No gem shows the engraving on it, when held up to the light, to as much advantage as does a fine sard.

The best examples are brilliantly transparent, and very fine in colour: perhaps the most beautiful are those which are of a golden yellow tint.

Early use of sard.

Both the sard and the carnelian are very commonly used for engraved gems of all periods, including the cylinders of Assyria, and the scarabs of the Phoenicians, the early Greeks and the Etruscans. According to Pliny, signets made of sard, as well as those of sardonyx, had the advantage that the wax did not adhere to them when an impression was made: see *H. N.* XXXVII. 104 and 105. He also tells us that certain kinds of sard were usually backed with gold or silver foil.

According to Theophrastus (*Lap.* 30) the sard was of two principal kinds; the *female*, of transparent red tint, and the *male*, of a brownish colour.

Sardoine.

The latter is now commonly known as the *sardoine*; it is sometimes very dark in tint, almost black, unless it is held up to the light, when it appears of a deep translucent red. It occurs more commonly among Roman than among Greek engraved gems.

Chalcedony.

CHALCEDONY was also a very favourite stone for gem-engravers of all periods, especially those of early times. The most beautiful sort of chalcedony is of a semi-translucent milky white or pale blue tint; fine examples of the latter are called *sapphirine chalcedony*: gems No. 7 and 11 in the Fitzwilliam collection are good examples of this quality of stone. Other kinds of chalcedony are of a translucent brown tint, such as No. 10 in the same catalogue. Other colours occur, but all specimens of chalcedony are to some extent translucent. If quite opaque the stone would come under the head of one of the varieties of *jasper*.

Plate I.

Jasper.

JASPER, ἴασπις, is an almost equally common material for antique signets, especially the Assyrian cylinders and the early *lenticular* and scarab gems. It is also common among gems of the later Roman Empire.

The *iaspis* of Pliny (*Hist. Nat.* XXXVII. 115) denotes specially the green varieties of *jasper*, and includes the translucent kind which is now known as *plasma*—"viret et saepe tralucet iaspis." Pliny tells us that one fine variety of jasper was called σφραγίς, as being κατ' ἐξοχὴν the signet-stone; see *H. N.* XXXVII. 17.

Jasper signets of the finest quality, he says, were set open in rings; that is, they were not backed with gold, but merely framed in a gold border—"praestantiores funda cluduntur ut sint patentes ab utraque parte, nec praeter margines quicquam auro amplectente." The meaning of the word *funda* σφενδόνη, has been explained above, see page 34.

The jasper used for gems is most commonly either the green or the red variety, but it also occurs of many other colours, yellow, brown, grey, white and black. The *black jasper*, known as *Lydian stone*, was used by goldsmiths as a touch-stone, *coticula*, to show the quality of gold by the colour of its streak marked upon the stone: see Pliny, *Hist. Nat.* XXXIII. 126. The red jasper appears to be what Pliny in one passage calls *haematites* (*Hist. Nat.* XXXVII. 169); but he elsewhere uses the same word for what is now called red *haematite*, an oxide of iron; see *H. N.* XXXVI. 129.

The red jasper used for cylinders and gems is frequently of the most brilliant blood-red tint. In Roman times it was believed to have occult virtues, especially when engraved with a figure of Serapis or some other Egyptian or Persian deity. As Pliny tells us "Totus oriens pro amuleto gestare eas traditur," *H. N.* XXXVII. 118. The same magical qualities were also attributed to the green jasper, on which figures of Horus or Harpocrates were frequently engraved during the Imperial period: see gems No. 20 and 105 in the Fitzwilliam Catalogue.

The *iasponyx*, mentioned by Pliny in the last named passage, was a stratified *onyx*, in which one of the layers resembled *jasper*; just as the *sardonyx* was a combination of the *onyx* and the *sard*.

The *plasma*, as is mentioned above, is a translucent variety of the green jasper: the word *plasma* is a corruption of *prasina*, leek-green.

Roman Imperial gems of very good workmanship some-

Plasma. times occur on *plasma* of a beautiful emerald tint, usually mottled with markings of a deeper green: one of remarkable beauty in the British Museum is engraved with a bust of Severus, very well executed considering its late date, and of very fine colour: No. 1627, *Brit. Mus. Cat.*

Bloodstone. The BLOODSTONE is a variety of *green jasper*, studded with specks of red, like drops of blood.

Akin to this is the HELIOTROPIUM of Pliny (*Hist. Nat.* XXXVII. 165) which is a variety of translucent green *plasma* with similar crimson spots, "porraceo colore, sanguineis venis distincta."

Both these stones were used by the late Roman gem-engravers, but not very commonly. Among the Greeks they were scarcely ever used for signet-stones.

Opal. The OPAL is a very beautiful form of *silica*, which derives its magnificent colours, not from the presence of any pigment, but from its laminated structure, which gives brilliant prismatic colours by breaking up the rays of light. The opal is described by Pliny (*H. N.* XXXVII. 80 to 84) as being next in *Value of opal.* value to the *emerald*. Enormous prices were paid by the Romans of the Empire for fine specimens of this gem. A large opal, mentioned by Pliny as being valued at two million sesterces, was the cause of its owner the Senator Nonius being proscribed and driven into exile by Marc Antony who coveted the possession of the gem. Though very beautiful as a jewel, the opal was quite unsuited to receive engraving, and was not used for signets, though there are a few Roman examples of its use for cameos.

III. Among the third, the *stratified* class of *silicon* stones, the most important are the following—

Onyx. The ONYX, ὀνύχιον, from ὄνυξ a finger-nail, Theoph. *Lap.* 2 ; and Pliny, *Hist. Nat.* XXXVII. 90 to 91. According to Sudines, quoted by Pliny, its name was derived from the fact that the *onyx* had one stratum resembling the human finger-nail, combined with one or more layers coloured like *sard* or *jasper*.

It should be observed that the word *onyx* is also used by Pliny to mean a quite different substance, namely *Oriental alabaster*; see *Hist. Nat.* XXXVI. 59 to 61.

Under the Roman Empire the onyx was a very favourite stone for signets, although an unstratified gem is really more suited for *intaglio* work. In the number and colour of its layers the onyx varies very much; like other stratified gems it was well suited for cameos, especially if it consisted of one white stratum on a brown or dark red one: the figures, being cut in the upper layer, appear in white on a dark background with very good effect, if skilfully treated.

As a rule the stratified forms of *silica* occur in nodules with more or less concentric layers formed round a nucleus, and it was therefore by no means easy for the gem-engraver to get hold of a sufficiently large piece with fairly level strata. In some cases large cameos were built up by joining together several pieces of onyx, as is the case with the celebrated Odescalchi cameo, six inches high by five wide, with busts of a Roman Emperor and his wife, or Mars and Roma. In this case the junctions are cleverly arranged so as to be concealed by the edges of dress, armour or necklaces[1].

The word AGATE is now used in a rather vague way to denote almost any *chalcedonic* stone with strongly marked layers of deposit.

According to Pliny the *achates* (ἀχάτης) was once highly valued, but in his time had fallen greatly in value. Its name was derived from the river Achates in Sicily, where fine specimens of it were found: *Hist. Nat.* XXXVII. 139.

Pliny mentions a great many different varieties of agate, each with its special name descriptive of the markings on it, such as *iaspachates, smaragdachates, haemachates, dendrachates* and the like.

Most of these stones, according to the *Magi*, had some occult virtue.

A variety of *onyx*, which was much used under the Roman Empire, is the *nicolo* as it is now called—a corruption of the Italian diminutive of onyx, *onycolo*. It has a bluish white layer on a dark brown ground. This is probably the Egyptian

[1] The Odescalchi cameo is now in the Hermitage Museum at St Petersburg: it was formerly taken for a work of Ptolemaic date.

gem called *Aegyptilla* by Pliny (*H. N.* XXXVII. 148), who describes it as being formed "in nigra radice, caerulea facie."

Sardonyx. The SARDONYX was the most highly valued form of *onyx*; it is described by Pliny, *Hist. Nat.* XXXVII. 85 to 89.

The name σαρδόνυξ, *sardonyches*, was derived from the stone having one layer like a *sard* superimposed on the strata of an ordinary *onyx*.

Thus, the true *sardonyx* may consist of strata of various numbers and colours, the essential point being that one of these layers should be of the colour and appearance of a sard.

Lucian (*Dea Syr.* 32) who mentions the Σαρδῷος ὄνυξ, "Sardinian onyx," was probably misled by not understanding the real meaning of σαρδόνυξ.

One of the earliest instances of this gem being named by any Greek writer is in Plato's *Phaedo*, 110 D, where reference is made to the fine colours of *emerald, sardonyx* and *jasper*.

According to Pliny (*Hist. Nat.* XXXVII. 88) the sardonyx, like the sard, is one of the very few gems to which the wax does not adhere when it is used as a signet.

Sardonyx beads. The finest kinds of sardonyx and of onyx were imported from Arabia and India, where, as Pliny tells us, this stone was commonly drilled by the natives, and worn, in the form of beads or cylinders, round the neck.

Antique gems, especially large Roman cameos, often have remains of a drilled hole through them; no doubt on account of the use of the stone on a necklace, before it came into the hands of the Roman engraver.

The sardonyx was but little used for Greek gems; like all stratified stones it is more suited for cameos than for signets. The Romans however used it commonly for both purposes.

Demostratus, quoted by Pliny (*Hist. Nat.* XXXVII. 85), tells us that Scipio Africanus the Elder was the first Roman who used the sardonyx for his signet, and that ever since that time it was very highly valued in Rome, coming next to the opal in point of costliness.

Value of gems. Pliny arranges the principal gems in the following order of value—1, *Adamas;* 2, *Pearl;* 3, *Emerald;* 4, *Opal;* 5, *Sardonyx*. This however refers, not to their value for engraving, but as decorative jewels. As stones to engrave upon, the *sard* and the *sardonyx* would probably rank first.

The importance of the sardonyx as a signet-gem is mentioned by Juvenal (*Sat.* XIII. 138), *Sardonyx gems.*

> "arguit ipsorum quos littera gemmaque princeps
> sardonychum, loculis quae custoditur eburnis:"

See also Juvenal, *Sat.* VII. 145

> "Ideo conducta Paullus agebat
> sardonyche."

The Emperor Claudius made the sardonyx specially fashionable, that and the emerald being his favourite gems.

This concludes the list of *Silicon* gems.

The TOPAZUS of Pliny (*Hist. Nat.* XXXVII. 107 to 109) is certainly not the brilliant yellow gem which is now called the *topaz*. Pliny's *topazus* was a green stone, often of large size, and soft enough to be cut with the file and to be injured by wear: § 109. Possibly under this name Pliny includes the modern *chrysolite* and the *peridot*, a gem of a fine yellowish-green tint. *Topazus.*

The statue, six feet high, made of *topazus*, which, according to Pliny, was dedicated in honour of Arsinoe, the wife of Ptolemy Philadelphus, in the "Golden Temple" in Egypt, was probably an instance of the use of paste or glass, like the "emerald" column in the Tyrian temple of Baal. It is however doubtful whether the name *topazus* was not sometimes used for an opaque stone, since Pliny speaks of the green turquoise as closely resembling it. *Glass statues.*

The CALLAINA of Pliny (*Hist. Nat.* XXXVII. 110 to 112) appears to be the green variety of the *turquoise*. *Green turquoise.*

The finest examples are said to be of an emerald colour. It was specially found in the Caucasus, and in Persia, where it is still very largely used for decorative purposes.

Pliny remarks that the *callaina* is injured by contact with oil, a fact that is true with regard to all turquoises. It is, he says, improved by being set in gold more than any other stone, and is easily counterfeited in paste.

The *blue turquoise* is evidently the stone which Pliny calls *Callais.*

Blue turquoise.

CALLAIS (*Hist. Nat.* XXXVII. 151)—"callais sappirum imitatur," that is, it resembles *lapis lazuli* in colour.

The *turquoise* is a hydrated phosphate of alumina, which derives its splendid blue or green colour chiefly from copper, but also from iron or manganese: it does not occur in a crystalline form, but is as hard as feldspar and takes a very high polish.

It appears not to have been used for Greek gems, but some fine cameos of Roman Imperial date are cut in it.

Turquoise cameos.

A very good example is No. 403 in the Marlborough collection, with heads of Livia and the young Tiberius cut in relief in a large *green turquoise*, which seems to have been valued by the Romans more than the blue variety. Probably the only ancient intaglios of turquoise are of Sasanian workmanship.

Lapis lazuli.

The SAPPIRUS of Pliny (*Hist. Nat.* XXXVII. 120) is not what is now called the *sapphire*, but is the opaque *lapis lazuli*, from which the fine *ultramarine* blue used in painting was manufactured.

Theophrastus (*Lap.* 23) calls it σάπφειρος κυανῆ, and describes it as being speckled with gold.

Lapis lazuli is a compound mineral of the *Haüynite* class, consisting of a silicate and sulphate of calcium, sodium and aluminium. It is of a magnificent deep blue colour usually mottled with white, and contains gold-like specks of iron pyrites.

Cyanos.

It appears also to have been known by the name *cyanos* (κύανος). Pliny describes *cyanus* as being called "a colore caeruleo," and mentions its gold specks—inest ei aliquando et aureus pulvis qualis sappiris"; *H. N.* XXXVII. 119.

Theophrastus (*Lap.* 55) mentions natural and artificial κύανος. The former came specially from Scythia and from Cyprus: the artificial kind was a product of Egypt, where it was invented at a very early period. Theophrastus also records that a certain quantity of κύανος formed part of the annual tribute paid by the Phoenicians: see also Pliny, *Hist. Nat.* XXXVII. 119.

Many examples still exist of Egyptian scarabs and signets

of other forms made of this artificial *cyanos*, which is an alkaline silicate, coloured a deep blue with carbonate of copper; the same compound was used as a pigment from very early times, as for example in the paintings of Egypt and those at Mycenae and Tiryns.

Artificial cyanos.

In Camiros and elsewhere in Rhodes and other Greek islands signets of this artificial *cyanos* have been found in the shape of rams' and lions' heads, pierced for suspension, with the signet-device cut on the flat underside. This artificial *cyanos*, when used as a pigment, is called *caeruleum* by Pliny, *H. N.* XXXIII. 161, who says that the best quality came from Egypt, where it had been invented by one of the kings.

The real *sappirus* or *lapis lazuli* was not unfrequently used for Egyptian scarabs and for Assyrian cylinders.

Lapis lazuli.

During the Greek period, except in Egypt under the Ptolemies, it was rarely used by gem-engravers, but it was not uncommon for the gems of the Roman Empire.

A good many well-cut *intaglios* and cameos in *sappirus*, of late Roman workmanship, still exist, though it is not really suited for the purpose of signets, on account of its inferior hardness and the great difficulty of finding a piece that is homogeneous in colour, most *lapis lazuli* having its deep blue much broken up by white.

Pliny refers to this when he says it is "inutilis sculpturis intervenientibus crystallinis centris," *Hist. Nat.* XXXVI. 120. Sasanian gems are occasionally cut upon very fine pieces of Persian *lapis lazuli*.

MAGNETITE (Latin *magnes*) is a hard metallic oxide of iron, $FeOFe_2O_3$, almost black in colour, with a strong metallic lustre when polished. It frequently has the power of attracting iron and then is known as natural *loadstone*.

Magnetite.

According to Pliny, who describes the *magnes* (*Hist. Nat.* XXXVI. 126 to 128), it was called by the Greeks *sideritis*, from its power of attracting iron, σίδηρος; the name *magnes*, according to Nicander, was derived from a shepherd called *Magnes*, who accidentally discovered it by feeling the iron nails in his boots stick to the stones on which he was walking.

HAEMATITE is another ore of iron, a sesqui-oxide, very

Haematite.

Haematite. similar to magnetite except that it is of a deep red tint like blood, and does not attract iron; it is described by Pliny (*Hist. Nat.* XXXVI. 129)[1].

Haematite, finely powdered, was used by the gem-engravers to give the final polish to their work. It was also largely used for medicinal purposes.

Early signets. *Magnetite* and *haematite* are both used very frequently for Assyrian cylinders, for the so-called Hittite gems, and for other signets of an early period.

Among the later Greeks these stones were rarely used, but they are not uncommon among the gems of the later Roman Empire. Fine specimens are very hard and close in grain, and have, when polished, almost the lustre and colour of steel. Both *magnetite* and *haematite* sometimes occur in the form of crystals.

Magnetite was also used for necklace beads and similar decorative purposes by the Egyptians, Phoenicians and other early Oriental races.

Steatite. STEATITE, or *soapstone*, is a silicate of magnesia; though not ranking among the hard stones usually used for ancient gems, it was an important material in early times. It was specially used for Egyptian scarabs, and not unfrequently for Assyrian cylinders and signets of the "Hittite," Phoenician and early lenticular classes. The softness of steatite, and the consequent ease with which it was worked, made it a favourite material for early races who had no harder substance to engrave with than flint or obsidian. For the same reason serpentine and limestones of various colours were commonly used for the primitive "Hittite" gems.

Granite. GRANITES and BASALTS of various colours were occasionally used for some of the same early classes of signets for which the softer steatite was employed, especially for Egyptian scarabs and Oriental cylinders.

The very fine, hard greenish-grey basalt of Egypt was very suitable for a signet-stone, being very close in grain and

---

[1] Pliny's use of the word *haematitis* to mean *red jasper* is mentioned above, page 145.

even in texture. It was sometimes used for this purpose in *Basalt.*
Egypt as late as the Ptolemaic period.

Examples of the green basalt of Mt Taygetus being
used for lenticular gems are mentioned above at page 20.
This beautiful stone is an almost pure form of feldspar,
coloured by a minute proportion of carbonate of copper[1].

PASTE gems, *gemmae fictitiae* or *vitreae*, were made by the *Paste gems.*
Greeks and Romans with very great skill. The material
of which they were composed was a pure, hard glass, without
any admixture of lead—what is now called "flint glass," a pure
alcaline silicate with the addition of lime. Roman pastes
usually contain, in 100 parts, about 70 of *silica*, 18 of *soda*,
8 of *lime*, 2 of *alumina*, and small quantities of *metallic oxides*,
to which the colour is due. Modern pastes are usually made
with nearly 50 per cent. of oxide of lead; and they are therefore much softer and more liable to decomposition than the
old ones. A fragment of an antique paste will scratch a
modern one, as easily as rock crystal will scratch flint glass.

The colours of ancient pastes are often very magnificent, *Colours of pastes.*
especially the ruby red, the sapphire blue, the emerald green
and the orange yellow. Ancient pastes in Italy are often
bought by jewellers to sell, when cut in facets, as real gems.
The chief pigments used to colour the ancient pastes were
various metallic oxides and salts. Blue, green and ruby red
were produced by different oxides and salts of *copper*.

Manganese produced an amethyst-purple. Another blue
was given by *cobalt*; yellow was produced by *carbon*.

Opaque white, used in making the white stratum of
imitation onyx, was produced by *oxide of tin*. The various
colours used for glass are mentioned by Pliny, *Hist. Nat.*
XXXVI. 198.

Pliny gives directions for distinguishing between pastes *Tests for gems.*
and real gems (*Hist. Nat.* XXXVII. 198 to 200); the chief
of these tests depend on the superior hardness, weight and
coldness of the true gems.

A splinter of obsidian (natural volcanic glass) or a file

[1] On the precious stones of the Greeks and Romans see Corsi, *Pietre antiche*, Rome, 1845, pp. 168—292.

Tests for paste.

will, he tells us, scratch a paste, but will not touch a real stone: unfortunately, he goes on to say, dealers in gems (*mangones gemmarum*) usually will not allow purchasers to put their stones to the scratching test (*limae probationem*); and if they did, there was always the risk of deception by means of the slice of real stone fitted at the back of the paste; see above, page 137.

Another test, mentioned by Pliny, is the presence of air bubbles in the body of the paste: there are however some very fine examples of antique pastes, such as that in the Marlborough collection, described above at page 116, in which no bubbles are visible[1].

Such pastes are very rare; in most cases a careful examination will detect minute bubbles in ancient imitations of gems, even though in colour and purity of "water" the paste may be quite equal to a fine example of a genuine stone. In fact, in point of richness and beauty of colour antique pastes are, on the whole, superior to the genuine stones which were used by the gem-engravers.

Crystal glass.

Colourless paste or glass was made to imitate rock-crystal, especially in the form of cups and bowls: these, Pliny says (*Hist. Nat.* XXXVII. 29), were imitated with wonderful skill, so that it was difficult to distinguish between the real crystal and the glass; yet, he remarks, the excellence of the imitations did nothing to diminish the price of the genuine crystal: see also *Hist. Nat.* XXXVI. 198 and 195: in the latter passage Pliny tells us that Nero paid no less than 6000 sesterces for two small cups of glass, probably examples of elaborate cutting with the lapidary's tools, such as those mentioned at page 118.

Amber.

AMBER: a considerable section of Book XXXVII. (30 to 53) is devoted by Pliny to a description of amber, *sucinum*,

---

[1] A great deal of the superior beauty of ancient glass is due to the presence of these minute air-bubbles, each of which catches the light and radiates it out from the body of the glass, thus making it internally *luminous*, not merely transparent.

The absence of air-bubbles in modern stained glass is one reason of its being so much less beautiful than the glass of mediaeval times, which has the same peculiarity as the pastes of the classical period.

though it does not properly come under the head of precious stones, and was much too soft to engrave for use as a signet.

Roman finger-rings cut out of amber have occasionally been found, but these had an engraved gem or paste set in the bezel. It was also used for cameos, especially for those which were set in honorary *phalerae*, for drinking-cups and even for statuettes, for which large prices were given[1].

According to Pliny (§ 51) amber could be stained to imitate various gems, and more especially the amethyst.

His account of its origin is quite correct, *Hist. Nat.* XXXVII. 42: amber is a fossil gum, which has exuded from a tree of the pine tribe—an extinct conifer, which modern botanists call *Pinites Succinifer*. The name *succinum* was derived from *sucus* (arboris), "tree-sap."

Amber was the ἤλεκτρον of the Greeks (Plato, *Tim.* 80 C)[2]; it was used in the early prehistoric period by almost all the races of Europe, and is found in tombs of the bronze and iron age over a very wide area. Homer (*Od.* XV. 460) mentions a gold necklace, with pendants of amber, which was offered for sale to the Queen of Syra by a Phoenician trading-captain. Throughout the Greek period it was largely used as an ornament in all sorts of gold jewellery.

In Pliny's time amber necklaces were commonly worn by the women of the North of Italy beyond the river Po. The curious electric properties of amber are noticed by Pliny (§ 48), who speaks of it attracting, when rubbed, bits of chaff and straw, as the magnet attracts iron filings.

Most of the amber used in Europe came from the shores of the Baltic, but it was also found in the Red Sea and in certain parts of the Mediterranean.

The existence of very early trading routes from the North to the South of Europe is indicated by the frequent discovery of amber from the Baltic in the prehistoric tombs of various southern localities.

---

[1] At *Hist. Nat.* XXXVII. 49, Pliny remarks that an amber statuette of a man often cost as much money as would have purchased a living slave.

[2] The word ἤλεκτρον also means an alloy of gold and silver, such as was largely used for the early coinages of Western Asia Minor, especially Lydia and Ionia.

Lyncu-rium.

A variety of amber called *lyncurium* is mentioned by Pliny, § 52; he says that it could be used for engraving like a gem, but that is probably an error.

Choice of stones.

With regard to the choice of special stones for the engraving of certain subjects, it may be observed that in Roman times and even among the later Greeks stones of certain colours were sometimes selected by the engraver with a reference to the subject he was about to cut on it.

Thus the *green beryl* or *aquamarine* was considered suitable for nymphs or deities of the sea, and the *green jasper* for pastoral scenes, such as cattle feeding.

Several of the epigrams on engraved gems in the Greek *Anthologia* refer to this fitness of colour and material to the subject cut on the stone.

Magic virtues.

Other stones were selected for mystic religious reasons; as, for example, the blood-red *jasper*, which was commonly used for heads and figures of the Graeco-Egyptian deities Serapis and Horus.

It would not, however, be safe to press this point very far. It was probably quite an exceptional thing for the colour of a gem to have any allusion to the subject which was engraved upon it.

THE COMPARATIVE HARDNESS OF GEMS.

The following table indicates the different degrees of *hardness* of the stones used for engraved gems, with the addition of some others for the sake of comparison. The number opposite each represents its hardness according to the scale now adopted by mineralogists generally.

1. *talc*, lowest degree of hardness;
2. *crystals of gypsum*;
2½. *amber*;
3. *transparent calcite and steatite*;
4. *fluor-spar (murrhina)*;
5 to 5½. *lapis lazuli*;
5½ to 6. *opal*;
6. *turquoise*, and *feldspar* such as *green basalt* and *red porphyry*;
6½. *haematite, magnetite* and *peridot*;
7. *rock-crystal*, including the coloured varieties, such as *amethyst*; the other varieties of the *silicon* gems, such as *chalcedony, sard* and *onyx*, are slightly less hard than the crystalline forms;
7 to 7½. *carbuncle* or *garnet*;
7½ to 8. *beryl* in all forms, such as *emerald* and the sea-green *aquamarine*;
8. *topaz*;
9. *sapphire, ruby* and other crystalline forms of *alumina*;
10. *diamond*, the hardest of all known substances.

APPENDIX.

DESCRIPTIVE CATALOGUE

OF THE

ENGRAVED GEMS

IN THE

FITZWILLIAM MUSEUM, CAMBRIDGE

BY

J. HENRY MIDDLETON

DIRECTOR OF THE FITZWILLIAM MUSEUM, SLADE PROFESSOR OF FINE ART,
AND FELLOW OF KING'S COLLEGE, CAMBRIDGE

CAMBRIDGE:
AT THE UNIVERSITY PRESS.
1891

CATALOGUE OF THE ENGRAVED GEMS IN THE FITZWILLIAM MUSEUM[1]

1. Archaic glandular gem; *stag* with curved horns, running; below are two branches: rude archaic work on *green chalcedony*, pierced lengthways; date possibly 8th century B.C. or even earlier.

2. *Eagle* flying, holding a serpent in his beak and with one claw; fine glandular gem, of *green chalcedony*, pierced; similar in type to No. 1, but of better execution; probably of the 7th century B.C. *Plate I.*

A similar eagle flying with a serpent in his beak occurs on various early silver coins of Chalcis in Euboea; see *Zeitschrift für Numismatik*, Vol. III. pp. 216 and 217; and *Numismatic Chronicle* for 1890, Pl. III. No. 23.

The eagle and serpent is also a frequent type on coins of Elis of the 6th and 5th centuries B.C.; see Head, *Coins of the Ancients*, Plate 14, Nos. 26 to 28. The eagle bearing a serpent, hare or some other animal, was commonly regarded as an omen of victory sent by Zeus; see Homer, *Il*. XII. 218. In his letter to the High Priest Onias, Areius King of Sparta states that his royal signet is an eagle bearing a serpent in its claws; see Josephus, *Ant. Jud*. XII. 5. It was a common practice for the writer of a letter, both among the later Greeks and the Romans, to mention at the end of it, what

---

[1] All are from Colonel Leake's collection except Nos. 3, 3*, 4, 8, 42, and the Poniatowski gem, the last in the Catalogue.
Unless described as cameos, all are intaglios.

was the design on its seal, as a guard against forgery and to prevent the letter from being tampered with in any way.

Plate I.   3. *Phoenician scarabaeoid* of *blue paste*, surface corroded, found at Camiros in the island of Rhodes.

The design represents an *enthroned deity* holding up a cup; behind is the kneeling figure of a worshipper; in front is an Egyptian cartouche containing illegible hieroglyphs. This is a very characteristic example of Phoenician work, with figures of half Egyptian and half Assyrian type: given by Prof. Middleton. Other paste scarabaeoids of the same type from Camiros are now in the British Museum, Nos. 140 and 141 in Mr Smith's Catalogue.

3*. Phoenician scarab of dark *green jasper* engraved with a design of Egyptian style, two seated figures of the hawk-headed deity Chonsu, also called Nefer-hetep, each holding a lotus-tipped sceptre, between them is the sacred Egyptian asp; above is the winged sun-disc, emblem of the god Ra. This is a good typical example of a Phoenician signet of the 5th or 4th century B.C. It is much worn with use.

Plate I.   4. *Scarab of Phoenician style* in red *agate*, the underside engraved with the sacred beetle of Egypt with outspread wings, within a "cable border." In the field is the inscription, in letters of the 5th century B.C.—ΚΡΕΟΝΤΙΔΑ ΕΜΙ, meaning "I am the signet or device (σῆμα) of Kreontidas." Examples of early gems with the names of owners are mentioned above at page 67. The inscription is not reversed, but is to be read on the gem itself, which may possibly be older than the date of Kreontidas; the style of cutting of the letters suggests that the name is an addition by a different hand from that of the original engraver of the scarab. This very interesting gem was discovered in 1840 in a Greek tomb in the island of Aegina, probably the tomb of Kreontidas. It passed at once into the possession of Mr George Finlay, the well-known historian of mediaeval and modern Greece, who described it in a paper published in the *Bull. Inst. Corr. Arch.* 1840, pp: 140, 141. At his death it became the property of Mr W. Finlay, who in 1877 bequeathed it by will to the Fitzwilliam Museum. The device is a favourite one on Phoenician scarabs; Pliny, *Hist. Nat.* XXXVII. 124, mentions the superstition that the scarabaeus beetle, engraved on an emerald, had certain magical virtues.

5. Scarabaeoid, pierced: *a Greek hero*, nude, wearing only a Corinthian helmet, is about to fit a greave (κνημίς) upon his leg. With both hands he bends the bronze apart; the Greek greaves having no means of fastening except the spring of the metal. This is well shown on the leg from a colossal bronze statue, now in the British Museum, on which the bronze greave is carefully represented, and modelled to imitate the muscles of the leg itself; see *Jour. Hell. Stud.* Vol. VII. p. 189 and Plate LXIX. This very fine gem, of about 500 B.C., is remarkable for its spirited drawing and very skilful treatment of the nude figure. In style it resembles the pediment sculpture from the temple in Aegina. *Plate I.*

It is surrounded by a "cable border," part of which has been ground away at some time, probably by a jeweller in setting the gem.

The stone is *rock crystal* of great purity and brilliance, possibly from Mount Taygetus in Laconia. Col. Leake obtained it in the Peloponnese. Gems of this period are rarely cut on colourless *rock crystal*, though it is often used for Assyrian cylinders, and sometimes for the early *lenticular* gems. No. 435 in the British Museum has the same subject, though treated rather differently.

6. *Female figure*, wearing long *chiton* and *himation*, stands before a small altar of fire, holding in one hand a *patera* containing some offering, and in the other hand a small *oenochoe* or wine jug. Fine Greek work of c. 480—450 B.C., or possibly archaistic work of later date, very minutely cut on a thin slice of *burnt agate*. *Plate I.*

7. *A maneless lion* or lioness, which has sprung upon the back of a bull, and is fixing its teeth in the bull's shoulders; very fine Greek work of the 5th century B.C., noble in style, broadly modelled and very spirited in design. A large scarabaeoid of fine *sapphirine chalcedony*, pierced for suspension. *Plate I.*

In early Greek art, that is from the pre-historic "Mycenae

period" down to the 5th century B.C., the lion occurs very frequently; more especially on vases of the so-called "Oriental style" with encircling bands of animals. Bands with lions attacking bulls are very common. Herodotus, VII. 126, tells us that certain districts of Thrace were full of lions and wild bulls, and in the previous section, VII. 125, he records that, during the Persian invasion of Thrace, many of the camels used as beasts of burden in the army of Xerxes were killed by lions: cf. also Aristotle, *Hist. Anim.* VI. 31.

In later times the lion became extinct even in the mountainous regions of Thrace, and hence, probably, the reason of its becoming comparatively rare in Greek art. A somewhat similar design to that on this noble gem occurs on silver coins of the 6th century B.C. struck at the Thracian Acanthus; see Head, *Coins of the Ancients*, Plate IV. 7.

The same subject, on a colossal scale, is repeated in more than one early limestone (*poros*) group recently discovered on the Acropolis of Athens, and now preserved in the Acropolis Museum.

8. *A cow* with head turned back towards its calf, which is sucking; a fine early Greek design, similar to that on coins of the 5th century struck at Dyrrhachium in Illyria, and in the Island of Corcyra, during the 6th and 5th centuries B.C., and elsewhere. Large scarabaeoid of almost *colourless paste*, pierced: the surface of the paste is corroded by decomposition.

In Oriental cults the cow and calf were frequently used as types of the Nature Goddess, Astarte, whom the early Greeks associated with Hera.

9. Head of *Herakles*, bearded, with short curly hair, apparently of the 4th century B.C.

Large scarabaeoid in almost *colourless glass* or *paste*, pierced, like No. 8. Both these paste gems have been formed in the usual way by pressing a lump of hot, soft glass into a mould: the edges, back and ground of the front were then cut into shape on a lapidary's wheel.

This scarabaeoid and No. 8 were probably pendants of a necklace, as they are far too large for rings.

10. *A youth*, nude, leaning on a jagged staff, bends *Plate I.*
downwards to caress his dog, which looks up affectionately at
his master; within a cable border. A gem of exceptionally
beautiful design and workmanship, of the best period of
Greek art, the middle or latter half of the 5th century B.C.
The modelling of the nude form is extremely skilful, and the
details are most minutely worked. Gems of this date are
very rare, especially examples as large and carefully executed
as this. A scarabaeoid of *clouded chalcedony*, of a yellowish
brown tint, pierced.

The design on this remarkable gem is similar to that on
some of the sepulchral *stelae* of Athens, dating a little before
and after 400 B.C.; most of these are reliefs of life size or
near it, and were found in the cemetery outside the Dipylon of
Athens. Another gem with almost exactly the same design,
but slightly inferior workmanship, was found in a tomb in
Cyprus by Cesnola, and is illustrated in his *Cyprus*, 1877,
Plate XXXIX. No. 6.

Another subject which occurs on the Attic *stelae* is engraved on a gem in the British Museum (No. 473), which
bears the nude figure of a youth, seated, and holding his oil-
flask ready for the bath.

11. *An Athenian lady*, wearing the *chiton poderes* and *Plate I.*
its girdle with the *himation* across her knees and a veil
over her head, is seated in a chair with lathe-turned legs;
with one hand she raises a corner of her veil. In front of
her stands an attendant girl, wearing the long *chiton* and
over it the short *chitoniskos*; she holds in one hand a wreath,
and in the other a mirror which she presents to her mistress.
In the field at the top is the inscription ΜΙΚΗΣ, probably the
lady's name; at the side, behind the seated figure, in very
minute letters, is the name ΔΕΞΑΜΕΝΟΣ, the signature of
the gem-engraver, cut so as to be read on the stone itself.
A scarabaeoid of fine *sapphirine chalcedony*, pierced; a "cable"
border surrounds the whole design; see above, page 68.

This gem is a very large and beautiful example of Athenian
work of the 4th century, probably before 350 B.C. Its design,
like that of No. 10, is precisely the same as those on some

sepulchral reliefs from the Dipylon Cemetery of Athens. Toilet scenes in one form or another are among the most frequently recurring subjects on the tomb-stelae of Attica. It may be that this beautiful gem was engraved and worn in memory of a dead wife or sister. In addition to its great beauty as a work of art and the comparatively large size of the composition, the fact of its being signed by the artist makes this gem one of the most important examples of the kind in the world. Genuine artists' signatures on gems are extremely rare, though forged ones are common enough, and it is a remarkable coincidence that two of the very few other gems, which, like this, have an artist's name of undoubted genuineness, are both signed with the same name Dexamenos; see Newton, *Essays on Archaeology*, 1880, p. 396. One of these is a minutely executed representation of a crane flying, with the inscription in microscopic letters—ΔΕΞΑΜΕΝΟΣ ΕΠΟΙΕ ΧΙΟΣ, "Dexamenos of Chios made (me)." The other gem has a standing crane, with the name ΔΕΞΑΜΕΝΟΣ alone, as on the Fitzwilliam scarabaeoid.

Both these gems with cranes were found, together with other objects of Attic workmanship dating probably from the first half of the 4th century B.C., in one of the numerous tombs which have been opened at Kertch in the Crimea, the ancient Panticapaeum. They are now in the Hermitage Museum at St Petersburg, and are illustrated in the *Compte-rendu de la Commiss. Arch.*, 1861, Plate VI., No. 10; and *ib.* 1865, Pl. III., No. 40.

The coincidence of date, the minute workmanship, and the close similarity of the letters in the inscriptions make it highly probable that both the gems from Kertch and that in the Fitzwilliam Museum are the work of the same Chian artist. It is very improbable that there should have been at the same date more than one gem-engraver of the same name and of such exceptional ability as was the artist of the Fitzwilliam and the Kertch gems.

A fourth gem, with the signature ΔΕΞΑΜΕΝΟΣ ΕΠΟΙΕ, exists in a private collection in Athens; it is a male bearded head, apparently a portrait: see *Compte-rendu de la Comm.*

Arch., 1868, Plate I., No. 12: it is said to have been found at Kara in Attica, but its genuineness is doubtful. It was not known till after the discovery of the gems by Dexamenos in the Kertch cemetery, and its inscription may very possibly have been copied from the one with the flying crane. The Fitzwilliam scarabaeoid, on the other hand, was in the possession of Colonel Leake long before the other gems of Dexamenos had been discovered, and its genuineness cannot be suspected.

On the various gems by Dexamenos, see Furtwängler, *Jahrbuch Arch. Inst.*, 1888, p. 199 to 204.

12. *A female figure*, fully draped, stands talking with a nude youth, who leans upon his staff—possibly Electra and Orestes: of good Greek style, but careless workmanship, on a fine *orange sard*. In point of technique this gem is an interesting example of the extensive use of the diamond-point, especially in the drapery of the female, and in the hair of both figures. *Plate I.*

13. Scarabaeoid: *a bull walking*: fine Greek work of the 5th or 4th century B.C. On a convex *bluish white chalcedony* with brown patches. *Plate I.*

14. *Bull standing*; behind is a cow facing in the opposite direction; well and minutely executed on *banded chalcedony*; possibly Greek work of the 4th century B.C. *Plate I.*

15. A true scarab in *carnelian*, pierced, the device on it is a *Siren*, standing, playing on the double flutes. The Siren is represented as a human figure with bird's feet, tail and wings; a similar figure occurs on a curious four-lobed pendant gem in the British Museum, No. 549 in Mr A. H. Smith's Catalogue. Scarabs of this type are often found in Etruscan tombs, being either Greek imports or native copies of Greek designs. Forgeries of modern date are also very common; the Fitzwilliam example may perhaps be one of these. It is set as a seal in a modern gold mount.

16. *Man on horseback*, with spear, pursuing a stag with branching horns which is already wounded with another spear. The hunter wears a curious hood over his head with horn-like projections at the back; the rest of his dress is not *Plate I.*

very distinct, but it appears to consist of trousers and a short tunic. He sits on a large fringed saddle-cloth, and appears from his costume to be of semi-barbarian type, not unlike some of the figures of Scythians represented on objects of Greek workmanship found in the tombs of Kertch. It is a well executed design, possibly of northern Greek workmanship. The horse closely resembles that on coins of various Macedonian kings.

This important gem is a large scarabaeoid of *clouded chalcedony*, with agate layers at the back: it is pierced for suspension. Set in a modern seal-mount.

17. Fragment of a large and very fine gem with a profile *male head*; only the back of the head with its crisp curls remains: probably of the 4th century B.C.; engraved on *sardonyx* with a raised border in a white layer.

18. Fragment of a large gem of good later Greek style, probably 3rd century B.C. The subject appears to be *Pegasus* or some other winged horse *trampling on a serpent*, but only the front portion remains; the rider and most of the horse are wholly lost. Cut on a fine orange yellow *sard*.

Plate I. 19. *Artemis* in long *chiton*, with scarf-like drapery floating behind her, is walking, holding a dead fawn by the forelegs, and in her other hand a bow and two arrows; she wears shoes tied with a knot above the ancle. Work of good style, probably copied from some statue of Praxitelean type, cut on a deep *orange sard*.

Plate I. 20. *Horus* (the Greek Harpocrates) seated on a lotus flower, with one finger pointing to his lips, and in the other hand a flail, on dark *green jasper*. Good work of the Ptolemaic period of Egyptian style, probably of the 3rd century B.C. On the back, in much later characters, is rudely scratched the mystic word ABPACAΞ, added by some Gnostic owner.

The letters of ἀβρασάξ or ἀβραξάς (as Greek numerals) make up the number 365. According to the Gnostic creed there were 365 orders of angels, each of which occupied a separate heaven; each heaven being superior to the one below and inferior to the one above it. It was especially the followers of the Gnostic Basilides who used this mystic word,

denoting the whole Hierarchy of Heaven, and also the
supreme Ruler of the universe. The *Abraxas* deity is frequently symbolised by a human figure with a cock's head and
serpent legs; this type is intimately connected with the sun-
god Mithras. The name and symbol of *Abraxas* were
supposed to have great talismanic powers, protecting the
wearer from disease, accident and misfortune generally. Its
medical virtues, when cut on the right stone, were very highly
valued, and believed in for many centuries; to a great extent
even throughout the mediaeval period. See above, page 123.

21. *Aphrodite*, half nude, leaning against a short pillar; *Plate II.*
she holds a helmet in one hand, and a long staff or spear in
the other; against the pillar a round shield is set. It is
engraved with great delicacy and minuteness on *black jasper*.
This figure, like No. 19, is probably taken from some celebrated Greek statue; the design occurs very frequently on
gems; the collection in the Paris Bibliothèque contains no
less than nineteen examples.

22. *Eros*, as a graceful winged youth, seated on a rock, *Plate II.*
holds up a wreath; his torch is stuck into the ground before
him: fine Graeco-Roman work on *sardoine*, minutely executed
with much taste and skill.

23. *Aphrodite*, fully draped in *chiton* and *himation*, stands
leaning against a short pillar. In one hand she holds a bird,
probably meant for a dove, with the other hand she raises a
corner of her *himation:* very rude work, mostly done with a
coarse wheel, on a large, slightly striated *carnelian*. This
gem, though of very poor workmanship, is of interest as being
probably a copy of some celebrated Greek statue.

24. *Hunting scene* in two tiers; at the top, a horseman,
riding at full speed, aims an arrow at a lion which approaches
him. Below, a similar horseman aims a long spear at a wild
boar. Both of the hunters wear a tight tunic and trousers,
and on their heads a hood of Oriental fashion. Instead of a
saddle the horses have a large fringed cloth over their backs,
and their long tails are tied up with a knot.

Persian work, of the Sasanian period, about the 4th century A.D., on a large scarabaeoid of *clouded chalcedony*, pierced,

25. *Silenus mask*, full face, of Greek workmanship, very minutely cut on *nicolo:* set in a modern ring, on which is engraved the word "Epirus," i.e. the district where Col. Leake bought the gem.

26. Enthroned figure of *Jupiter*, extending one hand over a small fire-altar; in the other hand he holds the long sceptre or *hasta pura*. Early Roman work on fine *opaline chalcedony:* in a modern ring.

27. *Jupiter enthroned* holding in one hand the *hasta pura*, and in the other a small figure of Victory bearing a wreath: at his feet an eagle. Roman work on a *carnelian*, in modern ring setting.

This design, which is common on Roman gems and on the reverses of Imperial denarii, is derived originally from the celebrated gold and ivory statue of Zeus at Olympia by Pheidias, which is copied on the reverses of various Greek coins, such as the tetradrachms of Alexander the Great.

28. Standing figure of *Bacchus*, nude, pouring wine from a cantharus to his panther; with the other hand he holds the thyrsus: rude Roman work.

This is a very common design on Graeco-Roman and Roman gems: e.g. two gems in the British Museum; Nos. 945 and 946 in Mr A. H. Smith's catalogue: Nos. 62 and 63 in the Fitzwilliam collection have the same subject. *Striated, bluish chalcedony*, in modern setting.

29. *Winged Victory*, half draped, resting one foot on a rock; she points to her face with one hand, and in the other holds a palm branch. Roman work on a *pale topaz* or *citrine* with both sides cut *en cabochon*. In modern ring setting.

30. *Winged Victory* holding in one hand a wreath, and in the other a palm branch: rude Roman work, probably of Republican date, on a very *pale sard:* in modern ring setting.

31. *Winged Victory* with wreath and palm branch, as on No. 30. Roman work of the Republican period on fine *chalcedony*, in modern ring setting.

This fine gem much resembles the sard set in a gold ring, which was found in 1780 on the skeleton hand of Cornelius Lucius Scipio Barbatus, consul in 298 B.C., whose sarcophagus is in the Vatican. This ring passed into Lord Beverley's collection, and is now in the possession of the Duke of Northumberland. It is of great value, not only from its historical interest, but also as being a dated example of early Roman glyptic art, which helps to fix the period of other similar gems. See above, page 47.

32. Profile *bust of Diana* with a crescent on her head, between *busts of Castor and Pollux*, each with a star over his head. The Dioscuri wear the usual *pileus* or egg-shaped cap encircled by a wreath, and a chlamys over the shoulder; their heads are very similar to those on silver coins of Bruttii of the 3rd century B.C.; see *Brit. Mus. Cat. of Greek Coins of Italy*, No. 8, p. 320. *Plate II.*

Fine *sapphirine chalcedony*, in modern seal setting inscribed "Morea" where Col. Leake bought it.

33. *Minerva* standing, wearing the long chiton and a helmet; she holds one hand extended, and in the other her spear and shield. Very good Roman work on a deep red *carnelian*, in modern ring setting. *Plate II.*

The original of this design appears to have been the Athene Parthenos of Pheidias: it is a common subject on Roman gems; the extended hand usually holds a statuette of Victory, which on this gem is omitted. The design seems copied, not directly from the statue, but from the representation on various Greek coins.

34. Nude figure of *Bonus Eventus*, standing: with one hand he pours a libation on to a small fire-altar: in the other hand he holds two ears of wheat. Roman work of the first century A.D. on a *nicolo-onyx*. This design is common on reverses of Imperial denarii during the 1st and 2nd century A.D. In a modern ring setting.

35. *A chariot drawn by two ants:* the driver is a rabbit, who holds the rein in one paw and a whip in the other. Roman work of early Imperial date, on a *carnelian*, in modern ring setting. This fanciful type of design occurs frequently on Roman gems, and also among the wall paintings of Pompeii, possibly in some cases with a satirical meaning.

36. *Nude hero* with crested helmet, and sword slung *Plate II.*

round him, kneeling on one knee; he works with a graver and hammer (?) on a metal cuirass. Rather coarse Graeco-Roman work on a fine transparent *chalcedony*. Acquired by Col. Leake in the Peloponnese. In modern ring setting, on which is engraved "Morea."

Plate II. 37. Profile *bust of Hermes* wearing a small petasus and chlamys fastened on the shoulder with a fibula; of good Greek style. *Paste*, imitating orange sard: in modern seal setting.

38. Profile *portrait of beardless youth* with long hair. In the style of good Roman work of early Imperial date, in fine *red jasper*. In modern seal setting; the gem itself may possibly be a modern copy.

39. Cameo *head of Medusa*, very rude work in *onyx* of two layers; the back is roughly shaped by flaking off chips: in modern ring setting. The cameo also is perhaps modern.

40. Portions of *two gold ear-rings* of very beautiful Greek workmanship: one is in the shape of a lion's head skilfully modelled: on the shank is a delicate scroll pattern formed in that minute *granulated* work, which the Greek jewellers executed with such wonderful skill. The other is a pendant, with a miniature figure of *Eros*, a marvel of minute execution: it was acquired by Col. Leake at Pella. Gold ear-rings, with an exactly similar figure of *Eros*, were found by Cesnola in a tomb in Cyprus; see Cesnola, *Salaminia*, 1884, p. 41, fig. 39.

41. *Ring* wholly in *glass*, probably of Greek workmanship: the bezel is of orange-yellow paste with a thin layer of white under it to imitate *sardonyx;* the rest of the ring is of a pale purple paste. Obtained by Col. Leake in Thessaly.

42. *Ring-shaped bead* of *magnetite:* on it is rudely cut a man driving a spear through a lion: Assyrian work of early date. Given by Prof. Middleton; bought at Beyrout.

43. Large cameo *head of Hera*, wearing a *stephanos*, in very high relief on an *onyx* of two layers, opaque white on a transparent chalcedony layer. Graeco-Roman work of good style, but coarse execution, said to have been obtained by Captain George Keppell " near Kula." In his *Narrative of a*

journey from India to England, 1827, Vol. II. p. 226, Captain Keppell mentions his visit to an eminence called Kula Noo, in Tartary, near the town of Kuba on the banks of the river Deli, which rises in the Caucasus and runs into the Caspian Sea; he does not, however, mention this cameo.

In modern gold setting inscribed " Ruins near Kula."

44. *Large ring*, wholly of silver, with large oval bezel on which is soldered in relief in gold letters the inscription ΑΤΤΥΛΑΣ — probably the owner's name. This ring is clearly of late date: Dr Waldstein has suggested that it may possibly bear the name of Attila, the great general of the Huns and Goths 434—454 A.D. in spite of the spelling Ἀττύλας instead of the usual Ἀττίλας or Ἀττήλας: see *Journ. Hellen. Stud.* IV., p. 162. On the inside of the hoop some recent sacrilegious hand has cut the word " Thessaly " in large letters, a record of the district where it was bought by Col. Leake.

45. The goddess *Roma*, in *stola*, *pallium*, and helmet, seated on a heap of armour holding a spear in one hand and in the other a small figure of Victory bearing a wreath. In the field behind, Q. MAX cut so as to read on the gem itself. Early Roman work on *carnelian*. This common type of the goddess Roma is derived from the Greek Athene, as represented on such coins as the tetradrachms of Lysimachus struck c. 300 B.C., with the deified head of Alexander on the *obverse*. Mr King suggests in his Catalogue (Case II., No. 28) that this was the signet of the celebrated Quintus Fabius Maximus, one of the earliest Roman conquerors of the Greeks, but the name was too common for any certainty as to the ownership of this special gem.

46. A seated figure of *Roma* (like that on No. 45) with sword and spear, holding Victory in her outstretched hand. Coarse Roman work on an *orange sard*, deeply cut.

47. Minute figure of *Athene* advancing, holding spear and shield: *orange sard*, a fine Greek design, which probably represents some important statue.

48. *Mars* in short chiton and crested helmet stands, holding a spear in one hand; with the other hand he supports a round shield, resting it on the ground.

Bold Roman work on *carnelian*, chipped on one side.

Plate II. 49. Bust in profile of the *winged Victory;* behind her is a palm-branch. Very fine early Roman work on *chalcedony;* chipped. The hair, wing and palm-branch are executed in a stiff but very delicate way with the diamond or corundum point: it is a very interesting example of the best sort of Roman work during the later Republican period. The same design occurs on several denarii of the Republic, and on the obverse of both gold and copper coins struck by Julius Caesar in 45 B.C., with the *legend* C. CAESAR DIC. TER.

Plate II. 50. *Bust of Diana* in profile, with bow and quiver slung across her shoulder. Her chiton is fastened with a fibula on the shoulder. Round the head, in coarsely formed Greek letters, the owner's name ΘΡΕΠΤΟC, cut so as to be read on the impression.

Good Graeco-Roman work on *carnelian*.

51. *Female head* in profile of the Amazon type; behind is a double axe, in front the inscription FELICI S..., part broken away.

Fine Graeco-Roman work on *grey jasper*.

Plate II. 52. *Venus Victrix* leaning against a *cippus*, with drapery round the lower part of the body: in one hand she holds a *hasta pura* or long sceptre, and in the other hand a helmet. On the ground in front is a cuirass. Coarse Graeco-Roman work on a convex striated *agate*. This design is probably copied from some well-known Greek statue.

Plate II. 53. A *cornu-copiae, dolphin and trident* grouped crosswise in a very graceful way. Very fine Roman work of the time of the early Empire on a dull semi-opaque *sard;* possibly the symbol of some general who, like M. Agrippa, was remarkable for success both by sea and by land.

54. Nude figure of *Ganymede* seated on a rock: he gives Jove's eagle drink out of a *patera*. Graceful design, poorly executed on a small *carnelian*. It is probably a Roman copy of some fine Greek design.

Plate II. 55. A *Triton* holding a trident, represented as a male figure with fish-tails in serpentine coils instead of legs. Good Roman work of early Imperial date on a yellowish *chalcedony*.

56. *Cupid* standing; in one hand a torch, with which he singes a butterfly held in the other hand: symbolical of the hot fever of love. A Roman design on very fine *red jasper*. *Plate II.*

The same design occurs among the "Marlborough Gems" (No. 142 in Mr Story-Maskelyne's Catalogue), and it is repeated on many other gems.

57. Minute figure of *Fortuna* standing, holding in one hand a cornu-copiae and in the other hand a rudder: a frequent design on Roman denarii of Imperial date. On *red jasper*.

58. *Roma* seated on a heap of armour: very rude Roman work on an orange *sard*.

59. *Vulcan* seated, working with a hammer on a helmet placed on an anvil: very rude Roman work on mixed *jasper and chalcedony*.

60. *Mercury* standing with the caduceus in one hand, and in the other a purse and a cock: in the field is a scorpion and a goat. Rude Roman work on *carnelian*. This is a not uncommon type of astrological gem, representing its owner's fortunate horoscope: cf. *Marlborough Gems*, No. 172 in Story-Maskelyne's Catalogue, London, 1870.

61. *Mercury* standing, with the caduceus in one hand and a purse in the other: very rude Roman work on yellow *sard*: a very common subject both for gems and for sculptured reliefs of the Imperial period.

62. *Bacchus* with the thyrsus in one hand and in the other a cantharus: at his feet a panther: rude Roman work on *sard*: cf. No. 28.

63. Minute figure of *Bacchus* holding the thyrsus and a cantharus, with the panther at his feet (like No. 62): the whole figure is enclosed by a vine. Poor Roman work on *amethyst*, a stone which was supposed to give its wearer the power of drinking large quantities of wine without his becoming intoxicated: hence its name from ἀ-μέθυσος. Pliny (*Hist. Nat.* XXXVII. 124) expresses his disbelief in this superstition.

Dionysiac subjects were very frequently engraved on the amethyst, especially during the Roman Imperial period.

64. Winged figure of *Nemesis* in *stola* and *pallium*, *Plate II.*

standing holding a caduceus over a conical object like the *meta* of a circus. The Romans had no very fixed method of representing Nemesis: on gold and silver coins of Claudius, she is represented as a winged woman holding a caduceus, with a serpent on the ground. On other coins she appears with different symbols.

Very rude Roman work on a convex orange *sard;* the use of the drill-point and the wheel is very evident, owing to the want of skill of the engraver.

65. *Portrait of Socrates,* of the usual Silenus type, on *carnelian.* Graeco-Roman work, if not a modern imitation: broken across: in Mr King's Catalogue the fragments are numbered separately 12 and 46 in Case I.

Plate II. 66. Profile *portrait of Nero,* laureated, executed in a fairly good, bold style on *carnelian.*

67. Very rude *profile head* with radiated crown, perhaps representing *Apollo Helios:* coarsest kind of Roman work on *carnelian.*

68. *Head of the youthful Hercules,* rudely worked, the hair executed with the drill-point. On *red jasper,* broken at the bottom.

69. *Silenus* seated on a rock, plays the lyre in front of a small shrine set on a rock: behind him is a wreath with long streaming fillets. Rude Roman work on orange *sard.* No. 993 in the British Museum has the same subject.

70. A *goat* standing under a tree: in the field, on the other side, is a lizard. Roman work, very well and delicately executed on the convex surface of a *sardonyx.* A very remarkable example of minute work.

71. A *Faun seated* on a crate or basket; in front of him is a goat, which he caresses with one hand: in the other hand he holds a river-rush. Delicate Roman work on *sard.* The same design occurs on a gem in the British Museum, No. 1056.

Plate II. 72. A *hippocamp* or sea-horse, swimming. Fine Roman work on a convex *carnelian,* deeply cut; edge chipped.

Plate II. 73. A *horse* standing to graze; above it, a star within a crescent: very fine Roman work on *carnelian.* As Mr King suggests (Cat. p. 14, No. 26) this may be the portrait of a favourite race-horse; the star and crescent being the owner's badge, which was frequently branded on the horse's skin.

74. *A lion walking* under a tree, holding some object in its mouth. Very fine and minutely executed Roman work on *white jasper* mottled with pink; the colour has been altered by fire. *Plate II.*

75. *Hound running* at full speed; in the field above is a curved knobbed stick, such as was used to knock over small game. Coarse Roman work on olive green *plasma*.

76. *Crab holding in its claws a shell;* very minute work on *sard*. This design occurs frequently on Roman gems: in some cases the crab holds a fish or a shrimp in its claws.

77. *An ant*, rudely cut on an *onyx* of four layers.

78. *A hound attacking a rabbit;* above them is a flying eagle: rude Roman work on *yellow jasper*. The same subject occurs on many gems of Imperial date, e.g. one in the British Museum, No. 1958 in the Catalogue.

79. *A cock*, holding in its claw an ear of wheat: Roman work, cleverly executed on a very small *chrysoprase* or *plasma* of pale emerald green colour.

80. *Cupid riding on a dolphin:* coarse Roman work on *carnelian*.

81. *A satyr and a goat* on its hind legs, dancing face to face: behind the satyr is an ear of bearded wheat: Roman work on a *sard*. About a third of the gem is missing. The design is one which occurs in Pompeian paintings.

82. *A wolf or bitch giving suck to an infant:* above is an eagle with outspread wings. The animal resembles the "wolf of the Capitol" suckling Romulus and Remus: possibly one of the twins was omitted on the gem for want of space; or perhaps the subject is that which occurs on coins of Cydonia in Crete, having, on the *obverse*, the infant Miletus (the brother of Cydon the founder of Cydonia) suckled by a wolf. Rude Roman work on a fine *sard*.

83. *The eagle of Jupiter* standing with outspread wings. Coarse Roman work on a *sardonyx* with roughly chipped back.

84. *A bull walking*, on yellow *paste*, a cast of a good gem.

85. *A winged male figure*, nude, in crested helmet, armed with spear, sword and shield. Coarse work on a pale yellow *sard:* chipped.

86. *Cupid sitting on the ground* with his hands bound behind him; a butterfly hovers in front of him: symbolical design. Fine Roman work on *sard*.

87. *Cupid with a hound in a leash:* very coarse Roman work on dark green *quartz crystal*, or *plasma*.

88. *Profile head of a youth* on *sard*, coarsely cut: part broken away.

89. *Head of Pan*, with small horns: in the field below is his *syrinx* (pan-pipes): Roman work on *red jasper*, chipped: cf. the small head of Pan on late Macedonian tetradrachms.

90. *Gryllus:* a parrot standing on a branch: its body is made up of a Tragic and a Comic mask: Roman work on convex *chalcedony*.

Pliny, *Hist. Nat.* XXXV. 114, uses the word *gryllus* for a class of grotesque figures first used in painting by Antiphilus of Alexandria. The word also means a cricket, but with regard to gems is used to express any grotesque monster which is made up of several masks or portions of other animals.

91. *Comic mask:* Roman work on dark olive-green *plasma*, slightly executed.

92. *Comic mask:* Roman work on a convex orange *sard*.

93. *Comic mask:* Roman work on yellow *jasper*.

94. *Bearded male head and female head*, conjoined: Roman work on *sard*, possibly representing Jupiter and Juno.

95. *Scarabaeoid* with a rude representation of some sort of shrine (?) deeply cut on the convex surface of a fine piece of very transparent *chalcedony*.

96. *Three horsemen* wearing high crested helmets: two riding side by side, the third galloping in the opposite direction. Roman work, minutely cut on *carnelian*.

97. *Seated female figure* with one hand extended over a small circular altar placed in front of a rock, on which stands

a small shrine; a tree grows out of the rock: rude Roman work on *sard*.

98. *Female figure pouring a libation* (?) on to a small circular altar at the foot of a tree. On the other side of the tree a female, seated in a chair, holds an infant on her knee: very minutely executed: broken in two places; part of the seated figure is missing. This design possibly represents the fostering of the infant Zeus by the Nymphs Adrasteia and Ida, daughters of Melisseus, in the island of Crete. Good Roman work on dark red *carnelian*.

99. *A nude male figure* wearing on his head a petasus, stands holding in his arms a stag with curved horns: below a small figure reaches up towards the stag. Behind the principal figure is the word AVCTVS. The lower part, about a third of the gem, is missing: rude Roman work on *orange sard*.

100. *Two male figures* wearing tunics standing, between them an infant is kneeling on the ground: minute, but poor Roman work on *carnelian*; broken. Mr King in his Catalogue, Case I, No. 42, explains this subject as representing "Diomede and Ulysses debating about the fate of Astyanax"; but the gem belongs to a late period when subjects of that class were no longer selected.

101. *Nude female figure* stooping towards a large vase *Plate II.* which stands at the foot of a column: behind her is a tree and on the other side a warrior in full armour, with sword and round shield: on orange *sard*; the upper part broken away. Coarse work very deeply cut. Subject doubtful: a gem in the British Museum (No. 1463) has a similar design.

102. *Full-faced bust of Mercury*, wearing the petasus and holding a caduceus: coarse Roman work on dark *carnelian*: the marks of the drill and wheel are very conspicuous.

103. *Bust of Harpocrates* with his finger on his lip; very rudely cut on *chalcedony*: late Roman work.

104. *Profile bust of Jupiter Serapis* with the *modius* on his head; in the field the letters $\begin{smallmatrix}&\text{H}\\\text{K}&\\&\Lambda\,\text{E}\end{smallmatrix}$. Very good Graeco-

Roman work on *sard*: it has been reduced in size to fit in a small ring-bezel.

Plate II. 105. *Eagle with outspread wings;* and above, a small *bust of Serapis* with radiated head; round it is the *legend* ЄIC ΖЄΥC CΑΡΑΠIC, "One God Serapis." Good Roman work of the second century A.D. on *red jasper*. This type of gem is common; varieties of the inscription are ЄIC ΘЄΟC CΑΡΑΠIC, and ЄIC ΖΩΝ ΘЄΟC, attestations of the Divine Unity, like that of the modern Moslems.

106. *Gnostic scarabaeoid* on green *plasma*: on the front the late Egyptian sun-god Cnoubis, represented as a serpent with lion's head surrounded by rays of light. On the back is the hieroglyphic symbol ϟϟϟ surrounded by the legend ΧΝΟΥΒΙC. The whole is a common type of Egyptian gem during the Roman Gnostic period, 3rd and 4th centuries A.D. The name of this deity is written variously as ΧΝΟΥΦΙΣ, ΧΝΟΥΜΙΣ and ΚΝΗΦ; he appears to be a late development of the early Egyptian deity Chnemu, the World-Creator or Moulder. He is called "Maker of all things that exist, Creator of things that are, the origin of evolutions, the father of fathers and mother of mothers." He is also "Father of the gods, moulder of men, begotten of the gods, maker of Heaven and Earth and Hell, of water and mountain."

In later times Chnemu became associated or identified with the sun-god Ra and with Osiris. With the Gnostics he was a form of Hor-Apollo—the Demiurgos or Spirit which "pervades the universe." This note I owe to Mr E. A. W. Budge. The medical properties of this design when engraved on a green jasper or plasma (*jaspis*) are explained by Galen, *De Simp. Med.* IX. See above, page 145.

107. *A cornu-copiae and a small globe*: coarse Roman work in banded *chalcedony*.

108. *A cornu-copiae, a cock, and a stalk of bearded wheat.* Minute Roman work in brilliant *amethyst*.

109. *A human-headed locust*, walking with a pole across his shoulder, from which are hung a hare, a rabbit and a lobster; in the field a serpent and a scorpion. Fanciful

Roman work of the first century A.D. on a *banded agate*. A talismanic gem with magical properties.

110. *A hand extended:* round it the legend MNHMONEYE, on *sard;* a common type of Roman memorial gem; in many cases the hand is pinching an ear, which the Romans regarded as the seat of memory; cf. Virgil, *Ecl.* VI. 3 to 4, *Cynthius aurem vellit.*

111. *A grotesque nude figure,* walking with a staff, and bearing on his back a dead crane; probably referring to the old story of the battle of the Pygmies and the cranes. Minute Roman work on *carnelian*, if antique.

112. *A man with a mattock* breaks up the ground at the foot of a cross, on *sard:* of doubtful antiquity.

113. *A rude palm-branch:* by it the letters Є : the rest
C A
of the inscription is broken away: late Roman work on dark *carnelian*. The inscription was perhaps meant for Ἰησοῦς νικᾷ.

114. *A dolphin set in a basin* on a tall pedestal in the form of a twisted column : the whole is apparently a fountain. Coarse late work on *carnelian.*

115. *Male figure standing by a cippus:* very rudely cut on a small pink *amethyst.*

116. *Scarab* cut in a fine emerald-coloured *plasma;* a bead from a necklace with no engraved device.

117. Two fragments: *sard* and three-banded *agate.*

MODERN GEMS.

1. Copy in dark red *paste* of the celebrated *signet of Michelangelo* in the Bibliothèque in Paris: No. 2337 in M. Chabouillet's Catalogue.

The original was engraved for Michelangelo by his friend Piero Maria da Pescia, who worked in Rome for Leo X., and was one of the ablest *intagliatori* of the Renaissance[1]. The boy fishing in the *exergue* is a rebus of the artist's name *Pescia*, derived from his birth-place, a small town of that name in Tuscany. The main design represents

---
[1] See above, page 126.

a Bacchanalian festival, and contains no less than eleven figures—one of the greatest marvels of microscopic workmanship that has ever been produced. A great many paste copies of this wonderful gem exist. The original was bought by Louis XIV., with the rest of the important Lauthier collection, and so it passed into the Bibliothèque Royale, where it is still preserved. In the last century it had a very narrow escape of being stolen. The Curator of the Bibliothèque was exhibiting the royal gems to the Baron Stosch, an enthusiastic collector of engraved stones, when suddenly the Curator observed that Michelangelo's signet-gem had vanished, after a suspicious movement on the part of the Baron. The Curator immediately sent for an emetic, and forced Baron Stosch to swallow it; with the fortunate result that in a few minutes the gem was heard to fall into the basin provided for the purpose; see Des Brosses, *Lettres sur l'Italie*, II. p. 27[1].

2. *Female head* in profile in the white layer of an *onyx*.

3. *Female full face*, wearing a diadem and necklace; on grey *jasper*.

4. *Profile bust* of a bearded man wearing a turban, on a very fine *bloodstone;* i.e. green jasper with red spots.

5. *Peasant blowing a cow-horn*, on *sard*.

6. *Male Bacchanal* with a thyrsus, dancing, on *banded sard*.

7. *Eagle's head* on *dark green chalcedony*.

8. *Head of M. Agrippa;* cameo on *onyx*, good modern work.

9. *A veiled lady* standing, holding an urn; cameo on *sardonyx*. A poor modern work, probably meant to represent Agrippina with the ashes of Germanicus.

---

[1] Baron Stosch, who was a Hanoverian spy on the Pretender's doings abroad, had a large collection of engraved gems, including some genuine antiques and many forgeries; a very interesting catalogue was made of them by Winckelmann, printed at Florence in 1760. Stosch died in 1757: he is the *Annius* of Pope's satire—

"False as his gems, and cankered as his coins."

The Stosch gems are now in the Berlin collection, which contains more than 5000 gems, antique and modern.

10. *Head of Ariadne* with ivy wreath; small cameo on *onyx* of three strata. one *jasper* layer between two of *chalcedony*.

11. Gem from the Poniatowski collection. Large figure of *Venus*, half draped, seated on a rock, and balancing a stick on one finger. Cupid flying upward grasps at the stick. In the *exergue* is the name AYΛOY: on a fine large *carnelian*, cut to an octagon shape and mounted as a ring. What is possibly the original of this design exists in the British Museum, No. 2296, cut on a *burnt chalcedony*, a fine gem of the later Renaissance period, inscribed AYΛOC, not AYΛOY as on the Poniatowski copy. This is an exceptionally fine specimen of the celebrated Poniatowski gems, which were engraved early in this century by various clever artists, such as Pichler Junr., Girometti, Cerbara and others, and passed off as antiques by Prince Poniatowski, who died in 1833. Most of them have, like this gem, the name of a supposed ancient gem-engraver: this particular name *Aulus* occurs on many of them. The very graceful design on this gem seems originally to have been taken from some Roman wall-painting; the execution is very skilful and the design is essentially pictorial in character. As modern works of art many of the Poniatowski gems have considerable merit, but in style they are very unlike ancient gems. The fact that they were generally accepted as antiques in the early part of this century is a striking example of the low state of archaeological knowledge at that time. The nucleus of Prince Poniatowski's collection consisted of about 150 ancient gems inherited from his uncle Stanislaus, King of Poland; by the help of modern engravers the Prince increased his collection to no less than 3000 gems. The forged artists' names were mostly added by one clever engraver named Dies. The whole collection was dispersed in 1839. At one time single examples of the Poniatowski gems were valued at as much as a thousand pounds, but after their spurious nature was discovered they seldom fetched more than from three to four pounds each, although, in many cases, they were really worth far more as exceptionally fine specimens of modern gem-engraving.

PLATE I. AND II.

The following Plates are reproductions by the autotype process of the most important of the gems in the Fitzwilliam Collection.

As they are taken from impressions of the gems in plaster, they represent the design as it appears on the seal made by the gem; not as it is on the intaglio itself.

For the sake of clearness each gem is enlarged, in linear dimensions, to one and a half times its real size, and also because a reproduction of the same linear dimensions *in plano* of a rounded surface not only appears but really is smaller than the original. The higher the relief, the greater the loss of visible surface when it is represented *in plano*.

Plate I. contains examples of work of the earlier periods, ranging from glandular gems of pre-historic times down to gems of late Greek or Graeco-Roman style.

Plate II. contains other examples of Graeco-Roman work, together with Roman gems from the period of the Republic down to that of the later Empire.

Though on the whole the process employed in these Plates is a fairly satisfactory one, yet it must be remembered that much of the delicate beauty and refinement of modelling in the best of the gems is necessarily lost in the process of reproduction.

The *numbers* on the Plates refer to the numbering of the gems in the preceding Catalogue.

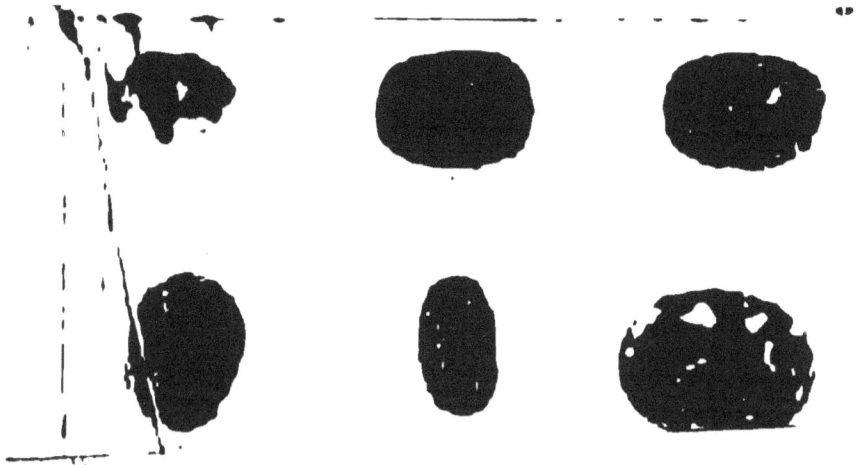
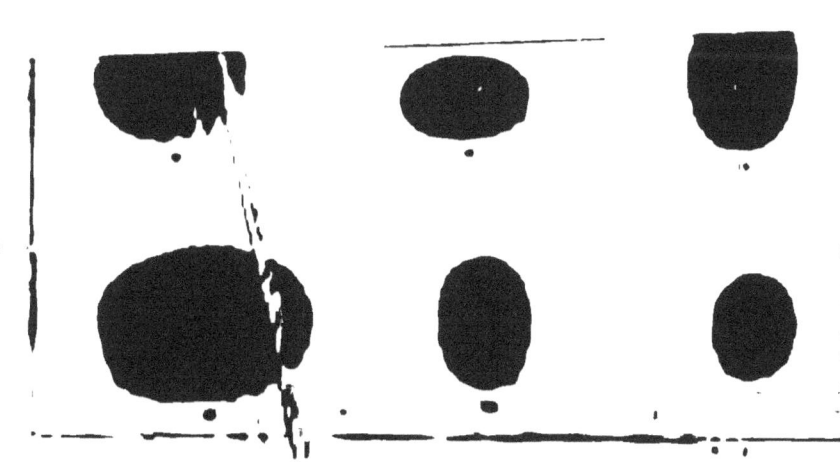

PLATE I. AND II.

The following Plates are reproductions by the autotype process of the most important of the gems in the Fitzwilliam

ERRATUM.

In the description Plate I *for* "Roman" *read* "Greek"

down to that of the later Empire.

Though on the whole the process employed in these Plates is a fairly satisfactory one, yet it must be remembered that much of the delicate beauty and refinement of modelling in the best of the gems is necessarily lost in the process of reproduction.

The *numbers* on the Plates refer to the numbering of the gems in the preceding Catalogue.

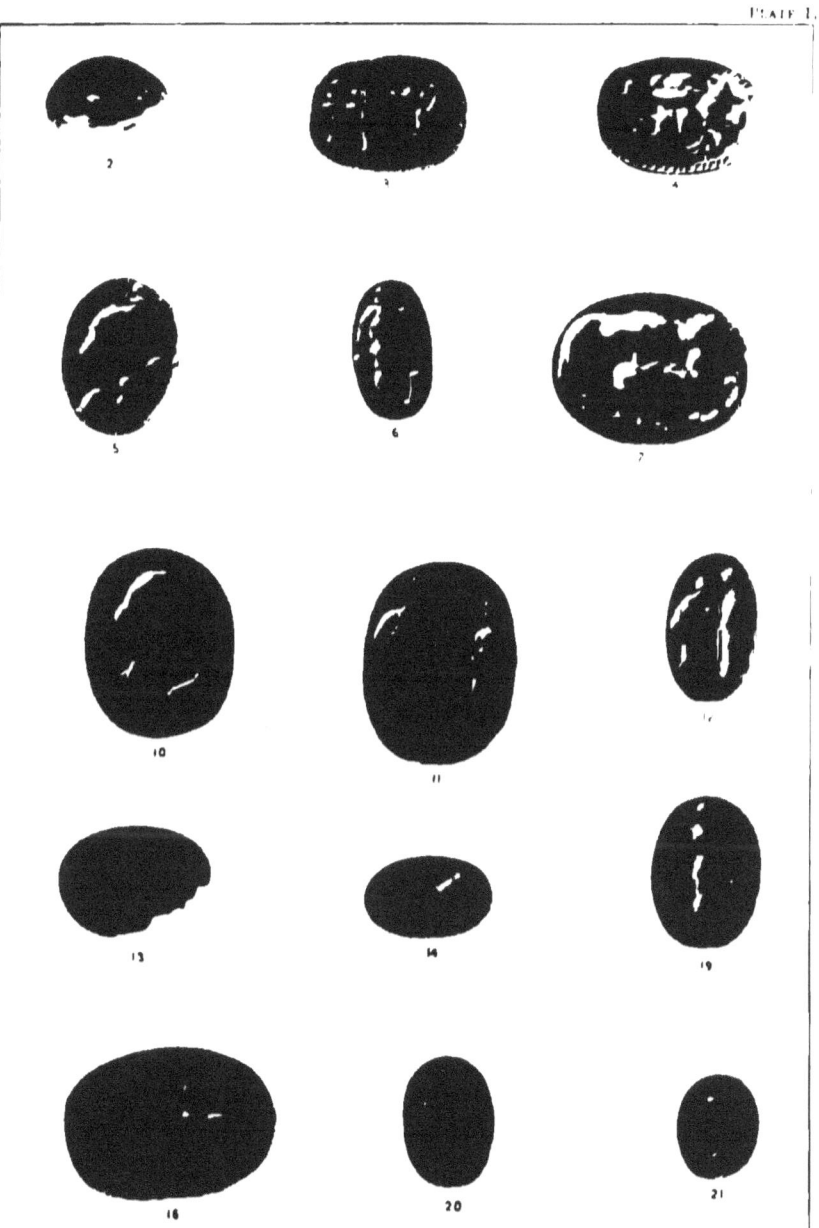

GEMS OF THE ROMAN PERIOD.

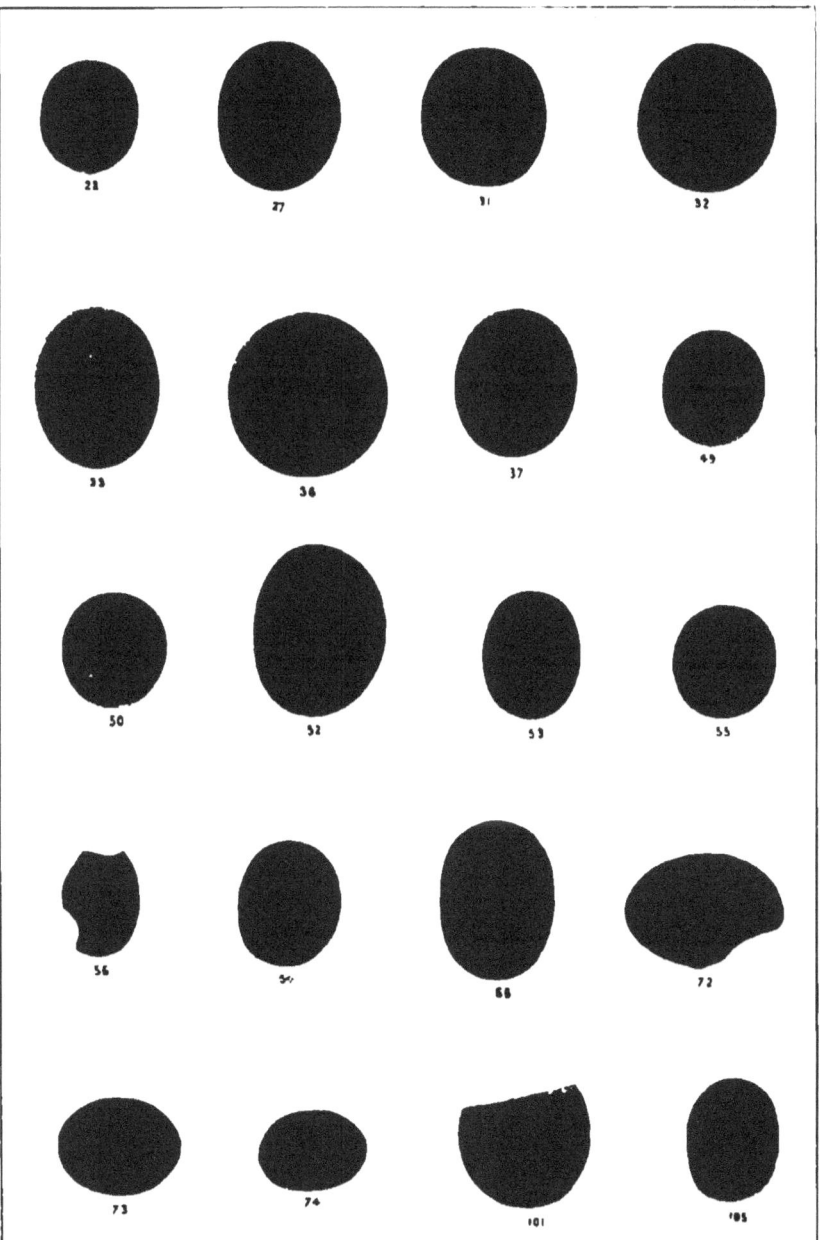

GEMS OF THE ROMAN PERIOD.

INDEX.

Aaron's breastplate, Gems on, 66 *note*, 131

Abraxas the mystic sun-god, 56; the word, engraved on gems, 94, *App*. x, xi

Abundantia, Figure of, on gems, 54

Achilles playing the lyre, on a gem, 79

Acropolis of Athens, Discoveries on, 15, 26

Adamas, The, 129 131

Aegaeae, Eutyches of, 75

Aegina, Phoenician scarab found in the Island of, 14, 15, *App*. iv

Agate, 147; large cameo patera of, 62

Agathopus, Gem signed by, 80

Agrippina, on modern cameo, *App*. xxiv

Alexander, Head of, on gems, 41; on coins of Lysimachus, *ib*.; used for signet by Augustus, 50

Alexandros, Name of, on gems, 82, 83

Ambassadors, Gold rings worn by, 50

Amber, 154—156; rings made of, 155; use in prehistoric times, *ib*.

Amethyst, The, 142, 143

Amulet gems, 145

Amymone, Figure of, on emerald gem, 40, 135

Anichini, gem-engraver, 126

Ant, Representation of an, *App*. xix; chariot drawn by two ants, *App*. xiii

Antaradus in Phoenicia, "Hittite" signet found at, 10

Anteros, Gems signed by, 81

Antiphanes, Passage from, on scarab ornaments, 21

Antiphilos the Graeco-Egyptian painter, inventor of the *gryllus*, 55

Antoninus Pius, Portrait head of, used as a seal by Louis I., 121

Anthrax, 132

Aphrodite represented on gems, 40, *App*. xi

Apollo, Bronze statue of, by Kanachos, copied on gems, 42

Apollo Helios, Probable representation of, *App*. xviii

Apollo Sauroctonos, Representation of, on gems, 42

Apollolotos, Gem of, 68, 69

Apollonides, gem-engraver, 71

Apollonios, Gem signed by, 78

Apotheosis of Augustus, 61; of Germanicus, *ib*.

Aptera, Coin of, 92

Aquamarine, variety of beryl, 136

Arcadia, Signed coins of, 92

Archaic glandular gems, 18 21, *App*. iii

Arcius, *King of Sparta*, Signet of, mentioned in a letter, *App*. iii

Ariadne, Head of, 92, *App*. xxv

Aristippus, Head of, 115

Aristophanes, Passage from, on the custom of securing doors with a seal, 36, 37; on magic rings, 23

Artaxerxes, name of various Sasanian kings, 58

Artemis, Figure of, on gem, 77—78, *App*. x

Ashmolean museum, Gems in, 10, 13

Asklepios, Head of, on gem, 82

xxviii INDEX.

Assyria, Signets of, 2—6
Astrion, 132
Astrological gems, 55
Athenades, Signet signed by, 73
Athene, Head of, 60, 68; bust of, 76; figure of, *App.* xv
Athenion, Cameo signed by, 84, 85
Attalus II., *King of Pergamus*, Collection of engraved gems made by, 33
Attulas, Name of, on ring, *App.* xv
Augustus, Sardonyx of, 34; Apotheosis of, 61; portrait bust of, 63; head of, on cameos, 65, 76, 86; the Sphynx, head of Alexander the Great, and his own portrait used as signet by, 49, 50
Aulus, Name of, on gems, 82, *App.* xxv
Austria, Eagle of, taken from Oriental device, 11—12

Babylonian cylinder, Figure of an early, 4; cylinders, produced under Darius and Xerxes, 5
Bacchanal, *App.* xxiv
Bacchus, Figure of, *App.* xii, xvii
Baphion, Lenticular gems discovered at, 20, 21
Basalt, 152, 153; gems made of, 20
Bead, Ring-shaped, *App.* xiv
Bean-shaped gems, 18
Belli, Valerio dei, gem-engraver, 126
Beryl, The, 136—138
Betrothal ring of St Joseph and the Virgin, Supposed, 96
Beverley, *Lord*, Scipio's ring formerly in the possession of, 47, *App.* xiii
Bezel, Meaning of the word, 34
Bloodstone, The, 146
Boethos, Cameo signed by, 85
Bonus Eventus, Figure of, 54, *App.* xiii
Bow and arrow, Hero with, figured, 26
Bow and drill, Illustration of a man working with, 105
Bracelet, Signet worn as, 3
Brutus, Portrait-head of, on ring, 73
Bull, on gem with name of Hyllus, 77; attacked by lion, *App.* v; and cow, *App.* ix; walking, *App.* xx

Cable or guilloche border, 15
Cabochon form of gems, 39
Caesar, Julius, Gift of ring-gems to the temple of Venus Genitrix by, 36; head of, on gem, 79; Victory on coin of, *App.* xvi
Callaina, The, 149
Callais, The, 150
Calpurnius Severus, Gem of, 74, 75
Cameo gems, 59—65
Cameos with artists' names, 84—89
Camiros, Gem in the Fitzwilliam Museum from, 13, *App.* iv; glass cylinders found in the tombs of, 5
Cannae, Gold rings from, 52
Capua, Gold ring found on the site of the ancient, 73
Caracalla, Portrait of, on sapphire, 132
Carbuncle, The, 138, 139; cups of, 139
Carlisle gems in the British Museum, 49, 78, 81, 87
Castel Bolognese, G. da, gem-engraver of the Renaissance, 126
Castor and Pollux, Busts of, *App.* xii
Cellini, Benvenuto, 86, 127, 133 *note*; gem bought by, 135
Centaur, Figure of a wounded, on Greek gem, 28
Cesati, Aless., gem-engraver, 82, 83, 126, 127
Chalcedony, 144
Chariot drawn by two ants represented on gem, *App.* xiii
Charles V., *King of France*, Signet of, 124; cameo given to Chartres Cathedral by, 62
Chaton, Meaning of, 34
Cheops, Ring of, 31
Chersonesus, Rings found on the fingers of a Queen of the, 33
Cherubim and palm-tree, 3
Chester collection of signets, 10, 11
Chios, Sphinx on coins of, 49
Christian gems, Devices on, 57
Claudius, Portrait of, on rings, 42
Clay seals, 5, 6, 27
Clazomene, Tetradrachm of, 92

Cnoubis, Representation of, on Egyptian gem, 56, *App.* xxii
Cock, Representation of a, *App.* xix
Coins, Portraits on, 40, 41; Artists' names on, 89—96
Cologne, Gems on shrine at, 124
Colyns, Thomas, Prior of Tywardreth, Signet of, 42, 43
Comic mask, *App.* xx
Concord, Collection of gems in the Temple of, 35, 36
Concordia, Figure of, on gems, 94
Condalium, Meaning of, 31
Conical Signets, 6; figures of, 7, 9; how worn, 8, 9
Constantine, Decadence in time of, 57
Cornu-copiae, *App.* xvi, xxii
Corundum (emery), 133, 134
Cow, on gem by Apollonides, 71 *note*; on gem in Fitzwilliam Museum, *App.* vi
Crab on a gem, *App.* xix
Crete, Signed coins of, 92
Cronius, gem-engraver, 71
Crystal, Quartz, used for gems, 25, 141, *App.* v; stained to imitate jewels, 137; cups made of, 141—142; used for cautery, 141
Crystalline silica, 140—142
Cupid, Figures of, on gems, 85, *App.* xvii, xix, xx
Custos annuli, Office of, 53
Cyanos, real and artificial, 150, 151
Cydonia, Tetradrachm of, 92
Cylinder, Early Babylonian, figured, 4
Cylinders, 1—16; materials of, 2, 3; worn as bracelets and necklaces, 3, 5; general use of, *ib.*; how engraved, 3, 4; their inscriptions, 4; Babylonian, produced under Darius and Xerxes, 5; found in the tombs of Camiros, *ib.*
Cyprus, Glass rings from tombs of, 117
Cyrene, Gems lavishly worn in the Greek colony of, 33
Cyriac of Ancona, Ancient gem described by, 76

Dactyliothecae, 33, 36
Darius, Babylonian cylinders produced under, 5
Dedicatory inscriptions on gems, 96
Dexamenos, Gems signed by, 28, 71, *App.* vii—ix
Dexilla, Dedication of articles of jewellery by, in the Parthenon, 31—32
Diamond (adamas), 129, 131
Diamond, Eyes of, in Greek statuette, 130; set in Roman rings, 131
Diamond-Point, The, 111, 113
Diana, Bust of, on gem, *App.* xiii, xvi
Diomede, Figure of, 68, 74, 75, 98, 125
Diomede and Ulysses, Figures of, 74, *App.* xxi
Dionysus, Representations of, 14, 40, 115, *App.* xvii
Dioscuri figured on Roman gems, 48; *App.* xiii
Dioskourides, Gems signed by, 71, 75, 79, 86; mosaic signed by, 79 *note*
Divine Unity, Profession of the, on gems, 94
Dolphin, Representation of a, 67, 135, *App.* xxiii
Domenico de' Cammei, gem-engraver, of the Renaissance, 126
Donatello, admirer of ancient gems, 124
Drill, The gem-engraver's, 103—109
Drill-cut scarab, figured, 107

Eagle represented on jasper, *App.* xxii; Emperor borne by, 61; Jupiter and the, 61; head of, on chalcedony, *App.* xxiv; flying, on a glandular gem, *App.* iii
Ear-rings, Gold, *App.* xiv
Ectypae, Cameos, 59
Egypt, Cylinders used as signets in, 5; their materials, *ib.*; clay seals found in, 6; Scarabs of, used for sealing bottles, 37; and offerings, 27
Electra, Probable representation of, on gem, *App.* ix
Emerald, The, 134—136; ring of Polycrates, 35, 69; portrait of Alexander on, 71; dolphin on, 135; used by

xxx INDEX.

Nero in theatre, 134; by gem-engravers as rest for their eyes, *ib.*
Emery, Use of, 104, 107—108; best, from Naxos, 105, 133
Epicurus, Portraits of on gems, 41
Episcopal rings, 122—123; crozier set with gems, 123
Epitynchanus, Gems signed by, 83
Eros, Figure of, on gem by Phrygillos, 91; *App.* xi; on ear-rings, *App.* xiv
Etruscan tombs, Gems from, 44—46; scarab with rude drill-work figured, 107; scarabs, 35—46
Euainetos, Coins by, 30, 89, 90
Euarchides, Coin signed by, 91
Eucleidas, Coins signed by, 90
Eumenes I., Portrait head of, 41
Euodos, Portrait of Julia by, 49, 63, 74, 123, 137
Euphrates Valley, Cylinder signets used primarily by the races of the, 3
Entyches, Gem signed by, 75, 76
Evans, A. J., on signed coins, 90
Exakestidas, Coin signed by, 91
Explanatory words on gems, 93
Ezechiel's list of gems, 110, 131

Facet-cut gems, 39
Fauns on gems, 24, *App.* xviii
Felicitas, Figure of, on gems, 54
Felix, Gem signed by, 75
File, Use of the, 113, 114; used to test gems, 137
Fire drill, 104
Fitzwilliam Museum, Catalogue of engraved gems in the, *App.* iii—xxv
Flamen Dialis, Hollow ring worn by the, 51, 52
Foiled gems, 116, 138; and pastes, 116
Foppa, Amb., gem-engraver, 126
Forgeries of gems, 99—102; of artists' signatures, 72; of stones, 117, 154
Fortnum, Dr Drury, Collection of Christian rings of, 57
Fortuna, Minute figure of, *App.* xvii
Francia, Francesco, the painter, Gems engraved by, 126
Frog engraved on seals, 50

Funda, Meaning of, 34

Gaios, Gem with name of, 87
Gallene, Swimming figure of, 71
Galvanic rings, 56
Ganymede, Figure of, 127, *App.* xvi
Garnet, The, 138
Gem-engravers, Tools used by the ancient, 103—114; names of, 66—93
Gem-engraving, The technique of, 103—120
Gems, Antique, Materials used for, 129—156; characteristics of ancient, 97—102; in mediaeval times, 121—128; of the Silicon family, 140; engraved gems treated as personal ornaments, 1; greetings on, 95; artists' names on, 72—75, 98—102; comparative hardness of, 157; inscriptions on, 66—89; polishing of, 114; variety of shapes of, 38, 39
Germanicus, The Apotheosis of, 61; Head of, on gem, 83
Gistubar, Figure of, strangling a lion, on a Babylonian cylinder, 4
Glandes, sling-bullets, 18
Glandular gems, 18—21, *App.* iii
Glass rings, 117, *App.* xiv
Glass, Various methods of working, 119
Gnaios, Signature of, on gem, 75
Gnostic Aeons, Names of the three, on gems, 94
Gnostic belief concerning the Orders of Angels, *App.* x, xi
Goat, Representation of a, *App.* xviii
Gold signets, 17, 31, 73, 119—120; among Parthenon treasure, 32
Gold, Store of, in throne of Jupiter, 52
Gorgon's head on cameos, 59, 60
Granites, 152
Greaves, Method of fitting, shown on gem, 25, *App.* v
Greco, Il, 82, 126
Greece, Common practice of wearing gems in, 33
Greek coins, Indication of Magistrates' names on, 24; with artists' names, 89—93

INDEX.   xxxi

Greek gems, 17—42; subjects on, 24;
—— signet-gems, badge of owner on,
   23, 24
—— use of the Signet, 22, 23, 37
—— vases, Warriors badges on, 24
Greetings inscribed on gems, 95
Gryllus, Figure of a, *App.* xx; used for
   Roman signet-gems, 55
Guilloche border on gems and coins, 15

Hadrian, Sale of the collection of gems
   formed by, 53
Haematite, 145, 151, 152
Haggai, Gem of, 66
Hand, A, extended, *App.* xxiii
Hardness of gems, Table of, 157
Harpocrates, Figure of, on gems, 55;
   Bust of, *App.* xxi
Hea-band figured on cylinders, 4 *note*
Heliotrope, The, 146
Hellen, Name of, engraved on gems, 82
Hera, Possible representation of, on
   ring, 54; cameo head of, *App.* xiv, xv
Heraklaea, Bronze tables of, 13, 14;
   coin of, 29
Herakleidas, Ring signed by, 73
Herakles, Representations of, 24, 80,
   81, *App.* vi
Heraldry of ancients, 19, 20
Hercules and Cerberus on cameo, 86;
   head of, *App.* xviii
Hero with bow and arrow figured, 26
Herodotus on signet-cutting, 111
Hermes, 77, 78, 119; bust of, *App.* xiv
Hermes Psychopompos on gems, 57
Herophilos, Cameo signed by, 86
Himera, Representation of the Nymph,
   on tetradrachm, 90
Hippias, Signet-ring made by the Soph-
   ist, 114
Hippocamp, Representation of, on a
   gem, *App.* xviii
Hittite Signets, 6, 7, 10, 12; how worn,
   7; their devices, 11
Horse, Representation of a, on a gem,
   App. xviii, xix
Horsemen, Three, figured on carnelian,
   App. xx

Horus, Figure of, used for signets, 55;
   representation of, *App.* x
Hound, Running, *App.* xix
Hunting scenes, represented on gems,
   App. x and xi; on gold signet from
   Mycenae, 17
Hyacinthus, The, 132
Hyllus, Gems signed by, 76, 77

Indulgentia, Figure of, on ring, 54
Inscriptions on gems, 66—89
Inscriptions, Talismanic, 94
Io, Head of, on gem signed by Dios-
   kourides, 79
Iron rings, 51; used in Rome for be-
   trothal, 51 *note*
Isis, Figure of, on ring, 54; worship of,
   in Rome, 55
Island gems, 18; their dates, 10; de-
   signs, *ib.*; their material, 21
—— scarabs, 12; their material, *ib.*;
   devices, 18, 19
Ismenias, Emerald bought by, 40
Isocrates on use of seals, 34

Jasper, 144, 145
Jewellers' tricks, 117, 154
Jewellery, Greek, 135, 136, 138
Jugurtha, Engraving of the surrender
   of, used as a signet by Sulla, 53
Julia, Signed portrait of, by Euodos, 49,
   63, 74, 123, 137
Juno, Figure of, 48, 55; bust of, 63
Jupiter, Figure of, on gems, 48, 55, 62,
   App. xii; eagle of, *App.* xix; head of,
   60; head of, used as a portrait of St
   Oswald, 122
Jupiter Ammon, Head of, on ring,
   54
Jupiter Capitolinus, Gems in temple of,
   35, 36
Jupiter Serapis, Bust of, *App.* xxi, xxii
Jus annuli aurei, 50—51

Kallimachus, said to have first drilled
   stone, 108
Kamarina represented on coin, 91
Kanachos the sculptor, 42

Kertch, Gems &c. found in tombs at, 60, 72, 73, *App.* viii, x
Kimon, Coins by, 30, 89—91
King, C. W., List of works of, *Pref.* x
Kleito, Dedication of jewels by, in the Parthenon, 31—32
Köhler, Treatise of, on scarabs, 45
Kreontidas, Name of, on scarab gem, 67, *App.* iv

Laocoon, True position of the lost arms of, 42, 43; represented on a gem, 42
Lapis lazuli, 150, 151; imitation of, in paste, 65
Lenke, Col., Collection of gems and other works of art of, *Pref.* ix, x
Lenticular gems, 18—21; ditto in collection of Mr A. J. Evans, 20; ditto showing the use of the wheel, 110
Leo X., gem-collector, 126
Leonardo, Camillo, author of a work on gems, 126
Leonardo da Milano, gem-engraver of the Renaissance, 126
Letters, Precautions in seals of, 22—23; inscription on seal of, 67
Lima, a gem-engraver's tool, 113
Lion, Maneless, on gem, *App.* v, vi; representation of a, *App.* xix; common in early Greek art, *App.* v—vi
Lion and Stag on Greek gem, 28, 30
Livia, Figure of, on gem, 63, 83; block of crystal dedicated by, 141; cameo head of, on turquoise, 150
Locust, Human-headed, *App.* xxii, xxiii
Lothaire I., Crystal signet of, 121, 122
Louis I., Ancient gem used as signet by, 121
Louis IX., Cameo given by, 61
Luynes, Duc de, Collection of scarab gems made by the, 16
Lyncurium, variety of amber, 156
Lysimachus, Head of Alexander used on the coins of, 40, 41

Maecenas, Head of, 75, 77; official seal of, 50
Maenads on gems, 24

Magi, Superstitions of the, 142
Magic wheel (ἴυγξ), 33
Magical gems, 123
Magistrates' names on coins, 24
Magna Graecia, Gold signet-rings from tombs in, 31; ditto signed by their engravers, 73
Magnes, natural loadstone, 151
Magnetite, 151, 152
Man on horseback represented on gem, *App.* ix, x
Marc Antony, Device on gold coin struck by, 53; opal coveted by, 146
Marcellus, Dedication of gems in the temple of Apollo by, 36
Marcus Aurelius, Portrait head of, used as seal by Charlemagne, 121
Maria, Giovanni, gem-engraver, 126
Marlborough gems, 74 *note*; modern gems among, 128
Mars, Representation of, *App.* xv
Massaro, Matteo dal, gem-engraver, 126
Maximianus Herculeus Augustus, Glass cup bearing the name of, 119
Mediaeval use of ancient gems, 121—123; gem-engravers, 124—127; collections of gems, 124
Medici Family, Badge of the, 131
Medici, Lorenzo de', Name of, on gems, 77, 80; as a gem-collector, 125—126
Medici, Piero de', Gems of, 125
Medusa, Figure of, on cameo, 63; head of, 38, 60, 64, 132, 135, *App.* xiv; Forged artist's signature on gem with head of, 75
Melos, Aphrodite of, 42 *note*
Mercury, Figure of, 77, 78, *App.* xvii; bust of, *App.* xxi
Metal signets, 17, 73, 119—120
Michelangelo, Copy of the signet of, *App.* xxiii, xxiv
Mike, Gem of, 68, *App.* vii
Minerva, Head of, on cameo, 86; figure of, 48, 55, *App.* xiii
Mithradates, Collection of Greek gems in Rome formerly belonging to, 36; coin portrait of, 41
Mnesarchus the gem-engraver, 70

INDEX. xxxiii

Moretti, Marco, gem-engraver, 126
Moslem signets, 58
Moulds for paste gems, 115
Muse playing on lyre, signed by Onesas, at Florence, 80
Mycenae, gems found in, 17, 18; their devices, *ib.*; gold signets from, 17

Naples, Patera cameo at, 62, 63; gold signet at, 73; signed cameo at, 84
Naxium, emery, 133
Nemesis, Winged figure of, *App.* xvii, xviii
Nero, Portrait of, *App.* xviii; emerald used by, in theatre, 134
Neuantos, Coin signed by, 92
Nico, Dedication of gem of, in the temple of Aphrodite, 32, 33
Nicolo, variety of onyx, 147
Nikander, Gem signed by, 74

Obsidian, used for statues, 142; to test gems, 153
Odo, *King of France*, Signet used by, 121
Offa, *King of Mercia*, Signet of, 121
Onatas, Gem signed by, 88
Onesas, Gem signed by, 80
Opal, The, 146
Onyx, The, 146, 147
Orestes, Probable representation of, on gem, *App.* ix

Pacorus, *King of Parthia*, Engraved portrait of, on gem, 23
Palm-branch, *App.* xxiii
Pamphilos, Signature of, on amethyst, 79—80
Pan, Figure of, on coin, 97; head of, on jasper, *App.* xx
Papal rings, 122
Paris, Inventory of precious objects in the Sainte Chapelle at, 61; gems in the Bibliothèque in, 61, 62, 74, 77, 79, 83; signet of Michelangelo in, *App.* xlii—xliv
Paris, Judgment of, cameo signed by Anteros, 81

Parthenon, Gems deposited in the treasury of, 31—32
Pasiteles, sculptor and gem-engraver, 71
Paste cameos, 64, 65
Paste gems, The technique of, 114 119; how to distinguish them from real gems, 153, 154; materials of, 153; made to imitate crystal, 154; bubbles in, *ib.*
Paul II., Collection of gems of, 125
Paul III., *Pope*, Portrait of, 127
Pebbles, Gems shaped like, 18—19; used for voting, 107 *note*
Pegasus, Probable representation of, on gem, *App.* x
Persephone, Head of, on coin, 91
Perseus represented on gems, 14
Persian gems, 6, 7, 58
Peruzzi, a mediaeval gem-engraver, 124
Pescia, Piero Maria da, gem-engraver, 126, *App.* xxiii
Phalerae cameos, 60, 62, 63, 142
Phanes, Coin of, 67
Pharaoh's signet, 1
Pheidias, Gems of the age of, 28; forged name of, on gems, 93; Athene of, copied on gems, *App.* xiii
Philemon, Signature of, on gem, 80, 81
Philistion, Coins signed by, 29
Philoctetes, Figure of, on cameo, 85
Phoenician gems, 12—16; devices on scarabs, 13—15; scarab figured, 14; scarabaeoid, *App.* iv
Phrygillos, Gem and coins with signature of, 91
Pisanello, painter and medallist, 127
Piscatoris, Sub annulo, 122
Pistrucci, Benvenuto, 102
Plasma, 145
Plautus, Passage from, on use of signet-impressions, 22
Pliny on gem-cutting, 106
Poison rings, 52
Polish of gems, 114
Polycrates, Signet of, 35, 36, 69, 70
Pompey, Devices on the signets of, 53
Poniatowski collection, Gem from, *App.* xxv; its history, *ib.*

Portland Vase, 117, 118
Portraits on gems, 40, 41
Pottery, disc-stamps used on, 6; incised lines on, cut with diamond-point, 113; ornamented with wheel-cut patterns, 119 *note*
Prase, 143
Prometheus, Legend of the ring of, 50
Protarchos, Cameo inscribed by, 85
Proverbial phrases on gems, 95
"Ptolemies, Cup of the," 62
Pyrgoteles, gem-engraver, 41, 70, 71
Pythodorus, Coin signed by, 92

Quartz crystal, 140—143

Ra, The Sun-god, 1, 2
Renaissance, Gem-engravers of, 126
Rings, Glass, 117, *App.* xiv; gold, 17, 73, 119
Rings, Large numbers of, worn by ladies of rank, 33; of the Romans described by Pliny, 50
Rock crystal, 141—143
Roger, *Abp.*, Signet used by, 122, 123
Roma, Figure of, 55, *App.* xv, xvii
Roman denarii, Magistrate indicated on, 24
—— gems, 47—57; subjects figured on, 48
—— names for rings, 51
—— use of gems as signets, 49
Romans, Rings seldom worn by the, in ancient times, 50
—— Signet-gems of the, used for sealing plaster stoppers of bottles, 37
Rossi, Giov. Ant. de', gem-engraver, 126
Rotellino of gem-engravers, 109
Ruby, The, 132, 133

Saladin, Badge of, 11
Salus, Figure of, on gems, 54
Samothrace, Use of gold signet-rings said to have originated in, 31
Sapor or Shapur, Portrait of, on Sasanian gems, 58

Sapphire, The, 132; white, 131
Sappho, Representation of, on Greek gem, 27; on vase, *ib. note*
Sappirus, 150
Sard used for ancient engraved gems, 129, 143—144
Sardoine, 144; gem with Eros cut in, *App.* xi
Sardonyx, The, 148, 149; made up of three stones, 137
Sargon I., Cylinder of, 4; date of, 5
Sasanian gems, 58; *App.* xi—xii
Satyr, A, represented on gem, 24, *App.* xix; head of, on cameo, 88
—— and wine-cup represented on a Greek scarab, 25
Satyreius, gem-engraver, 71
Savonarola, Fra Girolamo, Portrait of, by G. delle Carniuole, 126
Saw, used for cutting marble, 109
Scarabaeoids in Fitzwilliam Museum, *App.* iv—viii
Scarabaeus beetle, 1, 2, 2 *note*, *App.* iv—v
Scarabs, 1—16; set as rings, 1, 2; worn round the neck, 2; as charms, 2 *note*; materials of, 2; collection of, in the Fitzwilliam Museum, 2 *note*; date of the oldest, 2; used as ornaments by the Greeks, 21, 22; used for sealing plaster stoppers of bottles, 37
Scaurus, M. Aemilius, the earliest Roman gem-collector, 36
Sceptre, Gold, in the British Museum, 136
Scipio Africanus the elder, Sardonyx worn by, 148
Scipio, Ring of, 47, *App.* xii
Scopas, Forged name of, on gems, 93
Sculptor using a drill, represented on Roman relief, 104
Seal, Passage from Aristophanes on the custom of securing doors with a, 36, 37; used to secure voting-urns, 34; ditto wine-jars, 37
Seffrid, *Bp. of Chichester*, Abraxas gem used by, 123
Seleucus IV., *King of Syria*, Portrait

INDEX.

head of, used as a seal by Odo, *King of France*, 121
Semites, Cylinder signets used by the, 3
Semitic inscription on figured gem, 66
Semon, Inscription on gem of, 67
Serapis, Worship of, 53; "emerald" statue of, 135; bust of, *App.* xxii
Severus, Portrait of, on plasma, 146
Sicilian colonies, Early art-development of the, 30, 31
Sicily, Gems and coins produced by the engravers of, 29; coins of, with artists' names, 89
Sigillum, Meaning of, 51
Signatures of gem-engravers, 69—93
Signet-gems used for sealing plaster stoppers of bottles, 37
Signet-ring, Names used for the various parts of a, 34
Signets, 1—16; Use of, in wine-cellars, 37; conical, 6; cubical, 10; circular, 11; handled, 9; figured, 10
Silenus, Representation of, *App.* xviii
Silenus mask, *App.* xii
Silicon stones, 140—149
Siren, Device of a, on gem, *App.* ix
Sirius, Head of, on gem, 87
Smaragdus, 134—136
Socrates, Head of, on gems, 41, *App.* xviii
Solon, Law of, with regard to gems, 22
Solon, Name of, on gem, 75
Sospita, Juno, on coins and gems, 48
Sostratos, Cameo signed by, 87
South Kensington Museum, Waterton collection of rings in the, 53, 54
Sphynx used for a signet, 49
Stanislaus, *King of Poland*, Gems of, *App.* xxv
Star-sapphire, 132
Statues represented on gems, 42, 77, 99; cut in crystal, obsidian &c., 141—142
Steatite, 152; used for earliest scarabs, 2; and for Island gems, 21
Stelae, Attic, gems with similar designs, 25, *App.* vii
Stratified stones, 141

Sulla, Signet used by, 53
Surias, Gem signed by, 88, 89
Symbolum, Meaning of, 51; use of, 12

Taghacarne, gem-engraver, 126
Talismanic inscriptions, 94; rings, 23
Taygetus, Mt., Basalt from, used for gems, 20; rock crystal from, *App.* x
Tests for gems, 153—154; for adamas, 130; to distinguish ancient from modern gems, 98—102
Teukros, Name of, cut on gem, 82
Tharros, Scarabs from, 14—16
Thebes, Heraldic shield devices on vase from, 24
Theodorus of Samos, 35, 69, 70
Theodotos, Coin signed by, 91
Theophrastus on gem-cutting, 106
Thersis, Gem of, 67, 68
Theseus represented on gems, 24, 80—81
Threptos, Name of, on gem, *App.* xvi
Tools, invented by Theodorus, 69; of gem-engravers, 103—120; used by the Sophist Hippias, 114
Topazus, The, 149; statues of, 16
Tornus, a gem-engraver's tool, 103 *note*, 109; a joiner's tool, 69
Trajan, Gems sold by, 53
Triton, Representation of a, *App.* xvi
Tryphon, gem-engraver, 71
Tubular drill, used for gems, 108
Turkey, Manner of signing edicts by the Ottoman Sultans of, 37
Turquoise, The, 149—150
Tympanum of gem-cutters, 110

Ulysses figured on gem, 74
Ungulus, Meaning of, 51

Vasari on gem-engravers, 83, 116
Vases, Warriors' badges on Greek, 24; artists' names on, 93; incised lines on, 113
Velia, Coin of, copied on gem, 29—30
Venus, Figure of, on gem, *App.* xxv
Venus Victrix, Figure of, 133, *App.* xvi
Victory, Figures of, 47, 57, 87, 88, 115, *App.* xii, xiii, xv, xvi

Vienna, Great cameo of, 61; cameo of Herophilus at, 76
Voting-urns sealed up with signets, 34
Votive offerings sealed with clay, 37
Vulcan, Representation of, *App.* xvii

Walter, *Abp.*, Gold ring of, 123
Waterton collection of rings in the South Kensington Museum, 53, 54
Westminster Abbey, Ancient gems in, 65
Wheel, The gem-engraver's, 109—111
Wine-cellar, Use of signets in, 37
Wolf represented on sard, *App.* xix

Xerxes, Babylonian cylinders produced under, 5

Youth caressing his dog on gem, as on Attic stelae, *App.* vii

Zeus destroying the Giants, cameo at Naples, 84; head of, on a scarab of the finest style, 27, 112
Zeus, Fostering of the infant, *App.* xxi
Zeus Lycaeos, Head of, on coin, 92
Zeus Serapis, Head of, on gems, 55, *App.* xxii

FINIS

www.ingramcontent.com/pod-product-compliance
Lightning Source LLC
Chambersburg PA
CBHW020823230426
43666CB00007B/1083